Learn to Sail

Learn to Sail

Dennis Conner *and* Michael Levitt

Illustrations by Chris Lloyd

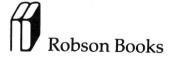 Robson Books

First published in Great Britain in 1995 by Robson Books Ltd,
Bolsover House, 5-6 Clipstone Street, London W1P 8LE

British Library Cataloguing in Publication Data
A catalogue record for this title is available from the British
Library

ISBN 0 86051 944 9

Printed in Great Britain by St. Edmundsbury Press, Bury St.
Edmunds, Suffolk.

Dedication

I would like to thank all my friends and colleagues that helped make this and some of my previous books possible. Amongst all the stars Ed du Moulin shines the brightest and Daintry Bell made all the work worthwhile.

Contents

Contents

x

Acknowledgments

The authors acknowledge the generous help of Ed du Moulin, who commented on this manuscript at each step of the way. Appreciated, too, is the help of Brian Doyle, of North Sails Cloth, who cast his engineer's eye on the technical material, and Ken Guyer for his comments on Chapter 13, Rules of the Road. Several of the photographs used in this book were gleaned from the photo archives of Sunfish Laser, Inc., and J Boats, Inc. For this we thank Peter Johnstone and Jeff Johnstone. The images were primarily the work of Onne Van Der Wal. Daniel Forster was kind enough to let us use a photograph that appears in Chapter 11. James "Beau" LeBlanc, of The Rigging Company, in Portsmouth, RI, supplied the lines used in photographs in Chapter 5. Peter Pell, of Thule, provided tips on carrying a boat on the top of a car.

Those who posed for photographs include Cutter Smith and Ann E. Marshall, of Sail Newport; Karen E. Callender, of Shake-A-Leg Inc.; and Molly and Linda Levitt, of Michael Levitt—or vice versa. Some photographs were taken on Steve Pettengill's boat, *À Tout À L'Heure*. Also thanks are due to George Witte, our editor at St. Martin's Press, and Meredith Bernstein, of the Meredith Bernstein Agency.

Learn to Sail

1 | Why Learn to Sail?

There are many sports out there competing for your attention, time, and money. A fundamental question you need to ask yourself—if you haven't already—is: Why learn to sail?

On the negative side of the ledger, it's not the fastest way of getting from here to there. Its speed is closer to walking than running. Sailing is not the most comfortable form of recreation. It is relatively hard to learn and hard to do. If you're the kind of person who doesn't find satisfaction in hard work, sailing is probably not the sport for you.

On the positive side, sailing is as close to nature as any of us will probably ever get. Most people are attracted to the world of water, wind, tide, and weather. For most, being a spectator is sufficient. A few choose to play there. That's sailing.

In sailing, you have to cooperate with the wind, waves, and tide, not try to beat them into submission or outgun them with more horsepower. I like that sense of being a part of nature, not always striving to be the master of it. A lifetime in sailing has taught me how difficult the elements are to master.

Sailing also engages the senses more completely than other sports. This is because you can't see the wind—the driving force. You can only see evidence of it. In some ways, it is like playing baseball without being able to see the ball. In sailing, you must use your eyes better, looking for more subtle clues: how the wind appears on the water; the direction of a flag or smoke; the angle of the ribbon telltales in the rigging; the angle the headstay makes to the horizon. There is a wealth of information out there once you learn to "see" it.

Also, you must better use your other senses, like touch and hearing, to solve the puzzle of the wind: its direction and strength. In sailing, you must be sensitive to how the helm feels in your hands; how the wind feels on the back of your neck; what is the sound the hull makes as it passes through the water; the sound of the wind in the sails. I've even won races by smelling a coal-burning power plant to the south of my position—meaning the new wind had begun to blow from the south—while the rest of the fleet was struggling in a dying northerly breeze.

Sailing is relatively hard to learn and hard to do. That appears on both sides of the ledger. The sport is a challenge, which I find holds my interest. I have been doing it for forty-seven of my fifty-one years, and it's a rare day that I don't learn something. Further, no two days are the same. These are some of the reasons why, for many, sailing becomes a lifetime sport. It has been for me.

Sailing gave me pleasure, challenge, competition, and my first taste of success long before I figured out why I even liked it.

My father was a commercial fisherman until World War II. He had a love of the sea, which he communicated to me. We lived in a small and ordinary house on a fairly busy street in San Diego's Point Loma neighborhood. San Diego Bay and the San Diego Yacht Club were a couple of blocks away. Naturally, I drifted down the hill to play in, around, and eventually on the bay.

I don't remember my father teaching me how to sail. Perhaps he did. During World War II, he sold his tuna-fishing boat, the forty-five-foot *Victor I*, and started building airplanes at the General Dynamics plant in San Diego. For more than thirty years he worked there, until he died.

When I was four, in 1946, my father gave me a nine-foot sailing dinghy, which he must have found abandoned in San Diego Bay. It was in such sorry shape that no one but a child could love it. And did I. I used to sleep with the sail, which was much patched and dirty, as some kids sleep with a favorite baseball glove. I was allowed to use the boat, to sail around the harbor, provided I wore an outsized life preserver. That was good because I couldn't swim then and can't swim now.

Thinking back on it, it seems strange to turn a four-year-old who couldn't swim loose on San Diego Bay, but if there is a more perfect—less threatening—place to learn to sail, I haven't found it. Also, in those days, being a parent was more casual—less institutionalized—than it is today, or at least it was in my house. It was a sink-or-swim childhood. Those who know me, know I learned to swim in life, if not in the water.

A round bottom and relentless leaks made the dinghy fundamentally unstable. It was always tipping over. When that happened, I wasn't big enough or strong enough to right it. Even if I could, its cotton sail would often rip. The small boat had a two-piece mast, probably for easy storage, and often when the boat tipped over, the mast's pieces would separate and rip the sail. With an overturned boat and a ripped sail, I'd have to wait, hanging on, until someone came along to rescue me. I don't remember being particularly scared by any of this, just frustrated that my day on the water was over and perhaps my month.

My family had no money for such things as sail repair. To get my sail fixed, I'd hang out at Herb Sinnhoffer's loft, which was within the boundaries of the San Diego Yacht Club. I wouldn't go away unless he fixed it. While there, I'd sweep floors, wash cars, make myself useful so he wouldn't throw me out. At the same time, I'd watch how Sinnhoffer made and repaired sails. I'd ask questions, make a pest of myself, and finally he would fix my sail just to get rid of me.

There were a host of others who had to suffer through my relentless personality. Ash Bown, for example, was a used-car salesman and probably the most gifted sailor at the San Diego Yacht Club. The San Diego Yacht Club was another place where I used to hang out. Since they couldn't get rid of me, the yacht club made me a junior member when I was eleven.

Ash Bown had a forty-foot boat called *Carousel*, and when I was older, I used to wait for him on the dock, to help him with his boat's mooring lines. My hope was that he'd take me sailing. Once he did, there was no shaking me. I was always at his house, talking about the sport; he was like a second father to me. His wife, however, was less enthusiastic about this arrangement. She'd often say to me, "Isn't it time you went home?"

I learned to sail, by sailing, watching, talking, and making a nuisance of myself. Obviously, this method of instruction has worked for me. In the forty-seven years that I have been doing it, I have sailed on winning America's Cup yachts four times; three of those times I was the skipper. I have won two Star World Championships and a Bronze medal in the 1976 Olympics. I have won the Etchells World Championship in 1991, two Congressional Cups, and four Southern Ocean Racing Conference (SORC) championships. In 1993, Brad Butterworth, my skipper, and I set a transatlantic-racing record of eleven days, eight hours in my 60-

foot Whitbread boat, *Winston*. This was my first crossing of an ocean. This broke the record set in 1905 by the 185-foot schooner *Atlantic*.*

L earning to sail involves training the body and the mind. Can you learn solely from a book like this, which is better at training the mind than the body? The responsible answer is no. However, learning theory from a book is at least as important as learning the physical movements: the wiggling of the tiller or wheel, or the trimming of the sails. When the conditions are benign, as they should be when learning, the physical moves of sailing just aren't that demanding. It's like skiing: It isn't that difficult to ski down the bunny slope—after a morning of lessons practically anyone can do it—but it's extremely difficult to ski down the expert slope.

While it is possible to learn to sail from a book alone, just as I learned mostly by sailing, I wouldn't recommend it. To do so would be as irresponsible as recommending someone solo an airplane after reading a how-to-fly book. The most direct and—more important—safest way to learn is to ascertain theory from a book and go out with someone who knows what he or she is doing. That can be an instructor giving a formal lesson, or a knowledgeable friend. Not only does an able teacher more than complement a text, but this person can help you if the weather suddenly and unexpectedly changes. In sailing, the bunny slope can change into the expert slope without much warning.

While that's true in the ocean, where the next stop can be Portugal or Hawaii, it's less true in a small lake, where the next stop is likely to be a neighbor's beach. The same wind blows less in a small, sheltered area, and the seas are smaller than in the open ocean. Also, inland, there is no tide and usually no current to worry about. Thus, learning to sail on a small lake can be a more casual affair.

On the other hand, if it is blowing fifty-five knots on the ocean and forty-five knots on a lake, you have a problem. This book is written then, for the most part, as if the next stop is Portugal.

Writing a book like this, you try not to give too little information because, as everyone knows, a little information can get you into big trouble. At the same time, provide too much information and the reader can lose his or her way. While I've tried to strike the right tone, if I've erred, it has

---

*Two sailboats, not involved in a race, have crossed the Atlantic in less time. They are *Procea*, a 244-foot monohull, which sailed transatlantic in eight days, three hours, and *Jet Services V*, a catamaran, which did it in six days, twelve hours.

been on the side of too much information. (Material that appears in foot-notes is a good example.) However, as I see it, it is better to be challenged by the information in this book than overwhelmed by the elements because you don't know enough. Instant sailing this isn't.

To learn to sail, I believe, you must learn to think like a sailor. You must know what to do, the maneuvers, like anchoring, reefing sails, steering through a tack, but also what to do when the unexpected occurs. In sailing, you must expect the unexpected. Given time, the unexpected gives way to anticipation. You can anticipate problems before they occur, which is the mark of a sailor.

The best way to learn to sail, I believe, is to train your mind and body at the same time. To get the most out of this book, try what you've read on the water with an instructor or competent friend. Read the book again, read something new, then, again, attempt what you've learned on the water. And so on. Read *Learn to Sail* carefully and take every opportunity to go out on the water. In a day of sailing, you'll have tried—if not mastered—most, if not all, of the skills you need to know.

The book is organized as if one were embarking on a day sail, to mirror your time on the water. In Chapter 2, The Language of Sailing, my coauthor, Michael Levitt, and I define some terms; obviously, we need a common language. You aren't, however, expected to memorize four thousand nautical terms—which there are. Fewer than one hundred terms are all recreational sailors ever use. Rather than memorizing, these sailing words will be defined repeatedly, as you move through the book, to help you commit them to memory. You'll grow comfortable with the language of sailing by seeing the words used in context. We'll also use mnemonics (memory aids) when appropriate and reference illustrations, including page numbers, should you need a quick review of a word or concept.

In Chapter 3, How Sailboats Work, we define the principles of the sport. There we show that sailing is the sport of fluid dynamics and geome-try. If that statement lacks romance, understanding this and a few basic principles from high school science can facilitate learning to sail.

In Chapter 4, First Steps, we teach you how to think like a sailor. In sailing, there normally isn't anyone telling you when and even whether to go. You must decide this in view of the weather, your boat, your ability, and that of your crew. Beyond fluid dynamics and geometry, we also show that sailing is the sport of weather. A theme of this book is introduced here: Sound planning, skillful execution, and the ability to revise your plans are keys to this sport. We also address such "housekeeping" chores as moving the boat to the water and launching it from a trailer.

Some assembly is necessary in sailing. In Chapter 5, Rigging: The Ties That Bind, we teach you how to tie the knots and to assemble the pieces of a boat. In Chapter 6, Cutting Loose, we undo those ties that bind us to land by taking leave from a beach, launching ramp, mooring, or dock. The principles of steering are also addressed. Under the supervision of an instructor or sailing friend, you are also encouraged to steer a boat on a reach (or with the wind perpendicular to the boat) and tack (bring the bow through the eye of the wind).

In Chapter 7, we describe how to sail upwind and make progress directly into the wind through tacking. If you get confused when learning to sail—and you're going to get confused—the first question to ask yourself is: Where's the wind? The likelihood is you're trying to sail too close to it. In Chapter 8, we focus on steering and trimming sails on a reach, and in Chapter 9, illustrate how to sail downwind and gybe—or turn the back of the boat through the wind.

In Chapter 10, Day's End, the boat is put to bed. This, too, involves a host of housekeeping details, such as anchoring or docking and the folding of sails.

In Chapter 11, we describe the more advanced controls: the vang or kicking strap, sheeting angle, and halyard tension, and explain how to use them in more rigorous conditions. In Chapter 12, we describe how to avoid or to recover from emergencies, such as capsize, and in Chapter 13, we describe the rules of the road—what you need to know to avoid another boat—be it a powerboat or another sailboat.

If approached cautiously and knowledgeably, sailing is a safe sport. However, make a mistake and you can capsize—particularly if you sail a small centerboard boat that, unlike a keelboat, doesn't have external ballast, or weight, to help resist capsizing. This is one reason why many people learning to sail are more comfortable, at least in the beginning, in a boat with a keel. (See the next chapter.)

Everyone is familiar with the question: Which comes first, the chicken or the egg? That has particular relevance when writing a how-to-sail book or learning how to sail.

For example, a beginning sailor can capsize a boat at any time, yet he likely doesn't have the skills—an understanding of the wind and waves— to recover from it until fairly far along in the course of study. In this book, for example, recovering from a capsize and picking up a person who has fallen overboard are not addressed until Chapter 12. While that may be a logical place for it to appear in this book, it doesn't help you very much if you've tipped over having just finished reading and learning the skills addressed in Chapter 7. That situation is analogous to me at age four, not having sufficient weight to right my nine-foot dinghy following a capsize. While I survived it, it's not something I would wish for others. That's another reason why it's valuable to have aboard a more experienced sailor.

If capsizing comes late in this text, a subject we don't address very completely is navigation. The subject is too broad, and the methods, which range from piloting with a handbearing compass to navigating by satellite, are too varied for a learn-to-sail book. It is a complication on top of a complication. Most people learn to sail first and to navigate second. That generally isn't a problem if you learn to sail with people who know more about things like navigation or seamanship than you do, as you should.

Our learn-to-sail voyage is about to begin. It might last a lifetime, as it has for me.

2 | The Language of Sailing

For better or for worse, there is a language of sailing. In the eighteenth and nineteenth centuries, sailboats were the mechanical marvels of their time, as high tech then as an F-16 fighter aircraft is today. There was no time or place for imprecise language for the sailors high in the rigging of the 235-foot *Flying Cloud*, which in 1854 sailed from New York to San Francisco in eighty-nine days and eight hours. This record stood until 1989.

From an "arse" (part of a wooden block) to a "woolder" (a lever used to tighten lines around a mast), everything had a name. There are, for example, four thousand definitions in the book *Nautical Terms Under Sail* (Crown). Misunderstanding a command or being slow to respond to one could spell the difference between "smooth-sailing," which is good, and "foundering," which is bad.

As I said, for better or for worse, there is a language of sailing. The problem with the rich language is its complexity. In the eighteenth and nineteenth century, sailing ships were fundamental to commerce and to war, while today sailing is a sport, a pastime. The complexity of its language can intimidate people; even frighten them away.

Nevertheless, we start with terminology, because to learn to sail it is necessary that we share a common language. Further, by focusing on the words, it is necessary to start explaining some of the important concepts of sailing.

While there may be four thousand terms, as I said, fewer than a hundred of them are probably all recreational sailors will ever need to know. Also, as you don't need to be fluent in French to enjoy France, you don't need to be fluent in the language of sailing to enjoy it.

Throughout this book, we will use the proper terms and define them as we go along. First usage of words commonly used in the sport will be surrounded by quotation marks. Also, at the risk of belaboring it, we will define these sailing terms repeatedly, to help you commit them to memory. You'll grow ever more familiar with the words of the sport by seeing them used in context. Again, at the danger of overdoing it, we will associate sailing words with mnemonics, common terms, or expressions: For example, The boat left port. Port and left mean the same thing. I find such associations useful memory aids. Lastly, we will reference illustrations, including page numbers for figures found in other chapters, to help you recall a definition or a salient point.

What follows is a brief discussion and several illustrations of a few dozen common sailing terms.* We will address the rest as we go along. We don't expect you to memorize these terms at this point. Just begin to become familiar with them.

Types of Boats

While there are many ways to classify sailboats, keelboats (see Figure 2.1 left) and centerboard boats (right) are the most useful categories for those learning to sail. This distinction is appropriate because you're likely learning on one or the other. Also, there are differences as well as similarities in sailing these two types of boats. The differences will be highlighted in this text.

KEELBOATS

In profile, a keel is an underwater foil that provides lift, as a wing or sail does. This lift, or force, from the keel allows a sailboat to sail as close as 45 degrees into the wind. Without this lift, a sailboat couldn't sail any closer than about 120 degrees to the wind.

Figure 2.1, left, shows a J/22, a popular keelboat. The boat weighs 1,790 pounds, while the keel alone weighs 700 pounds. As such, the keel represents 39 percent of the total weight. This weight is no accident. A worker didn't come into the boatyard office and say, "Hey, Mannie! What

*Most of the terms are also illustrated. When omitted, they have been done so to keep the drawings from becoming too cluttered.

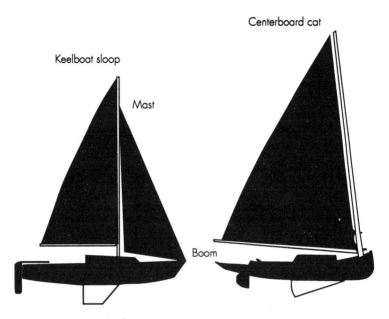

Keelboat sloop

Mast

Centerboard cat

Boom

Keel is fixed, while centerboard swings down.

FIGURE 2.1 *Comparison of a keelboat to a centerboard boat, and a sloop with two sails to a cat-rigged boat with one.*

do you want to do with that lead over there? The guys keep tripping over it." Wind in the sails causes a boat to "heel," or lean over. A keel, made of lead, which weighs 700 pounds per cubic foot, or steel, which weighs about 500 pounds per cubic foot, resists the heeling force from the sails.

Perhaps you have seen a child's inflatable punching bag with a weight on the bottom. Knock it over with a punch, and the weight at the bottom stands it upright again. That's how a keel works. This weighted fin below the boat resists the heeling forces of the sails. Because of the keel, a keelboat is much less likely to "capsize"—turn on its side—than is a centerboard boat. Many people learning to sail prefer them.

There are negatives to a keelboat as well. The weight of something and its expense go hand in hand. Also, the more something weighs, the slower it goes. In addition, a boat with a keel doesn't easily lend itself to being transported on a trailer, or to being launched at a ramp. This type of boat normally requires a hoist to lift it off a trailer and to drop it into deep water. (Hoists are far less common than are launching ramps.) Most often, keelboats are kept in the water, which is an added expense—although an added convenience. Further, this type of vessel requires careful navigation because if you run it "aground"—as running into the sea bed is known—the keel and the boat can be damaged. Finally, when run aground, it can require considerable effort to get off.

CENTERBOARD BOATS

Figure 2.1 right shows a centerboard boat. The centerboard is located on the *center*line of a boat. That is an easy way to remember the term *centerboard*.

A centerboard is only a fin that provides lift, allowing a boat to sail as close as forty-five degrees into the wind. Most commonly made of fiberglass or wood, it might weigh ten pounds. Contrast that to the keel on the J/22 that weighs seven hundred pounds. On a centerboard boat, crew weight primarily counteracts the heeling forces of the wind in the sails.

A centerboard can be raised and lowered depending on the angle of the boat to the wind. It is fully lowered when the boat is sailing at forty-five degrees to the wind—which is about as close to the wind as a boat can sail. It can be fully raised when heading in the same direction as the wind. With the board all the way up, there is a marked decrease in underwater resistance. While there are exceptions, a keel can't normally be raised or lowered.

Usually, the centerboard has a pin, holding it at the forward-lower corner. The centerboard pivots around the pin. If the centerboard hits something, it will normally pivot and do no harm.

A daggerboard (see Figure 2.2) is similar to a centerboard, except the board doesn't have a pin on the front and, thus, is unable to pivot. You push it straight down and pull it straight up. You need to be a little more careful about hitting the bottom with a daggerboard than with a centerboard.

With the board out of the way, a centerboard or daggerboard boat can sail in a foot, or so, of water. Should you run aground, you can often just lift the centerboard. Thus, navigation (i.e., worrying about the depth of the water) is less of a concern here than with a keelboat. Also, a centerboard boat is usually much cheaper to own. The vessels are easily transported on a trailer and launched, with the board up, at a common launching ramp. Such boats are easily and inexpensively stored in a backyard or garage. Also, a centerboard boat is faster and more responsive. This is due to a lack of weight and a lack of resistance caused by the ability to raise the centerboard when sailing downwind.

There are negatives to a centerboard boat as well. While properly

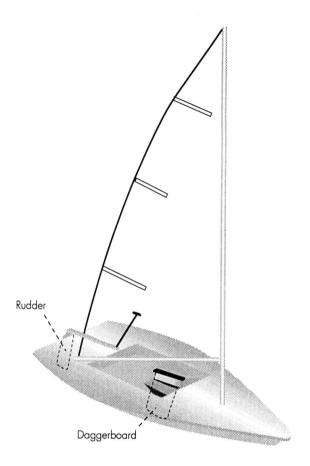

Rudder

Daggerboard

FIGURE 2.2 *A daggerboard is like a centerboard, only it doesn't pivot on an axis.*

balancing a boat is fundamental to sailing, it is more critical in a boat with a centerboard than in one with a keel. This makes the centerboard boat a good if sometimes demanding instructor. Many champion sailors got their starts in them; I am among them.

Rigs

A sailboat's rig comprises its sails and the tall mast and horizontal boom that support the sails.* A rig, due to its size, is the distinguishing feature of a sailboat. There are dozens of rig styles—similar to sailboat types—but

*There is a difference between "rig," as defined here, and "rigging," defined later. Standing rigging holds the mast, or "rig," up. Running rigging adjusts sails.

for our purposes we need only distinguish between one-sail catboats and two-sail sloops. The likelihood is you'll be learning on one or the other.

CAT RIG

A cat-rigged boat, or catboat (see Figure 2.1 right), has *one* sail—that is its most conspicuous attribute. With only one triangular sail, it tends to be oversized in comparison to the mainsail on a sloop (on a boat of similar size). The boom, the horizontal spar that supports the bottom of the sail, called a mainsail, tends to be longer, too. Because of the size of the sail, the catboat's mast, which supports the leading edge of the sail, is placed forward in the boat.

With one sail, a catboat can be less complicated to sail and, thus, to learn on than is a two-sailed sloop. However, the lack of a headsail on a catboat sometimes makes maneuvering difficult—particularly in close quarters or when it is windy.

SLOOP/RIG

A sloop (see Figure 2.1 left) typically flies two sails. Besides a triangular mainsail, as on most catboats, a sloop has a headsail—a second triangular sail in front of the mast. A headsail is a much more effective sail than a mainsail, which sits in the disturbed airflow behind the mast. Beyond contributing greatly to speed, a headsail also helps considerably in maneuvering.

A sloop also can fly a spinnaker (pronounced SPIN'uh-kuhr), a lightweight, often highly colored sail discussed later.

Parts of a Boat

The "stern," or back of the boat, is a familiar word to nonsailors as well as sailors (see Figure 2.3). The "bow"—pronounced as in when the *bough* breaks, is the front. The "hull," as depicted in the figure, is the body of a boat; it does not, however, include the mast, sails, and "rigging"—the latter being the wires and ropes that hold the mast and sails up. (See standing rigging and running rigging later.)

There is also the "topsides," any part of the boat's hull *above* the water, and the "underbody," any part of the hull that is *under* the water. The underbody includes the keel, or centerboard, and rudder.

A rudder has a series of "pintles," vertical bolts that allow it to be affixed

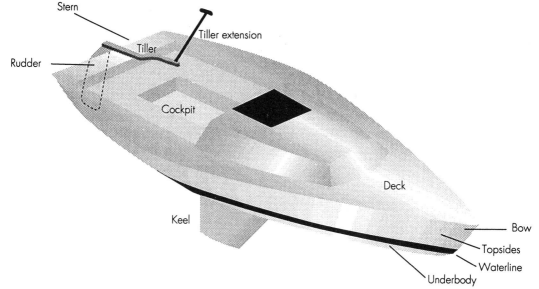

Stern

Tiller extension

Tiller

Rudder

Cockpit

Deck

Keel

Bow

Topsides

Waterline

Underbody

FIGURE 2.3 *Parts of a boat.*

to the hull through the "gudgeons"—metal clamplike devices. If words like *gudgeons* and *pintles* don't scare you off, nothing will. Every sailing book mentions them, so they are dutifully referenced here. If I've used those terms more than twice in my life, I'd be surprised.

The "waterline" is the horizontal dividing line between the topsides and the underbody. Look at a boat in the water, and you'll notice how the surface of the water seems to make a line on the hull—particularly when the water is flat. This line, or waterline, will vary according to the amount of weight in the boat, and where that weight is concentrated. If, for example, there is more weight forward than aft, the bow will be pressed down. Waterline is the sailor's equivalent of the carpenter's level. In practice, however, the waterline is a fairly broad line painted on the boat in a distinctive paint (black in Figure 2.3). It is where the designer calculates that the boat will float.

The "deck" is the platform extending from one side of a boat to the other. It is on the deck that you sit or stand. Usually, the deck is broken up by one or more "cockpits," recessed areas where sailhandling and steering are done. It is safer to work in a cockpit, because lower is generally safer than higher—except when in a flood or when chased by a grizzly. Also, in the cockpit is a wheel or alternatively a "tiller," used for steering the boat. A tiller looks like a long stick and is sometimes called a "stick." To make it longer, a tiller often has an extension, called—easily enough—a "tiller extension."

Directions

Knowing where things are or where to go, to get, or to do something is important in sailing. "Forward" and "aft" are familiar (see Figure 2.4); as is "aloft." "Below," not pictured, designates below or under the deck, which often means in the cabin. The meaning of "amidships" (not pictured) is fairly obvious, too; it means the *mid*dle of the boat, at its widest point. "Athwartships" means from one side to the other, or across a boat.

Another boat or object is "abeam" if it is at right angles to a fore-and-aft (longitudinal) line of a vessel. "Astern" is behind. "Overboard"—as in man overboard—is usually a bad place to be, as is "adrift," which means the boat is "unmoored," not affixed to land, and at the mercy of the sea. It denotes a loss of power, be it sail power or power from the engine.

Something can also be on the "port" or "starboard" side; that is, left and right, respectively, as you look forward (see Figure 2.5). As noted, you can remember the difference with the line: The boat *left* port.

A sail has a "leeward" (pronounced LUU'word) and "windward" side (see Figure 2.5), as does a boat, while there are "lee shores" and "weather shores." Leeward, or "lee," designates farther downwind, while windward and weather designates farther upwind.

When I was learning to sail forty-seven years ago, I would think of the wind as coming from the end of a hose, not as a moving wall, which it

FIGURE 2.4 *Directions on and off a boat.*

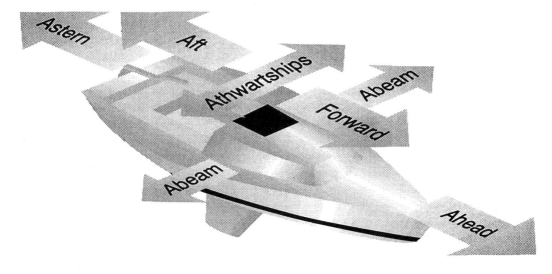

FIGURE 2.5 *Imagining the wind as spray from a hose makes it easier to see that the windward side is closer to the wind than the leeward side. Obviously, the two sides of a boat have many names: windward-leeward, port-starboard (as you look forward), and high-low.*

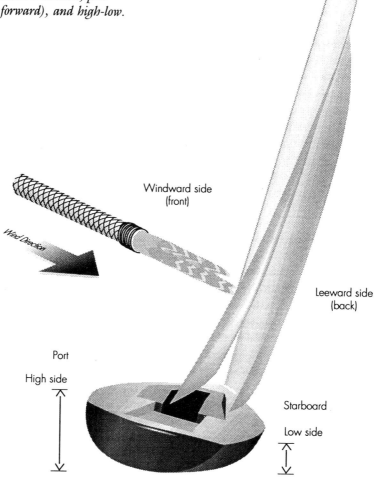

really is. Envisioning the wind coming from a hose allows it to be treated as a straight line (see Figure 2.5). This makes its relative direction to the boat's line of travel (or the wind's angle to the boat) easier to see.

Suppose you are abeam—perpendicular to that "longitudinal" line— of a boat. From this position, you turn a hose on a boat, and the *first* side the water touches is the windward or weather side. This side is, obviously, closer to the wind. An instant later it touches the leeward side, which is farther downwind. The windward side of the sails is the same as the windward side of the hull—again, it is closer to the wind. So, too, is the leeward side—it is farther from the wind.

The windward side of a sail is also often called the "front," and the leeward side, the "back." The weather shore is the shore upwind of a boat or, in this illustration, into the spray of the hose. The lee shore is downwind. Obviously, it is easier to go with the flow (downwind) than into the flow, or spray from the hose (upwind).

As described, a sailboat leans away from the wind, so when there is sufficient wind for the boat to heel, or lean, one side of the boat is *higher* than the other. The windward side is informally known as the "high side"; the reason why is apparent in the figure. The leeward side is the "low side." As a memory aid, note that the words *lee* and *low* are very similar. Also note that the sails are almost always on the leeward, low, or downwind, side.

Types of Sails

First, there are triangular sails: the mainsail and the headsail (see Figure 2.6). (As discussed, a cat rig only has one sail: a mainsail; a sloop has at least two sails: a mainsail, headsail, and sometimes a spinnaker. A spinnaker is a lightweight sail usually made of nylon used when sailing in a more downwind direction [see points of sail below].) A small headsail is a "jib," which rhymes with bib. A larger headsail is a genoa—pronounced like the city in Italy or the salami.

Parts of Sails

Returning to Figure 2.6, the bottom of a sail, or the edge closest to the deck, is the "foot," like your foot. The back edge of a sail—or the hypotenuse of the triangle—is the "leech," pronounced like a leech, the blood-sucking worm. The front part of a sail—or its leading edge—is called the "luff." "Luffing" is also the term used to describe the shaking, wrinkling, or bubbling of the front part of a sail. Luffing signals that the sails need more trim, or the boat needs to be turned farther away from the wind.

A mainsail and some headsails have "battens," which are wood, fiberglass, or carbon-fiber sticks that run horizontally and help to support the back end, or leech, of a sail. As noted, a mainsail also has a "boom"—a horizontal spar that stretches the foot, or bottom, of the sail.

The attachment points (i.e., grommets, rings, or eyelets) for the sails have names. The bottom-front attachment point of either a mainsail or

FIGURE 2.6 *Types of sails and parts of sails.*

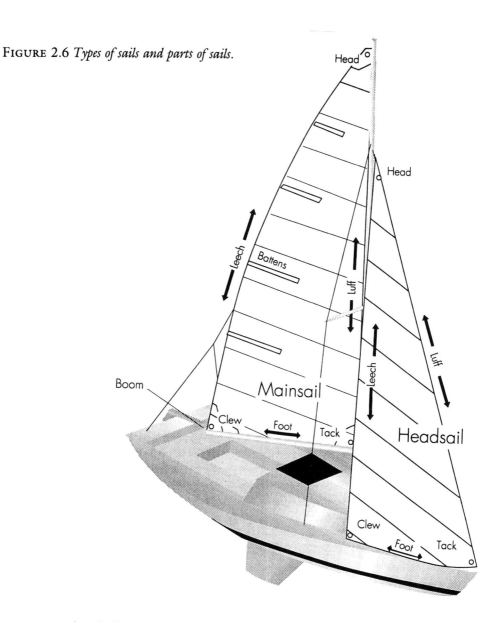

headsail is the "tack." The top ring of either sail is the "head." To confuse matters, a "head" on a boat is also the toilet compartment. The "clew"—as in I don't have a clue—is the eyelet at the back-bottom corner of a sail.

Standing Rigging

The *standing* rigging helps to keep the mast *standing*. Differing from "running rigging," discussed next, it is less likely to be adjusted when sailing.

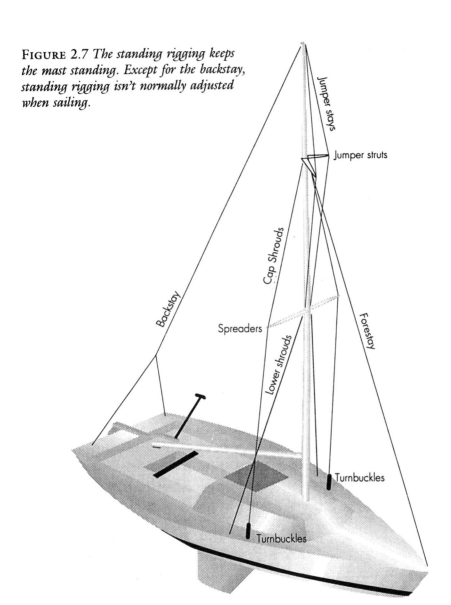

FIGURE 2.7 *The standing rigging keeps the mast standing. Except for the backstay, standing rigging isn't normally adjusted when sailing.*

Jumper stays

Jumper struts

Cap Shrouds

Backstay

Spreaders

Forestay

Lower shrouds

Turnbuckles

Turnbuckles

Standing rigging, which is most often made of wire, is generally divided into "stays" and "shrouds" (see Figure 2.7).

The "forestay" attaches to the forward, or front, part of the mast at or near the top and runs to the forward part of the deck, or bow. (It is also known as the "headstay.") The jib or the genoa normally attaches to the forestay by way of "hanks"—metal fasteners. Opposing the forestay is the "backstay," which runs from the top of the mast to the *back* of the boat. The backstay and forestay work to keep the mast from falling in the

The Language of Sailing

19

forward and backward directions. While considered part of the standing rigging, the backstay is often adjusted when sailing. It is used to bend the mast, which adjusts the shape of the mainsail and headsail (see Chapter 11).

The shrouds—pronounced as in *shroud*ed in mystery—are found on the sides of the mast and attach to the deck. They prevent the mast from falling off to one side or the other. Often they are divided into "cap shrouds" and "lower shrouds." "Turnbuckles" are used to adjust the tension of the standing rigging.

The "spreaders" are horizontal struts through which the shrouds pass. The spreaders run athwartships—from side to side. As the name indicates, the spreaders spread the angle of the shrouds—the wider angle allows the shrouds to support the mast better. (Some boats have two pairs of spreaders. If they do, they have intermediate shrouds as well as cap and lower shrouds. "Jumper struts," which are angled toward the bow, are found on many boats. Through the jumper struts run the "jumper stays," wire rigging that strengthens the top of the mast.

Running Rigging

Differing from standing rigging, the running rigging is adjusted when sailing. Hence, the designation running rigging. In this category are the ropes, or more properly "lines," used to adjust sails. (Just as people from San Francisco never say Frisco, sailors almost never say ropes.) A more precise term for a line that controls a sail is "sheet," as in bedroom sheet. This includes the mainsheet and genoa sheets, which control the mainsail and genoa (or smaller jib), respectively (see Figure 2.8). They either pull these sails in or let them out.

Also included are the "halyards" (pronounced HAL'yerds), which raise and lower sails. The halyard attaches to the top of the sail at the head. The "outhaul" tensions the foot of the mainsail. In this grouping, too, is the "boom vang" or "kicking strap" which holds the boom down.

Sailing Angles (Points of Sailing)

Earlier, I commented that it is helpful to think of the wind as coming from the end of a hose. Considered this way, wind direction can be represented as a straight line, as can the boat's direction of travel. These two lines, wind direction and boat direction, form an angle. Sailors think constantly about the vessel's angle to the wind, or sailing angles. Fortunately, there are only five angles that must be memorized: close-hauled, close-reaching, beam-reaching, broad-reaching, and running.

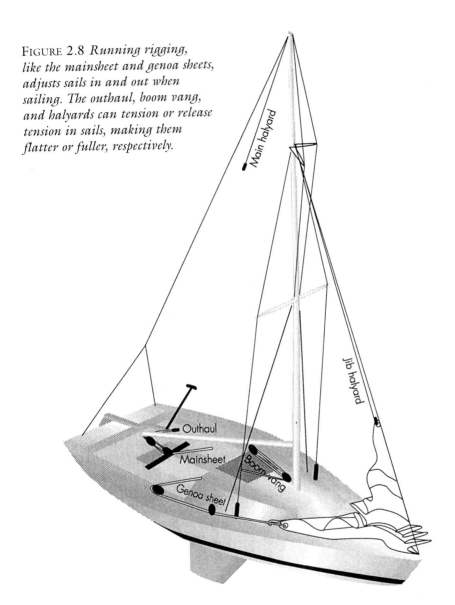

FIGURE 2.8 *Running rigging,*
like the mainsheet and genoa sheets,
adjusts sails in and out when
sailing. The outhaul, boom vang,
and halyards can tension or release
tension in sails, making them
flatter or fuller, respectively.

Main halyard

Jib halyard

Outhaul

Mainsheet

Boom vang

Genoa sheet

Let's start by putting the hose at 0 degrees, or at the top of the page (see Figure 2.9). It is blowing down, to the bottom of the page, or from 0 to 180 degrees. A wind is described by the direction from which it *comes.* Hence, a wind that comes from 0 degrees, as in the picture, is a "north wind." If the wind comes from 90 degrees (the right side), it would be an "east wind"; 180 degrees (bottom), a "south wind"; and 270 degrees (left side), a "west wind."

A sailboat can't sail directly into the wind. The closest it can sail is approximately forty-five degrees to the wind.* At a tighter angle than that the sails would not fill, and the boat would cease to make forward progress.

That means forty-five degrees on either side of the wind arrow is off limits to a sailboat. That represents an area of ninety degrees (the no-sail zone in the illustration). Note wind direction determines the makeup of

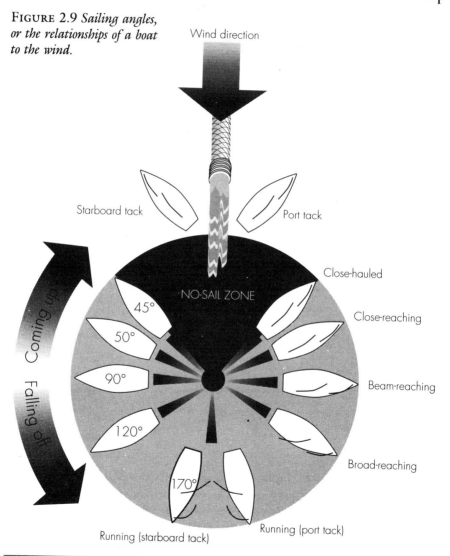

FIGURE 2.9 *Sailing angles, or the relationships of a boat to the wind.*

Wind direction

Starboard tack

Port tack

Close-hauled

NO-SAIL ZONE

Close-reaching

45°

50°

Coming up

90°

Beam-reaching

Falling off

120°

170°

Broad-reaching

Running (starboard tack)

Running (port tack)

*Some boats—such as racing boats—can sail a few degrees closer to the wind. Nevertheless, forty-five degrees is a representative, or good average, number.

the circle. If the wind was to shift ninety degrees to the right, an east wind, the no-sail zone would shift ninety degrees to the right.

Sailing as *close* to the wind as a sailboat can go, or at forty-five degrees to the wind, is known as sailing "*close*-hauled." That should be easy to remember.

After sailing close-hauled comes "reaching." A sailboat is reaching when its angle to the wind is from 50 to 170 degrees. That represents a broad band, so reaching is typically divided into "close-reaching"—when the boat's angle to the wind is about 50 degrees; "beam-reaching"—when the boat's angle to the wind is 90 degrees (a right angle); and "broad-reaching" —when the boat's angle to the wind is from 120 to 170 degrees.

Lastly, there is "running," which is or close to a dead downwind course, or from 170 to 180 degrees to the wind.

Notice that the circle has ten boats sailing ten angles rather than the aforementioned five. The right- and left-hand sides of the circle are mirror images. A boat can sail anywhere on this circle—even get to a point upwind, as will be apparent in a moment—by sailing on one "tack" or another.

A tack (not to be confused with the forward-bottom attachment point of a sail) is determined by which side of the boat the wind strikes *first*. All the vessels on the left-hand side of the circle have the wind striking the right, or *starboard*, side first. Hence, they are sailing on "starboard tack" (this is shown at the top of the illustration). Boats on the right-hand side of the circle have the wind striking their left, or *port* side, first. Thus, they are on "port tack."

Another comment about Figure 2.9. Sail trim, as shown primarily on the boats on port tack, is correct in the illustration. Note how the sails are trimmed the most (i.e., close to the centerline) when sailing close-hauled and the least when running.

While you doubtless won't understand all or even most of it yet, much of the theory of sailing is reflected in this illustration. This is an illustration to which you'll want to return.

Changing Course

Any course change that takes the *bow* of the boat *closer* into the eye of the wind is known as "coming up" (see Figure 2.9, left). As a memory aid, *closer* and *coming up* start with the letter C. Also shown in the figure, any course change that takes the bow of the boat *farther* from the eye of the wind is termed bearing away.

We are by now familiar with the no-sail zone, an area of 90 degrees total or 45 degrees on either side of the wind. If a boat strays into that area for too long, the sails can't fill, and the vessel will lose momentum and stop. It is, however, possible to use the boat's momentum to pass through the eye of the wind (see Figure 2.10), without stopping. The bow moves from 45 degrees to the wind (the close-hauled course) to 0 degrees (directly into the wind), and then to 315 degrees, where the boat can sail again on the opposite tack on a close-hauled course. An upwind turn through the eye of the wind is referred to as "tacking."

FIGURE 2.10 *Tacking is a type of turn where the bow, or front, of the boat crosses through the eye of the wind. By tacking back and forth across the no-sail zone, and sailing on a close-hauled course on one tack and then the other for an interval, a boat can make progress upwind.*

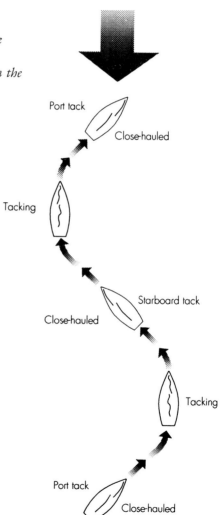

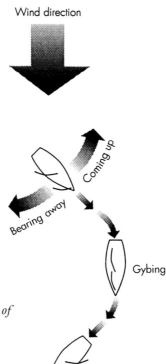

Wind direction

Coming up

Bearing away

Gybing

FIGURE 2.11 *Gybing is the opposite of tacking. By bearing away, the boat turns its back, or stern, through the eye of the wind.*

In tacking, the sails, which are, with few exceptions, always on the downwind side, will move from one side of the boat to the other.

The boat at the bottom of Figure 2.10 sails on a close-hauled course (forty-five degrees to the wind) on port tack (with the wind striking its port, or left, side first). After sailing on port tack for an interval, the vessel tacks, or turns its bow through the eye of the wind. Then it sails off on a close-hauled course on starboard tack. After sailing on starboard tack for a while, it tacks again and sails off on port tack. And so on. By doing this, the boat makes progress directly upwind. This zig-zag course is referred to as "beating."

If, by contrast, we bear away enough (turn away from the eye of the wind), the stern, or back, of the boat will cross the eye of the wind (see Figure 2.11). Again, the sails will shift from one side to the other. Note how the boat in the figure moves from port tack to starboard tack as it travels down the page. A downwind turn through the wind is called "gybing."*

---

*Recall the term for a small headsail is a jib, pronounced like the word *bib*. Gybe, however, is pronounced with a long I, as in your information doesn't *jibe* with mine.

3 | How Sailboats Work

Don't be intimidated when I say: Sailing is the sport of fluid dynamics. If that statement lacks romance, understanding this can simplify learning to sail. The fluids we are concerned with are water and air. While it may not seem so, air is a fluid, although it is 837 times less dense than seawater and 813 times less dense than freshwater.

When sailing, the sails *turn* the wind, or air, and the boat's underwater foils, or appendages—the keel (or centerboard) and rudder—*turn* the water. When both fluids are turned motion is the result.

Properly turning the wind by the sails, and the water by the underwater appendages, and balancing all the forces is almost the complete course in sailing. These things are the primary focus of world champions, world-cruisers, and day-sailors and should become a central theme, or image, for those who are just starting out in the sport.

Sailing is also the sport of geometry—the relationship of angles and points. While you can't see the wind, you must try to envision the angular relationship between the wind and boat. This, as shown in Figure 2.9, page 22, is divided into points of sail: close-hauled (with the bow of the boat at an angle of 45 degrees to the wind), close-reaching (50 degrees), beam-reaching (90 degrees), broad-reaching (120 to 170 degrees), and running (170 to 180 degrees).

While you can't see the wind, fortunately, the world is full of natural and manmade wind-direction indicators (see Figure 3.1). These include waves that typically (but not always) travel *downwind*, meaning the wind is

Wind direction

FIGURE 3.1 *Wind-direction indicators.*

usually behind (at a right angle to) the waves.* Remember, when describing wind direction, we are interested in the direction from which it *comes*—that is, a west wind comes from the west.

Other wind indicators include anchored boats and weather vanes that normally point *into* the wind. Additional indicators include flags, smoke and clouds that blow *downwind*. On boats, there are such "real-time" systems as telltales, which are ribbons in the rigging, that blow *downwind*; a masthead fly, or wind indicator, which is a weather vane–like device at the top of the mast, that points *into* the wind; and dedicated electronic indicators that present wind direction relative to boat heading on a dial or digitally.

Important, too, are weather reports on radio and television—although due to local influences and time delays, the wind may be very different where you sail. All such sources form the indispensable "Braille" of reading the wind.

Lacking the ability to see the wind means you have to use your senses better. For example, I like to judge wind speed and wind direction by

*Note, if a significant shift in wind direction is recent, there might not have been sufficient time for the waves to line up with the wind. Also, such things as currents, tides, and storms far offshore, if you're sailing on the ocean, can alter the direction of waves.

how it feels on the back of my neck. Often, before I sail in an important competition, I'll let my hair grow long. Then on the morning of the race, I'll have it cut short. This seems to increase my sensitivity on the back of my neck. As mentioned, I've even used my sense of smell to win races.

Similarly, sailors can sense if it is windy or rough by how the wheel or tiller feels in their hands; they can feel and see the boat's relative degree of heel. Sailors also listen to the wind: the whistle it sometimes makes in the rigging and the sound it sometimes makes in the sails. For example, a sail that isn't trimmed enough makes a sound similar to the snap of a flag in the wind. This is particularly true when it is windy. Without even looking, a good sailor would know if a sail needs to be trimmed by the noise it makes.

Blind people are able to sail. They do it by better utilizing the senses that they have. Those of us who aren't blind, but can't see the wind, can learn to sail, or learn to sail better, by more completely engaging our senses. That is key to the sport.

Sailing Downwind

Running with the wind—or sailing downwind—is as understandable as a kite tugging on a string on a windy day, or leaves scattering before the wind. A kite, leaves, or a sail block the wind and get pushed along in the downwind direction.

In truth, a sailboat wants to go downwind, even if you want it to go upwind. Like a ball running downhill, this can be thought of as a natural motion.

Bernoulli's Law

Sailing close-hauled, or at forty-five degrees to the wind, is more baffling. Leaves and a kite do not normally make progress into the wind. A sailboat can, however. It is this seemingly magical windward ability that allows sailors to return to where they started, or to cross oceans, no matter what the wind direction.

Upwind sailing works this way: When the wind meets a sail, the sail divides it. Some of the wind goes on the windward, or front, side, and some of it on the leeward, or back, side (see Figure 3.2). If the sail is trimmed in by the sheets, the sail *turns* the wind, as well as divides it. (Sheets, you will recall, are lines that control sails by pulling them in, or closer to the centerline, or letting them out.)

When the wind is forced to turn around a curved airfoil, like a sail, it doesn't travel at the same speed on both sides. Rather, the fluid travels faster on the back, or leeward side, than on the front, or windward side. (This difference in speed is shown in Figure 3.2 by the difference in the lengths of the arrows.)

While this speed differential on one side of a sail versus the other, or on the top of an airplane wing versus the bottom, is fundamental to sailing or aerodynamics, why this occurs fills page after page of engineering textbooks. The explanation is beyond the scope of a learn-to-sail book; indeed,

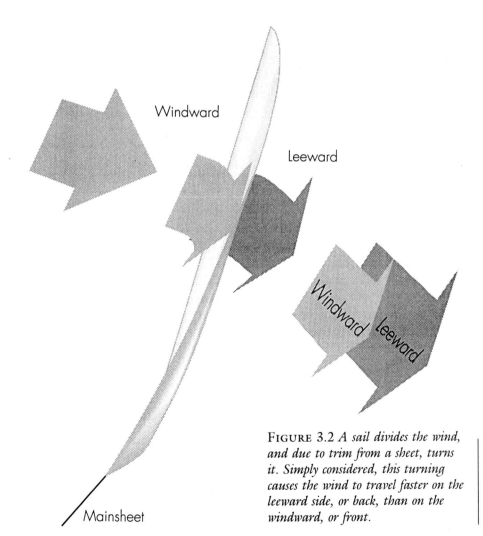

Windward

Leeward

Windward Leeward

Mainsheet

FIGURE 3.2 *A sail divides the wind, and due to trim from a sheet, turns it. Simply considered, this turning causes the wind to travel faster on the leeward side, or back, than on the windward, or front.*

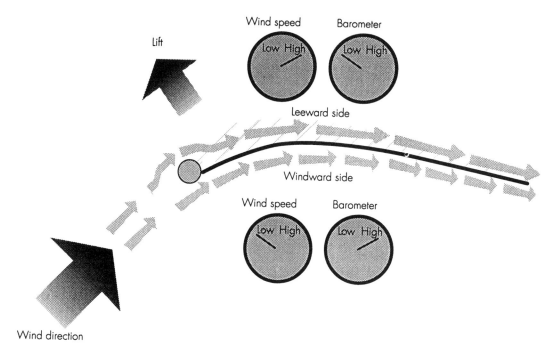

Wind speed

Barometer

Lift

Low High

Low High

Leeward side

Windward side

Wind speed

Barometer

Low High

Low High

Wind direction

FIGURE 3.3 *The barometers and wind speed indicators show the relationship between the speed of a fluid, like wind, and air pressure. Put low pressure (on the leeward side) close to high pressure (on the windward side) and a force is exerted: lift. Here, Bernoulli meets Newton.*

beyond the scope of most America's Cup crews, and skippers, or even the engineering fraternity. If you ever want to start an argument, ask two engineers *why* the wind travels faster on the back side of a sail than on the front, or faster on the top of an airplane wing than on the bottom.* This is one of the few places in this book that I just have to say this is *what* happens, not *why* it happens.

The result of this difference in wind speed on the back of the sail versus the front is a difference in air pressure. In 1738, Daniel Bernoulli, a mathematician from Switzerland, proved a relationship between fluid speed and air pressure. Bernoulli noted that the *higher* the velocity of a fluid, the *lower* its pressure. The converse is true, too: the *lower* the velocity of a fluid, the *higher* its pressure.

Applying Bernoulli to sails: on the back or "lee side" of a sail, the wind travels *faster* and, as a result, there is *lower* air pressure (see Figure 3.3). On

* For those who are interested in why, consult the book *The Art and Science of Sails* (St. Martin's, 1990), written by my good friend Tom Whidden and Michael Levitt.

the front or "windward side," the wind travels *slower* and, as a result, there is *higher* pressure. If you had two sensitive windspeed indicators on the front and back of a sail and two barometers, which show air pressure, you could measure this windspeed and air-pressure differential.

Newton's First Law

To move anything in nature, a force must be applied. Simply considered, this is Sir Isaac Newton's first law. A soccer ball remains at rest until you kick it, or the wind blows on it, or some other force acts upon it.

Place high pressure near low pressure, and a force is generated. The direction of the force is from high pressure to low pressure. An airplane flies because the wings move from high pressure to low pressure. Similarly, wind blows from high-pressure systems to low-pressure systems.

Returning to sails, the result of high pressure on the weather side and low pressure on the leeward side is a force, often termed "lift." (This, too, is shown by a thick arrow in Figure 3.3.) It is this force, or lift, that causes a sailboat to move.

You can experience this lifting force by sticking your hand out the window of a car traveling fairly fast. With your palm facing down and the back of your hand curved up like a sail or an airplane wing, your hand moves up, or from high pressure to low pressure. With the palm up, your hand moves down.

How effective is this pressure differential? you might ask. Watch a windsurfer—one of the fastest sail-powered vessels—travel at freeway-legal speeds (fifty-plus miles per hour) or, most amazingly, a Russian Antonov 225 cargo plane, which can take off with a cargo and equipment load of more than 1,100,000 pounds, and you'll see Newton and Bernoulli hard at work.

Sail Force + Underwater Foils Force = Upwind Sailing

With the force or lift from the sails, we have our sailboat moving, but it still isn't going upwind. Rather, it is sliding downwind, like leaves before the wind. To make progress against the wind, we need a *second* force, in a *different* direction from the force in the sails.

It shouldn't surprise you that this second force comes from turning of the water by the underwater foils: the keel (or centerboard) and rudder. These underwater foils divide and turn the water, creating lift, or forces, in

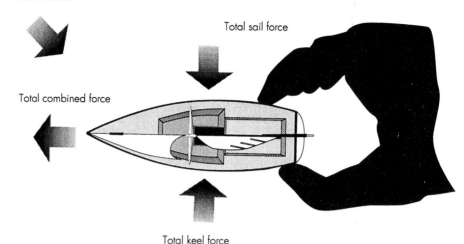

Wind direction

Total sail force

Total combined force

Total keel force

Similar to squeezing a watermelon seed, the keel, or centerboard, force and the sail force squeeze a sailboat, allowing it to sail as high as forty-five degrees to the wind.

FIGURE 3.4 *The watermelon-seed analogy, or why a sailboat can sail as close as forty-five degrees into the wind.*

their own right. As noted in the previous chapter, it is helpful to think of these foils as a boat's underwater sail plan. The total force from these underwater appendages is in the opposite direction to the total force of the sails. The combination of these two forces allows a boat to make progress against the wind.

Squeezing a watermelon seed between your thumb and forefinger is a serviceable analogy of how this works. When you squeeze a watermelon seed, it shoots forward. The squeezing of the boat by the sails and the keel forces (see Figure 3.4) allows it to sail as close as forty-five degrees into the wind. This, you will recall, is the close-hauled orientation (see Figure 2.9, page 22).

Why can't a boat sail closer than forty-five degrees to the wind? Because, if a boat tries to sail higher than that, such as forty-four degrees, the sails won't fill. The squeezing stops. Unfilled sails are analogous to an empty fuel tank in a car. In either case, you don't go.

Floating

Floating—or not sinking—is a concern of every sailor but, in particular, new sailors. Thus, it is worth exploring the principle. Two forces that act on a boat, indeed any object placed in water, are gravity and buoyancy (see Figure 3.5). Gravity—the natural pull of an object toward the center of the earth—is as familiar as Sir Isaac Newton's falling apple. Gravity, which gives an item its weight, tends to pull a boat down in the water. Buoyancy, which acts in a direction opposite to gravity, tends to push an object up.

Whether an item floats or sinks depends on whether it weighs less or more than the amount of water it displaces. A cubic foot of saltwater weighs 64 pounds; a cubic foot of freshwater weighs 62.2 pounds. An object will float if a cubic foot of it weighs *less* than 64 pounds, if in saltwater, or 62.2 pounds, if in freshwater.

Most woods will float, which is one reason why boat-builders have used wood for six thousand years. Today, very few boats are made of wood, however. The vast majority are fiberglass. Other alternatives are aluminum and, occasionally, steel.

Curiously, a cubic foot of fiberglass won't float. It weighs more than 95 pounds per cubic foot. A cubic foot of fiberglass, in fact, would sink like a stone. That's something of an overstatement because granite, for example, weighs 175 pounds per cubic foot—or nearly twice as much as fiberglass.

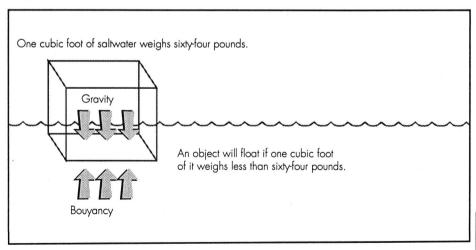

One cubic foot of saltwater weighs sixty-four pounds.

Gravity

An object will float if one cubic foot of it weighs less than sixty-four pounds.

Bouyancy

FIGURE 3.5 *An object will float in saltwater if a cubic foot of it weighs less than 64 pounds, the weight of one cubic foot of saltwater, or in freshwater if a cubic foot of it weighs less than 62.2 pounds.*

However, fiberglass boats don't contain any cubic feet of fiberglass. Within its volume, or three-dimensional shape, there is a fiberglass skin of about an inch or so in thickness, perhaps some wood furnishings, and mechanical systems, but most of the boat is air. Air weighs only .08 pounds per cubic foot.

Why a boat made of fiberglass floats—or for that matter one made of steel (493 pounds per cubic foot), or aluminum (168 pounds per cubic foot)—is analogous to why an empty tin can floats. Fill a tin can with steel (a tin can is ostensibly steel with a coating of tin), and it will, obviously, sink. Fill the can with water and it will sink, but keep the water out, and it will float.

As water flooding a tin can will cause it to sink, water flooding a boat, particularly one without added floatation, can cause it to sink. When sailing a larger boat in rough weather, sailors work to keep water from entering the cabin, or the below-decks area. This is done by closing hatches and "companionways" (doors to below-deck spaces), and, if necessary, bailing water from below decks. The danger of sinking is one reason why a leaky boat isn't desirable—indeed, can be dangerous.

Small centerboard boats, or dinghies, typically have foam built in during construction. Like a personal flotation device (PFD), this foam, which weighs about two pounds per cubic foot, provides added flotation or buoyancy. If such a boat tips over, the flotation from the foam keeps it comfortably afloat. Despite its load of water, the crew can hold on to a capsized boat for support, even stand on its centerboard to right it, without causing it to sink.

If there is a capsize, you can right these boats fairly easily, and off you go—a little wetter and perhaps wiser, but usually little the worse for wear. (Recovering from a capsize is discussed in Chapter 12.)

Heeling

While you can't see the wind, you can certainly see the effects of it—even measure it. When sufficient wind strikes the sails, it causes the boat to lean over or heel (see Figure 3.6). The more wind there is, and/or the bigger the sails, the more the boat heels. While this is a natural tendency, it can be frightening, particularly to the uninitiated.

Note, first, that heeling away from the wind is normal. A sailboat can heel twenty degrees, or even more, before requiring some significant corrective action. That twenty-degree angle, however, would likely be too close to the edge—so too close to capsizing—for the beginner. (Note how

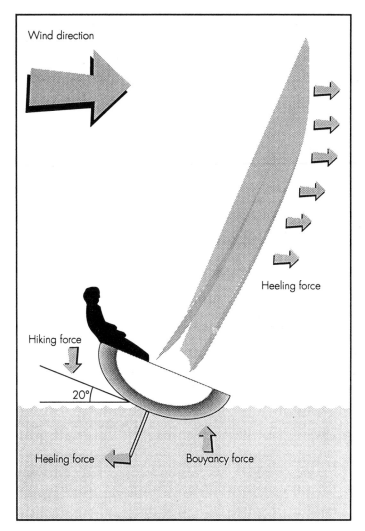

Wind direction

Heeling force

Hiking force

20°

Heeling force

Bouyancy force

FIGURE 3.6 *The wind pushing on the sails causes a sailboat to heel, or lean away from the wind: twenty degrees of heel is shown here. At some degree of heel, corrective action is required: weight on the rail or hiking, easing one or both sails, turning into the wind, reefing or changing to smaller sails.*

close the low side is to the water in Figure 3.6. This person might be more comfortable with a greater margin of safety, that is, fifteen degrees of heel or even less.)

There are things sailors can do, and the designer of your boat has done, to minimize heeling. As noted in Chapter 2, there are two types of boats:

PHOTO 3A *The farther from the centerline crew weight can be centered, the more effective it is in limiting heel. This is the principle of hiking.* (Photo courtesy Sunfish Laser, Inc.)

a centerboard boat and a keelboat. A centerboard boat depends to a large degree on moveable ballast, or crew weight, to keep it from heeling too much, even tipping over. When the centerboard boat heels away from the wind, the crew sits on the high side (see Figure 3.6). Weight on the high side decreases heeling.

If the boat continues to heel excessively, the crew may even place their feet under straps and lean out *farther*. This is called "hiking" (see Photo 3A). Hiking works because the farther from the centerline crew weight can be positioned, the more effective it is in limited heel.* Some boats even allow you to use a trapeze or hiking rack to increase the crew's distance from the centerline.

With few exceptions, keelboats don't use trapezes or hiking. However, weight on the rail is an appropriate response to excessive heeling in a keelboat, as well. For example, the Etchells is a thirty-foot, six-inch keelboat, raced by a crew of three. I finished second in the 1990 Etchells Worlds in windy Perth, Western Australia, with a combined crew weight of 800 pounds. That was an average weight of 266 pounds per man. We were the

---

* For those who remember their high school science, the measure of moment, or torque, is expressed in foot-pounds. Suppose there are two 150-pound crew members sitting on the rail, and the rail is three feet from the center of the boat. That is a righting moment of nine hundred foot-pounds, or $150 \times 2 \times 3$. Suppose they hike out so their weight is now centered four feet from the centerline. That is a righting moment of twelve hundred foot-pounds, or $150 \times 2 \times 4$.

heaviest crew by 75 pounds. I won the Worlds the next year in San Francisco—another windy venue—with an equally sizable crew.

With this weight, we could sail the boat flatter than could the lighter-weight crews. Particularly when it is windy, flatter makes a boat faster because when it heels less, the sail plan stands taller and the keel sits deeper. That translates to greater efficiency from both foils. The governing body of the Etchells class has since passed a rule limiting crew weight to 628 pounds.

Beyond weight on the rail, a keelboat has, by definition, fixed ballast, in the form of lead, iron, or steel, which resists heeling. As noted lead weighs seven hundred pounds per cubic foot. The weighted keel exerts a "righting moment"—a turning force or torque—that minimizes heel and decreases the likelihood of capsizing.

As described, a centerboard boat depends primarily on crew weight—or moveable ballast—to resist the heeling forces of the sails. This means that in a sudden puff of wind, the crew has to be quick to get their weight to the high side, otherwise the boat can capsize to leeward, or in the direction the sails are leaning. In a sudden "lull," the absence of wind, the crew has to be quick to get their weight off the high side, and into the center of the boat, otherwise the boat can capsize to windward, or in the direction the hiking crew is leaning. Puffs and lulls are fairly common in sailing.

Compare this to a keelboat that depends on moveable ballast (crew weight) *and* fixed ballast (keel weight). As such, a keelboat is much more forgiving of mistakes that have to do with improperly balancing a boat, or being slow to balance it, than is a centerboarder. Therefore, sailing a keelboat can be less physically demanding than sailing a centerboard boat.*

Beyond moveable and fixed ballast, there are things sailors can do to minimize heel. If your boat—be it a keelboat or centerboarder—heels too much, ease the sails. Another response to excess heeling is to turn the boat slightly into the wind (see Figure 2.9, page 22). This can be done instead of easing the sails, or at the same time.

Turning into the wind and easing sails are short-term solutions, however, to too much wind. A more complete solution to too much power from the sails and too much heeling is to decrease the size of the headsail and the main through a sail-shortening process known as "reefing". Alternatively, a headsail can be changed to one of a smaller size. Reefing and headsail changes are discussed in Chapter 11.

---

*There are exceptions to this rule, but the statement is generally true.

4 | First Steps

When learning to ski, you wouldn't start on an experts' run. Similarly, when learning to sail, don't take your first steps on a day that would test the mettle and abilities of an expert sailor. As the old saying has it: you have to learn to walk before you can run.

In sailing, there aren't signs with black diamonds designating experts' runs as there are in skiing. There couldn't be, as a change in the wind, for example, could turn the beginners' slope to the experts' slope without much warning.

Thinking Like a Sailor

A beauty of sailing—at least for me—is that the trail is unmarked, for the most part. There aren't, generally, signs or authorities telling you what to do and where and when you can do it, as there are in many other pastimes. The tradeoff for this freedom is that you must make intelligent decisions about where and even whether to go.

Fundamental to learning to sail is to think like a sailor. Ask yourself: Are the weather forecast and conditions I see appropriate to my abilities, my crew, and my boat, or beyond them? When in doubt, don't go. This question should be asked by the beginning sailor and expert alike, and asked each time you are planning a departure.

Weather being what it is, too few days are perfect—unless you live in San Diego. Therefore, you must decide how much this day and place vary from the best possible day and place. You want a perfect or nearly perfect day in the beginning. In other words, stick to the bunny slope when a beginner. However, as your abilities improve, you'll be able to handle—indeed enjoy—more advanced conditions. Of course, if you're sailing with an instructor or experienced sailor, as you should be when learning to sail, you can venture out in a wider range of conditions.

To help you decide where and even whether to go sailing requires a brief discussion of the conditions that delineate the playing field. In sailing, the playing field is defined by weather, seas, current, how complicated an area is to navigate in, the time of the year and time of the day, and communications (that is, is help readily available should you need it?).

This discussion also allows me to point out some things you should do, some things you should never do, and some things you should bring along to make your sailing safer or more enjoyable. Also described in this chapter is simply moving the boat to the water on a trailer or on the roof of a car. There is a wrong and right way to do that. It is important, I think, that you take your first steps into the sport with the proper attitude, equipment, and technique.

Weather to Go?

Earlier, I commented that sailing is the sport of fluid dynamics and geometry. It is also the sport of weather.

At any level, sailing is absolutely dependent on the weather. It sets the tone, from what you wear, to when, where, and even whether you go. Thus, to learn to sail, you need to begin to think about weather and become familiar with its patterns. If you aren't someone who enjoys the rich variety of weather, I doubt you'll ever be much of a sailor.

For sailors within UK coastal waters and northern Europe, an excellent source of weather information is provided by the BBC Radio 4 shipping forecasts, broadcast at 0033, 0555, 1355 and 1750 hours (UK clock times) on 198kHz (1515m and on local MF frequencies daily). Gale warnings are also broadcast at the earliest juncture after receipt and also after the next news bulletin. There is also an excellent automatic telephone weather service known as Marinecall, which is updated by the British Meteorological Office at least twice a day (three times in summer).*

When monitoring this source, as well as forecasts on television, radio, and in newspapers, pay close attention to wind speed, wind direction, air and water temperature, and barometer readings. Listen carefully for words such as *the passage of a cold front, a chance of thunderstorms, gale warnings,*

---

*With a VHF radio, Coast Guard and coastal radio station weather broadcasts can be monitored.

hurricanes and strong wind warnings.[*] These are the sailor's equivalent of a skier's black diamond; warnings that this day or this place can well be for experts only and maybe not even for them.

Another thing to consider is the amount of wind. When just starting out in the sport, you want some wind, maybe up to ten knots, not, however, a total absence of wind. Too much and you're on the experts' slope; too little wind, maybe under three or four knots, and there may not be sufficient power to make forward progress.

Also important are the temperatures of the air and the water. Most simply consider: Is it a warm, cool, or cold day? In most parts of the world, warm temperatures are better than cool or cold temperatures when sailing. This is because sailboats usually come with their own natural air conditioner: wind and spray, which can be remarkably effective.

You'll need to have good, waterproof foul-weather gear, and if it is cold, undergarments made of materials like wool, polypropylene, or some space-age fabric that continues to insulate even if it gets wet. However, foul-weather gear should never be left in a hot place as heat can ruin it.

Also consider: Is this late July or August, when the water is likely to be as warm as it gets in the Northern Hemisphere, or April or May, when it is likely to be cold? Again, warm is better, particularly if you sail a small centerboard boat that is close to the water and can capsize.

Cold must be considered the mortal enemy of sailors, should their boat capsize, should they fall overboard or be insufficiently dressed. The problem is hypothermia, a lowering of the core temperature of the body. Hypothermia starts when the body's temperature drops below ninety-five degrees Fahrenheit (thirty-five degrees Celsius). It is possible to become hypothermic in water that is seventy degrees or warmer. Some early symptoms include shivering, a loss of color, bluish lips, loss of muscle control, and a lackadaisical attitude. How quickly symptoms appear has to do with the temperature of the water or air and the length of the exposure.

If you suspect someone is suffering from hypothermia, remove his wet

---

[*]In sailing, wind speed and boat speed are traditionally given in knots, or nautical miles per hour. A nautical mile is a measure of distance that is 1.15 statute or land miles. So a ten-knot wind is actually a wind that travels at 11.5 mph. A strong wind warning is posted when winds are expected to be twenty-five knots or more or when dangerous sea conditions are likely. A gale is for winds from thirty-four to forty knots; "severe gale" is for winds of forty-one to forty-seven knots; a "storm" denotes wind speeds of forty-eight to fifty-five knots and a "violent storm" brings winds of fifty-six to sixty-three knots. A hurricane is for winds above sixty-four knots. Note that while the passage of a cold front is typically a dramatic weather event, the approach of a warm front—although it can be accompanied by rain—is usually not a problem for sailors.

clothes. Then wrap him in warm blankets or a sleeping bag to warm him *gradually*, not quickly such as by giving a warm bath. Warming a hypothermic person too fast can cause dangerous heart rhythms. Another person in the sleeping bag or under the blankets can help in gradually raising the temperature of the hypothermic person. Give the person warm but not hot liquids, such as milk or soup. Don't give alcohol or stimulants like coffee or tea, however. Immediate medical attention is imperative. If unchecked, hypothermia can result in death.

When listening to weather forecasts, also pay attention to what is said about the barometer and wind direction. A steady or slowly rising barometer, which indicates air pressure, means settled or fair weather. This can be a good day to go sailing. A rapidly falling barometer, though, combined with winds from the east, indicates unsettled, or foul, weather. That's a day to avoid—particularly when taking your first steps. A rapidly rising barometer indicates windy conditions, although generally fair weather. While this can make for challenging conditions for an intermediate or expert, it is not appropriate for the beginner.

Current Affairs

The ideal place to learn to sail shows an absence of tide or current. "Tide" is the *vertical* rise and fall of the water caused by the relative positions of the earth, moon, and sun. Tide is experienced on oceans, ocean bays, and on rivers, close to where they empty into oceans. "Current", or "tidal stream", is the *horizontal* movement of the water, which can be found on oceans, on rivers, even on lakes. Some causes of current are gravitational pull (i.e., water flowing downhill) or a strong wind blowing from the same direction for a day or two, whereas tidal stream is caused by the rise and fall of the tide. Both tidal stream and current can take a boat off course without your being aware of it. If you must learn to sail in a place where there is tide, do it with someone who is an experienced instructor or sailor. Further, start at times when the tidal stream is running slowly. The times of high and low tides are provided in some marine forecasts, newspapers, and on some VHF weather announcements. The water moves slowest an hour or so before, until an hour or so after the tide change. So, if according to the weather forecast, the tide will change at 1:00 P.M. little tidal movement, or a "slack water," can be expected from noon to 2:00 P.M. This is true whether the change is from high tide to low tide or low tide to high tide.

Some places have small tides: a few feet of difference between low and high water. Other places have considerably greater differences: more than five feet between low and high tide.* If you must sail in an area with tide, opt for one with a small difference.

Current, however, doesn't lend itself to prediction, as does tidal stream. Sailors should be aware of its existence and watch for its effects: that is, being taken off course. One sign of current is when anchored, or moored, boats don't face into the wind (see Figure 3.1, page 27). You should know that the current is strongest where the water is deepest, such as in a channel where deep-draft boats travel. It is also strongest around points of land.

The Bottom: Out of Sight, Not Out of Mind

You also want a venue that is easy to navigate in—that is, one without too many hidden rocks, shallows, shoals, or other navigational hazards. When learning to sail, you'll have enough to pay attention to without worrying about what's under the boat, which you usually can't see. Some areas start shallow, get deep quickly, and stay that way. There aren't many rocks, shallows, or other hazards lurking just under the surface that your boat might strike. Such a place is best when learning to sail.

If you aren't familiar with an area, sail with someone who is. Moreover, talk to people about hazards to navigation. Learn where the water is safe and where it isn't. Note navigational aids, like buoys. As there is a reason for traffic lights and stop signs, there is a reason that a buoy is placed where it is. For example, it might mark a rock, shoal, or wreck. Orient yourself with landmarks ashore. Additionally, find a chart of the area, if there is one. A chart shows navigational buoys, hazards, as well as the depth of the water.

When to Go?

Timing is important, too, when learning to sail. In most places, the wind tends to blow more in the afternoon especially in the summer—after the land has warmed up—than in the morning or early evening. (The temperature differential between the land and water affects wind strength.) Particularly if you sail in a place that can be windy, the morning can be the best time to take your first steps. This is because the temperature differential isn't as

*This information is often published in local newspapers and it appears in the *Macmillan and Silk Cut Yachtsman's Handbook* and *Reed's Nautical Almanac*, both published annually in Great Britain. Most good chandlers will sell or give you a tide table for the area. To work out variations in the depth of water between high and low tide, you must have a reference plane, which is known as chart datum (CD). The depth at any given position is denoted by a number on the chart which refers to the depth of water above, or below, if the number is underlined, CD. To this number must be added, or subtracted if the number is a negative one, the height of tide at the time in question (worked out from the tide table) to give the actual depth in that spot at the time in question. All numbers are in meters.

great. While early evening can be appropriate, too, the wind often blows offshore in the evening, or dies altogether, sometimes making it more difficult to return to land. Also, if you get into trouble at day's end, it can mean a long night waiting for help.

Similarly, there is typically less wind in the summer than in the spring and fall. Cold water and warm land, which characterize the spring and fall in many places, can make for windy and shifty conditions in terms of direction. Shifty wind, too, isn't desirable as it can easily confuse the beginner.

Also, if you're just learning to drive a car, you probably wouldn't want to drive in rush-hour traffic. Likewise, when you're learning to sail, you shouldn't make your debut in the middle of the Solent during Cowes Week.

On the other hand, you shouldn't make your first forays when there is no one likely to see you should you encounter difficulties. This speaks for sailing close to popular spots, such as in front of a busy club or close to a public beach—not far from the watchful eye of a lifeguard or other person. This can mean you'll be performing before an audience—something that many people don't find conducive to learning. However, should you get into trouble, such a public display is better than being out of sight and out of mind.

Safety First

As stated earlier, my father gave me a nine-foot dinghy when I was four. He allowed me to take the boat out in the harbor, provided that I wore a lifejacket. The lifejacket was this big overstuffed straitjacket that made swimming impossible. The boat would capsize, and there was absolutely nothing I could do to extricate myself except hold on to the boat and wait for someone in another boat to come along and rescue me. Since then, I've never been comfortable in the water and never learned to swim.

I retell this story for several reasons: My history aside, the first requirement in learning to sail is to be a swimmer. The second reason is to make the point that no matter how good a swimmer you are, never abandon a floating boat—no matter how close the shore appears.

My third point is to emphasize the importance of wearing a buoyancy aid or lifejacket when sailing. This is imperative if you sail a centerboard boat that can capsize, but it is a very good idea if you sail a keelboat, too, particularly in more rigorous conditions. While these boats are less likely to capsize, people can and do fall overboard. The U.S. Coast Guard says that 80 percent of boating deaths are related to failure to wear a buoyancy aid or lifejacket.

In the UK, there is no law governing lifejackets or buoyancy aids for the amateur sailor and his crew but the Royal Yachting Association (RYA) strongly recommend at least one lifejacket per person on a yacht, or one buoyancy aid per person in a dinghy or centerboard boat as a minimum, and at least one throwable lifebuoy on a keelboat or yacht. Boats used commercially, however (e.g. sail-training boats), are bound by regulations, as are all sail-training establishments in relation to such safety equipment.

Fortunately, buoyancy aids and lifejackets are more comfortable these days than when I started out in the sport. It is important to note that a buoyancy aid won't float an unconscious person face up. A lifejacket is most likely to do that provided that it is inflated.

A lifejacket that inflates automatically when it hits the water is probably the safest and most comfortable option.

Coast Guard Requirements

Beyond buoyancy aids and lifejackets, it is strongly advisable to carry certain other safety equipment, such as fire extinguishers. It is mandatory in a vessel over 7 meters (23 feet) long to carry navigational lights and sound-signalling equipment. Write or telephone the Royal Yachting Association on 0703 629962 for a list of recommended equipment. When sailing at any level or at any place, you absolutely should comply with the RYA recommendations and the law.

It is also essential to brief each crew member on the use and stowage of all the boat's safety equipment before setting off. A list should be posted in an obvious place.

EFFICIENT SOUND SIGNAL

According to the "International Regulations for Preventing Collisions at Sea" (known as the "Collision Regs"), recreational vessels of twelve meters (39.4 feet) or less must have a means of making "an efficient sound signal." This might be a whistle, bell, or gas-filled horn. While the requirements are vague for vessels of this size, an inexpensive hand-held gas horn, with a range of at least a half a mile, is probably best.

Boats larger than that are required to carry on board a power whistle or power horn, a bell and, in some cases, a gong. These sound-producing devices are used when meeting another vessel or when operating in fog. This is described more fully in Chapter 13.

FIRE EXTINGUISHERS

The Macmillan and Silk Cut Yachtsman's Handbook recommends the following: for boats up to 12 meters (30 feet) in length with cooking facilities and engine(s) "two extinguishers each not less than 3 lbs (1.4 kg) of the dry powder type". For similar-size boats with cooking facilities or engine only, one extinguisher of the above size and type. Foam extinguishers of equivalent capacity are another alternative but CO_2 extinguishers are too heavy for small-boat use. BCF (bromo-chloro-difluoro-methane) or BTM (bromo-trifluoro-methane) types are also acceptable but crew must be warned that the fumes they produce are dangerous in confined spaces and a notice to this effect should be displayed boldly near each extinguisher.

A fire blanket should also be carried for use on cooking-fat fires and so should at least one bucket with a "lanyard", or rope, attached. Never use water on a fat or fuel fire, or any burning liquid, as it will react dangerously and cause the fire to spread in all directions. It is also advisable to avoid using water on electrical fires. Finally, a bag of sand is very useful for smothering small fires.

Further details can be found in the British Home Office pamphlet "Fire Precautions in Pleasure Craft" (HMSO).

Always ensure that fire-fighting appliances are in-date and fully serviced.

VISUAL DISTRESS SIGNALS

Coast Guard-approved visual distress signals are also recommended if you sail in coastal or offshore waters, or on large rivers or lakes.

While some boats need not carry approved signals, know that if you need help and are visible to others, waving both arms over your head (see Figure 4.1), waving an orange flag (with a black square and ball), or a piece of orange cloth are commonly recognized distress signals.

---

*By law, you need not carry a fire extinguisher if your boat is not a commercial vessel or over 13.5 meters (45 feet) in length. However, if there is any place on the boat where trapped fuel vapors can collect, or if you have an engine, fuel, cooking gas, paraffin or pyrotechnics on board, you should carry at least one fire extinguisher.

FIGURE 4.1 *Waving both arms over your head is a commonly recognized distress signal. It is even more effective if you wave an orange cloth. Also, the higher you are, the more visible you will be.*

Note that there are two types of visual distress signals: "nonpyrotechnic devices" and "pyrotechnic devices," in the language of the Coast Guard. Nonpyrotechnic visual distress signals include the aforementioned orange distress flags and waving your arms—used during the day. At night, you can signal with a flashlight. Use the Morse code SOS-distress signal, which is three short flashes, three long flashes, and three short flashes (or . . . - - - . . .). If you sail on "inland waters," a lake, a high-intensity white light flashing at regular intervals from fifty to seventy times per minute is considered a distress signal. (See Rendering Assistance below.)

Pyrotechnic visual distress signals include hand-held red flares and parachute rocket flares—both of which are appropriate day and night. Also included are hand-held, or buoyant floating, orange smoke signals—used during the day only. If you do carry pyrotechnic devices, a minimum of two hand-held red flares for night or day use and two hand-held orange flares, for daytime only, are recommended if staying inshore (within three miles of the coast).

Pyrotechnic devices can be dangerous and should be used with caution. Know how to use them before you might need them.

Other Recommended Equipment

Essential on a yacht is at least one harness and lifeline per crew member, including the skipper. This enables all concerned to attach themselves to strong points on the boat by a long strap to allow mobility. These should always be worn in rough conditions when a man overboard is more likely.

A Red Cross St. John Ambulance *First-Aid Manual* and a first-aid kit should be carried aboard. Other first-aid books aimed at sailors include *Advanced First Aid Afloat*, by Peter Eastman, *The Ship's Captain Medical Guide* (HMSO).

A suitable anchor and long anchor chain or "warp" (rope) must also be aboard.* A paddle, or oars, should be carried in case the wind ceases to blow. A paddle is also useful to propel a boat away from a launching ramp or into deep water, where the rudder can be affixed to the boat (see the next chapter). Should the rudder break, use the paddle for emergency steering.

An assortment of tools is also a good idea; this should include a sharp knife, pliers, screwdrivers in assorted sizes and head types and a hammer. A bolt cutter is important should the mast ever break and you are forced to cut the shrouds to prevent the mast from damaging the boat. A flashlight also comes in handy, and a pump or bucket is a must. Tie the bucket to the boat, so it isn't lost if you capsize. Extra line is always a good idea as is a sponge, which can be used for bailing. Duct tape, too can prove invaluable.

Also essential are a spare anchor, heaving line, fenders, mirror, search-light, sunburn lotion, life buoy, a chart of the area where you're sailing, compass, boat hook, mooring lines, food and water, binoculars, spare batteries, sunglasses, marine hardware, extra clothing, including foul-weather gear, and extra parts.

For about £150, or so, a hand-held VHF radio can be a lifesaver if you get into trouble while sailing. This is particularly appropriate for the beginner. The Coast Guard monitors channel 16 on the VHF band.

---

*Anchoring is discussed in Chapter 10.

Obviously, before going to sea, you should know how to use the radio. Be warned that the Radiocommunications Agency requires a ship station license for all vessels equipped with marine VHF radios and the operator needs a "Restricted Certificate of Competence in Radio Telephony VHF Only" from the Department of Transport, for which he must pass a simple exam. This does not apply to Citizens Band Radio (CB).

In matters of life and death, start an *emergency* call on channel 16 with the salutation "Mayday" to get the Coast Guard's immediate attention.

There is coverage for portable cellular phones in most coastal areas. Have the Coast Guard's emergency number and that of the local police or rescue service handy—even programmed in your phone. From any telephone, the 999 emergency number will get you through to the Coast Guard.

Rendering Assistance

If at sea you receive a distress signal by any means and you are in a position to give assistance, you are obliged to do so with all speed, unless or until you are specifically released by the authority controlling the rescue (usually HM Coast Guard).

Passage Plan

It is a good idea to tell a reliable person where you will be sailing, when you intend to leave, and for how long you intend to be out. This is called a "passage plan."

They should have a complete description of your boat, its color, size, make, and rig type, and any other information that will help in its identification. A description of your car and its license number can be helpful in determining where you launched from if you trailer your boat. It is also helpful for the Coast Guard to know what safety or survival equipment you carry and whether you have aboard a marine radio, cellular phone, or CB. It is also helpful to know the names and addresses of people aboard, and if anyone has a medical condition.

If you haven't returned when you said you would, this person should contact the authorities. Obviously, you should contact the person holding the passage plan when you return.

Car-Topping

Sailors must know a variety of skills. One important first step is simply moving the boat to the water and then bringing it home again. You may never have to do this if you keep your boat at a marina or club year round. You may have to move your boat by car every time you use it if you keep it at home. The obvious advantage of keeping a boat at home is the tremendous cost saving. The savings are at the expense of convenience, however. If you opt to keep your boat at home, be warned that a boat in the backyard is not looked upon favorably by all neighbors. There may even be laws against it in some communities.

Small boats, like a windsurfer, the popular Sunfish, or a Laser, can be carried on the top of a car. This method of transport, known as "car-topping," makes for easier driving than pulling a boat on a trailer.

As a boat blowing off the top of your car is the last thing you want—it is also the last thing the person following you wants—match the rack to the weight you intend to carry. Also, match it to the car and attach it correctly. Better rack manufacturers have several models to fit most cars. Don't risk your £1,500 boat—or a £150,000 lawsuit—on a £25 rack. The rack should, also, be well padded so as not to damage the boat.

Note that with many roof racks, a Sunfish or Laser, which weigh about 130 pounds, are close to—if not over—the maximum specified loads. Be certain to get a maximum load from the store where you are buying such a rack and don't exceed it. Remember, too, that the mast and boom can add several more pounds to the total, so if you carry them on the rack, take their weight into consideration. You can better disperse the load by using a third or even a fourth support.

Most boats are oriented on a rack with the bow, or front, facing forward, and the boat upside down. This orientation provides better gas mileage and makes for less wind noise and a more stable ride for the boat and car.

Before lifting the boat, it should be facing forward, in the upside-down position, on the ground, and near to the car. Three strong people or four or more normal ones can lift a Sunfish or Laser and put it on top of a car. About thirty-five pounds of boat per person is a good rule. Lift the boat carefully with your legs, not your back, and with your back straight. Your head should be horizontal, not looking down or up. Balance the load between the front and the back supports.

If the trunk on your car isn't too long, a couple of people can put a small boat on the top of a car (see Figure 4.2) without too much trouble. First drive the car to the boat—the latter should be upside down with its bow pointed toward the back of the car. Then carefully lift the front of the boat and place it on the back support, which must be well padded. Then lift the back of the boat (see lifting technique, above) and gently slide it forward and onto the rack. Again, balance it between the front and rear supports.

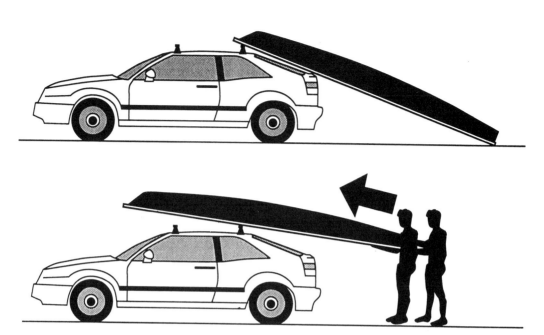

FIGURE 4.2 *How two people can put a small boat like a Sunfish or Laser on top of a car. Not all cars lend themselves to this method, however.*

With the straps, tie the boat tightly enough so it can't blow off, but not so tightly that it distorts the hull. Also, check the tension on the straps or ropes from time to time as synthetic materials, like nylon and Dacron (also called polyester), commonly used in strap or rope construction, stretch. While this is true all the time, it is particularly true when they get wet. It is also a good idea to tie the bow and stern to the front and rear bumpers, respectively.

Better racks have fittings to carry the mast and boom. Make sure that all such pieces are properly secured. When loading or unloading the boat, mast, and rigging, etc., be certain there are no close-by electrical overhead cables. If these pieces encounter cables, electrocution is possible.

Using a Trailer

In placing a boat on a trailer, position it upright (as it floats in the water), and with the bow, or front, forward. That may seem obvious, but when I crewed on my first Star boat in 1968, Alan Raffee, my skipper, and I didn't even know which direction to put it on the trailer. The first time we did it, we put the boat on backward. Nevertheless, we finished second in the

Olympic trials that year to Lowell North. If we had beaten North in the last race, we would have gone to the Olympics. North, the noted sailmaker, won that race and then a gold medal in the Olympic Games in Mexico.

Also, be sure that the boat is properly balanced on the trailer: side to side, and fore and aft. You want the car, or truck, to take some of the load. Make certain that your vehicle can pull such a load as many small- and even medium-sized cars can't. Carefully secure the boat to the trailer, the trailer to the car's hitch, and then use the safety chains. From time to time, check the ties holding the boat to the trailer and the trailer hitch.

Other practical and legal requirements include lights on the back of the trailer, indicating stopping and turning. Also, trailers must display number plates; make sure you have one with the same number as the car. If you pull a heavy boat, trailer brakes can be helpful, even a legal requirement. Cars pulling trailers might not be allowed on certain roads. You should check with the proper authorities to be certain you conform to all local laws.

Driving with a boat on a trailer requires some practice. You must take right turns a little wider, so the trailer doesn't jump the curb or hit a parked car. Remember, when pulling a trailer you are driving two vehicles rather than one, and frequently the vehicles are at cross purposes. If you are towing a keelboat, in particular, which sits higher on the trailer, you have to watch that your boat doesn't exceed the vertical clearances for bridges, tunnels, etc.

If going forward with a trailer has its challenges, backing up can be even more daunting. To get the boat to back *left*, the car has to back *right* (see the right-hand illustration in Figure 4.3). To get a boat to back right, the car has to back left (see the left-hand illustration). To get the trailer to back straight, both the trailer and car have to be in a straight line (see center illustration). The car's front wheels must be straight, too.

When backing a boat on a trailer, look over your left shoulder and don't turn the car's steering wheel too sharply, as the trailer can easily jackknife. If the car and trailer jackknife, go forward and start again. You have to get the trailer turning in the proper direction, but always be aware where the car or truck is heading, which is typically the opposite direction.

When backing, it helps considerably if you have someone directing you with words and hand signals from outside the car. Obviously, turn off the air conditioner and radio and open all the windows to hear the instructions more easily. All of this may sound daunting, but practice helps considerably. As a dress rehearsal, you might wish to practice driving with a trailer and backing it up at home before taking to the road or the launching ramp. On the road or at the launching ramp, it is often show time.

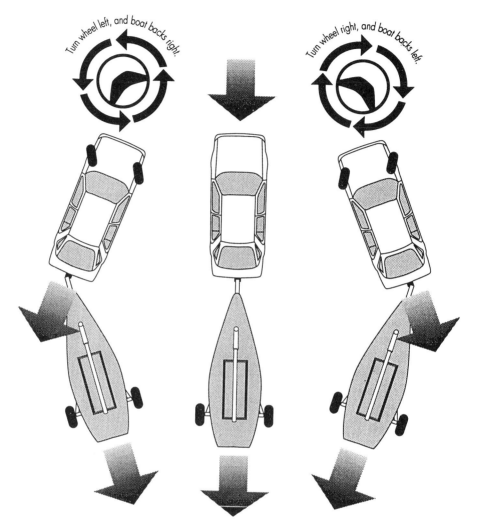

FIGURE 4.3 *Turn the steering wheel left to get the boat to back right and vice versa.*

It is best to launch a boat at a specially designed launch ramp. Such public-access ramps, common to many lakes and coastal communities, are typically paved, which helps the wheels of your car maintain traction, which is important. Also, if correctly designed, the ramp is oriented at the proper angle.

If the launching site is sandy, rather than paved, you can release air from the tires of your car to improve traction. Don't forget, however, to refill the tires before taking to the highway.

Better trailers allow you to extend the front end, or tongue. This makes the trailer longer, so the wheels of the vehicle need not go too deeply into the water or into it at all. Keeping the wheels of your car dry improves traction, which can be critical when pulling a trailer or the boat and trailer up the ramp. This also protects the wheels from the corrosive action of the water—especially saltwater. If you've extended the tongue to launch the boat, collapse it again before taking to the highway.

A boat on a trailer is normally launched with the mast up (see next chapter) and the sails rigged but not hoisted. So again, watch out for electrical wires. Also, if your boat has a drain plug or plugs and self-bailers, they should be in place and closed *before* launching.

Back the trailer into the water until the back end of the boat starts to float. Before pushing the boat off the trailer, take hold of the bow line to maintain contact with the boat. Once afloat, walk the boat or paddle it away from the launch area, to make room for the next boat. Then paddle it to a pier or temporary mooring or beach it. If two people are in a boat being paddled, one steers with the tiller, while the other paddles from a position ahead of the shrouds—the side stays that hold up the mast. If only one person is in the boat, it is easier—but not easy—to paddle the boat backward, or stern first, from the "transom," or back of the boat.

If you are beaching the boat, never leave it partway in the water and partway out. In this betwixt and between position, waves can damage it.

You can't have too many friends, or instant acquaintances, if you must lift a small boat and carry it into the water. As described, about thirty-five pounds of boat per person is a good rule of thumb—or back. A launching trolley, which the boat sits on, can make this easier. If the trolley has wide tires, it is less likely to get bogged down in sand.

Usually, keelboats require a hoist to lift the boat off the trailer and into the water. Be certain that your boat isn't too heavy for a particular hoist and that the boat is supported in the proper places. This should be done according to the boat manufacturer's instructions. As boats are typically hoisted with the mast up and the sails on but not raised, be sure that there aren't electrical overhead cables near hoists or launching sites. Make sure that no person or boat is directly underneath the hoist in case the boat falls.

5 | Rigging: The Ties That Bind

In sailing, as in most facets of modern life, some assembly is necessary. For example, the battens, which support the leech, or back, of the mainsail must be properly inserted. Then the foot, or bottom, of the mainsail must be fed into the boom, and its luff, or front, fed into the mast. The headsail also needs to be "hanked" (affixed) to the forestay or fitted into the groove there. The sheets, used to trim the sails, must be tied to the sail and run aft. To be perfectly candid, in sailing, *considerable* assembly is necessary.

"Rigging", as assembling the pieces of a sailboat is termed, is pleasant work, however. People who like boats don't seem to mind working on them. Also, working on or near the water is inherently satisfying—at least for me. As noted, if you're the kind of person who doesn't find satisfaction in work, sailing is probably not the sport for you.

With some familiarity, the job of rigging a sailboat goes very quickly. If you assemble a bicycle for your child on Christmas Eve, it's going to take two or three painful hours. If, however, you assemble ten bikes, by the time you get to the last one it's likely to take only thirty minutes. Rig a sailboat ten times, and it'll take minutes, not hours.

Knots

Much of the work in sailing is accomplished by pulling or easing lines (remember, with few exceptions ropes on sailboats are called lines) that are tied to sails. A fundamental skill in working with lines is tying knots that make the attachments.

Elsewhere, I have commented that sailing is a sport that is both very new and very old at the same time. For me, that is one of its attractions. You can be sure that sailors worried about tying effective knots nearly six thousand years ago. The earliest evidence of sailboats dates back to about 3900 B.C.

There are thousands of knots. Some are practical; some are decorative—called "fancywork"—some are both. During long passages, sailors of a bygone era had plenty of time on their hands, and fancywork was apparently a satisfying as well as useful way to fill the hours.

Fortunately, modern sailors need know only a half-dozen knots. They are the figure 8, reef knot, slipped-reef knot, clove hitch, bowline, and cleat hitch.

Knot Good, Knot Bad

It may come as a surprise, but not all knots are created equal. There are good, bad, and inappropriate ones. First, a knot has to be mechanically suited to the task. Then it should be fairly easy to untie. A knot that doesn't conform to these criteria is disparaged as a "granny knot" or "false knot."

Defining Terms

Before learning to tie knots, it is helpful to define some terms and actions, most of which are shown in Photo 5A. A line has two parts: There is the *free end*, which is also called the *bitter end*. This is the short end of the line, the part that is manipulated to form the knot. There is also the *standing part*, which is the long part of the line that will be under load. Between the free end and the standing part is the knot.

A *bight* (not shown) is an open curve in a line. If the bight crosses the line, or is closed, it becomes a *loop*. You have an *overhand loop* if the free end passes *over* the standing part, an *under*hand loop if it passes *under*. Also, one line can *twist* around another.

Following Directions

Properly tying knots is similar to following directions in your automobile. It makes a difference if you start with a right turn when you should have started with a left. For example, when you make a loop, note carefully in the illustration and instructions if it is an *overhand* loop or an *underhand* loop, or does the free end go *up* through the loop or *down*. In other

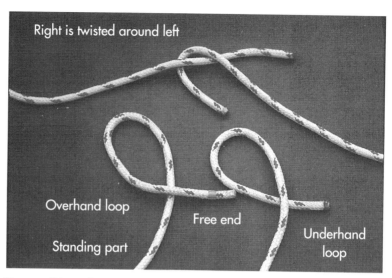

Right is twisted around left

Overhand loop

Standing part

Free end

Underhand loop

PHOTO 5A *Defining terms and depicting actions simplifies tying knots.* (Michael Levitt photo)

words, think of the illustrations as a road map—a three-dimensional one, however—and follow the directions carefully. To make this clearer, I have italicized prepositions, such as *over*, *under*, and *up*.

Once you've figured out the directions and have successfully tied a knot, practice it. Find your way to someone's house once, and you may not remember how you did it. Find your way to their house ten times, and you'll probably never forget it.

Figure of 8

A sheet, you will recall, is the name of a line that is used to trim sails. Often, headsail sheets have figure of 8 knots tied seven or eight inches from their free ends. This knot, sometimes called a "stopper knot", stops the end of the line from pulling out of the block. If it does pull out, it requires that the sheet be reled; at the very least, this is a nuisance.

The mast end of a halyard (the line used to raise and lower sails) often shows a figure of 8, too, after running through a cleat or mast-exit box. If it is a nuisance to reled a sheet, which has pulled out of a block at deck level, it is a major undertaking to reled a halyard, whose block is near to or at the top of the mast.

To tie a figure of 8: One, pass the line through the turning block for a headsail sheet or the base of a cleat for a halyard, for example—these

PHOTO 5B *A figure of 8 knot, also called a "stopper knot," stops a line, such as a sheet, from pulling out of a block, etc.* (Michael Levitt photo)

devices *stop* the line from pulling free. Two, make an *over*head loop with the free end (see Photo 5B left). It can be helpful if you hold the loop together between your thumb and two first fingers of your left hand, assuming you are right-handed. Three, twist the line around the standing part, which makes a second loop. And, four, then pass the free end *down* through the original loop. Tighten it. The knot is known as a figure of 8 because it looks like one.

Reef Knot

The reef knot, or square knot, is used to tie two lines of similar thickness and materials together. This is an appropriate knot if, for example, you need to lengthen dock lines, the anchor line, or a towing line.

To tie the reef knot: One, take one line in your right hand, one in your left. Bring the left-hand line over the right (see Photo 5C left). Two, then twist the former left-hand line around the back. (What I have described so far is the same knot you use to start a bow in shoelaces. Indeed, a square knot is little more than two of these knots, with care taken on whether the left goes over the right or vice versa.) Three, grab the new right-hand line with your right hand and repeat the motion: Bring the new right-hand line *over* the left-hand line and then twist it around the back. And, four, pull tight. The knot should look symmetrical. If you have successfully tied a reef knot, it shouldn't slip.

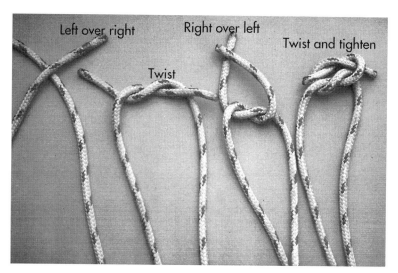

Left over right   Right over left   Twist and tighten

Twist

PHOTO 5C *The reef knot ties two lines of similar size and materials together. When tying it, I hear myself saying, "Left over right, twist. Right over left, twist."* (Michael Levitt photo)

Even if you tie it correctly, a square knot does not work well or at all with lines of different diameters, or if the lines are made of different materials.*

Slipped-Reef Knot

A variation of the reef knot is the slipped-reef knot. Use this knot, for example, to tie the mainsail to the boom. (This is necessary when the sail is down completely or down partially, as when it is reefed [see Chapter 11].) The slipped-reef knot is also used for tying an unhoisted headsail to the lifelines. A reef knot most often involves *two* lines, while a slipped-reef knot is typically used for *one* line that is looped around a mainsail and boom or around a headsail and the lifelines. It keeps sails under control—from being blown around by the wind.

To tie a slipped-reef knot, start as if tying a reef knot: One, take one end of the line in your right hand and the other in your left. Bring the left-hand end *over* the right (see Photo 5D). Two, then twist the former left-

*The sheetbend is the ideal knot to join two lines of different thicknesses or materials. Even though you can find it in any book on knots, it is omitted here because it isn't often used. In a pinch, you can tie lines of unequal diameters together with two bowlines (see below).

PHOTO 5D *Tying the slipped-reef knot, used for keeping sails under control, is very similar to tying a reef knot.* (Michael Levitt photo)

hand end around the back. This, again, is the first knot in tying shoes. Three, differing from a reef knot, make a *loop* in the new right-hand end, and with your right hand pass the loop *over* the left and then twist it. And, four, pull it tight.

A beauty of the slipped-reef knot, as the name implies, is how easily and quickly it unties. Just pull on the looped end and it slips free.

Clove Hitch

Use a clove hitch to secure a line around a piling, or post, or a fender around the "stanchion"—the upright pole that supports the lifelines. This is not a particularly complicated knot to tie, so Figure 5.1 should suffice.

Know that this is not a perfectly secure knot, however. It will be less likely to untie if the free end is not too short. A hitch at the end can help make the clove hitch even less likely to untie. To tie a hitch, take the free end *over* the standing part and *twist* it around the back. Bring the free end up through the resulting loop and pull tight.

Bowline

The bowline is probably the most commonly used knot in sailing. It forms a loop that won't slide; as such, the bowline is the opposite of a slip

Clove hitch

Pass the line once around
the post.

Pass the line around again over
the original line.

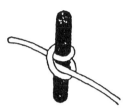

Tuck the line under the
crossing.

Tighten by moving both lines
together and
snugging both leads.

FIGURE 5.1 *The clove hitch is useful in tying a mooring line around a piling or a fender, which protects the boat from a dock or another boat, around a stanchion.* (Drawing courtesy Sunfish Laser, Inc.)

knot. A bowline is reasonably easy to untie—even after withstanding a tremendous load—but not while under load.

A bowline is used, for example, to tie sheets to headsails or for tying the stern line and bow line to pilings. (Note the difference in spelling between the knot *bowline* and the line *bow line*, the latter being the line that ties the bow, or front, of a boat to a dock or mooring. While a bow line is often tied with a bowline, they are not the same. Also, bowline [the knot] is pronounced BO-lynn, as in *bow* and arrow. Bow line [the line] is pronounced bough line, as in when the *bough* breaks—from that most unlikely lullaby.)

There are a few ways to tie a bowline. One of the easiest methods to learn is: One, make a small "*over*hand loop" in the line (see Photo 5E left). It is helpful if you hold the loop together between the thumb and middle finger of your left hand. Two, with your right hand, bring the free end *up* through the bottom of the loop. (Note: if you are tying the headsail sheets to the headsail, you would first pass the free end through the clew in the sail *before* proceeding with Step 2.) Three, continue with the free end in

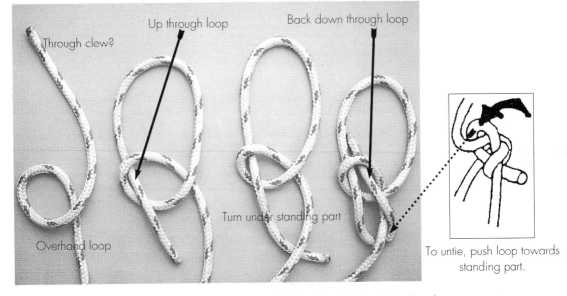

Labels on image: Through clew? — Up through loop — Back down through loop — Overhand loop — Turn under standing part — To untie, push loop towards standing part.

Photo 5E *For sailors no knot is more useful than the bowline.* (Michael Levitt photo; Sunfish Laser, Inc. illustration)

your right hand and make a turn *under* the standing part. And, four, take the free end *down* through the original loop.

Tighten the knot carefully by pulling on both the free end and the standing part. If the knot doesn't slide when tightened, you have successfully tied a bowline.

The knot is untied by pushing the loop forward in the direction of the standing part.

Cleat Hitch

Lines, such as sheets and halyards, that come off winches must be properly cleated. By properly, I mean so the line doesn't accidentally slip off the cleat. At the same time, it must be reasonably easy to undo. The cleat hitch is a good knot for this purpose. To tie a cleat hitch: One, make a complete loop around the cleat (see Photo 5F), passing *under* both horns. Two, make the second pass in a figure of 8 pattern. Three, rather than starting another figure of 8 crossing, make an *under*hand loop in the line. And, four, slip the loop over the horn as shown, making sure it is snug. Note how the free end completes the figure of 8 pattern.

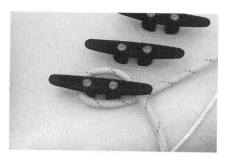

1) Make a loop, passing <u>under</u> both horns.

2) Make the second pass in a figure of 8 configuration.

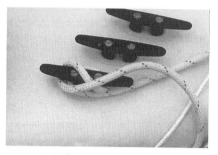

3) Instead of another figure of 8, make an underhand loop in the free end.

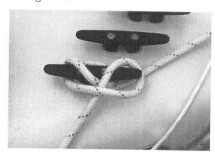

4) Slip the loop over the horn and snug line.

Photo 5F *The cleat hitch prevents a sheet or halyard from slipping off a cleat. If tying off a halyard to a cleat on the mast, put the underhand loop, which finishes the knot, on the top horn. Otherwise it can slip off.* (Michael Levitt photos)

Raising the Mast

Boats larger than eighteen feet usually require cranes and skilled operators to "step," or raise, the mast and to properly secure it. Masts on smaller boats, however, are often stepped by sailors. Before raising a mast make sure there are no electrical overhead cables with which the mast can come in contact. As noted in the previous chapter, sailors have been electrocuted when this has occurred.

In some boats, the bottom, or "butt-end," of the mast passes through the deck and sits on the bottom of the boat. This I will refer to as a "bottom- (or keel-) stepped" mast. With other boats, the mast sits on the deck. This is a "deck-stepped" mast. (The differences in stepping the two types of masts will be highlighted.)

To step a mast: One, lift the mast until it is vertical. To do this more easily, put the bottom (butt) end against a fixed object. Then, starting from the top of the mast, walk forward while pushing the mast hand over hand and over your head.

Two, with the mast held vertical, place its butt end on the step on the bottom of the boat or on deck, whichever is appropriate. (The "gooseneck," or attachment point for the boom, should be facing aft.) Typically, there is a fitting to prevent the mast from slipping off the step; if there is in your boat, have a second person lock the butt end in place.

Three, if a bottom-stepped mast, the mast is further held in place at deck level by the "partners." Make sure the mast is properly situated in them.

Four, while a crew member continues to support the mast, another person connects the shrouds, or side stays, and the forestay to the hull with the rigging fittings. Some boats also have a backstay, which goes from the top of the mast to the back of the boat. If your boat does, secure it in place.

Five, tighten the stays and shrouds (including lower shrouds if your boat has them) so the mast is exactly vertical (plumb) in the boat. You can check that the mast is plumb by running the main halyard to the stern quarter of the boat. Have a crew member hold it in position and then tension the halyard at the mast end and cleat it. This locks in the length for the measurement. Then run the halyard to the stern quarter on the opposite side. If the distance is the same—if the halyard just reaches—the mast is plumb. If it isn't vertical, ease or tighten the "turnbuckles", which adjust tension in the rigging, until it is.

Once the mast is plumb you need to tighten the rigging *considerably* so the mast doesn't lean to the side or bend *sideways*.* (Bending the mast *fore*

---

*There are too many boats and too many rigs to address adequately "tuning" the mast, as this is called. When learning to sail, you're going to need help doing this, so ask for it from someone who is knowledgeable about how to tune the type of boat you sail. Some general remarks can be helpful, however. How much to tighten the cap and lower shrouds (if your boat has lowers) has to be determined when sailing in twelve to fifteen knots of wind. When sailing, look up your mast to see if it's in a straight line. Kinks in the mast or *sideways* bend—normally caused by too loose shrouds—must be eliminated. Ideally, there should be no slack in the *leeward* cap shroud (i.e., the longest shroud on the same side as the headsail), when the boat is heeled twenty degrees—typical heel when it is blowing twelve to fifteen knots. (If adjusting shrouds when sailing, always work on the unloaded leeward shroud, never the loaded windward one. As it is the windward shrouds that do the work, however, this means you'll have to tack back and forth to see if your tensioning of the rig was correct.)

To adjust shroud tension, a crescent wrench holds the threaded stud, above the turnbuckle, stationary. A screwdriver turns the barrel of the turnbuckle. Always count the turns you take on the turnbuckle on one side so you can take the same number on the other side *after* you've tacked. (Don't forget to put the cotter pins, which must be removed before adjusting tension, back in before tacking.) Adjust the lower shrouds (again always work on the leeward side) so the mast is straight, or without sideways lean, when the boat is heeled twenty degrees. With too much tension on the *windward* lowers, the middle of the mast pops to windward and the top sags to leeward. Too little tension on the *windward* lowers, the middle sags to leeward and the top pops to windward.

and *aft* is common in most boats [see Chapter 11].) If you take the same number of turns on each of the shrouds while tightening them, the mast should remain plumb. Insert the "cotter pins" to keep the turnbuckles from coming loose on their own. Spread them to forty-five degrees.

Six, and lastly, the boom, the horizontal spar that secures the foot of the mainsail, is affixed to the mast at the gooseneck. The topping lift, a line that holds the boom up when the sail isn't hoisted, is attached. Alternatively, a boom crutch, gallows, or main halyard supports the boom.

Rigging the Mainsail

With a sloop, or a boat with a mainsail and headsail, sails are generally rigged and later hoisted from the back of the boat to the front. This means start with the mainsail and then the headsail.

To rig a mainsail: One, take it out of the sail bag. The sail bag should have the word *main* or *mainsail* stenciled boldly on it. If the bag is unmarked, a mainsail typically has batten pockets—slots along the back edge, or leech, for the insertion of battens. These are far less common on headsails. Headsails usually have hanks, or fasteners, at the luff, or leading edge, while mains never do.

Two, find the tack, or forward-lower attachment point, of the sail and the clew, the back-bottom attachment point. Before putting the sail on the boom, orient the sail so the forward part (tack) is facing toward the mast and the back (clew) toward the back. Affix the tack to the tack pin, where the mast and boom meet. While tack fittings vary, how they work is usually apparent.

Above the tack cringle, or hole, of the mainsail on some boats is a second cringle for the Cunningham. The Cunningham exerts a downward pull on the front of the mainsail, which makes it flatter (see Chapter 11). If your boat has one, it should be rigged.

Three, insert the "bolt rope" (excuse me, but rope is what it is called) on the foot of the sail in the slot on the boom and pull the foot toward the back end of the boom. It helps if two people do this job: One feeds the sail into the groove, while the other pulls it aft. Make sure the cloth at the foot of the sail runs smoothly into the boom; kinks or overlaps of cloth can make it impossible to feed the sail—even cause it to rip. (If the sail does kink, reverse the process until the kink clears and then continue feeding it into the slot.) Sometimes the foot of the mainsail runs on cars or slides. If so, the cars need to be fed onto the track. Make sure the cars aren't twisted.

Four, attach the clew to the outhaul fitting. Tighten the outhaul so there are no vertical wrinkles on the bottom of the sail.

Five, put battens in next; the openings are usually at the back, or leech, of the sail. Battens come in different lengths, so put the appropriate-sized one in the correct pocket. Their positions are typically marked on the battens. If not, match the length of the battens to the length of the pockets. The batten should be slightly shorter than the pocket. Some battens are shaped, with one end thinner than the other. If your boat has shaped battens, put the thinner edge in first.

Starting with the top batten and working down, push the first batten in. When it is almost all the way in, it will encounter a piece of elastic. Push it in a little farther, so the elastic stretches. This gives you room to secure the back of the batten under the back flap of the sail. Be sure the battens are properly seated under the flap, otherwise they can fly out of the sail. (Note while this is the most common procedure for inserting battens, there are other methods. If you can't figure out what your sailmaker intended, ask someone, like your sailmaker.)

And, six, if it is windy and there is a chance the mainsail will blow overboard, it should be bunched together and tied to the boom using nylon cord or line (see furling Photo 10B, page 175). The knot for this is the slipped-reef knot, discussed above.

Don't yet hoist the mainsail.

Obviously, a main is a complex sail to rig. Thus, many boats—particularly those that are kept in the water—don't remove their mainsail after sailing; rather the sail is furled and covered with a sail cover. If the mainsail is covered, remove the cover. Leave the sail ties on until you are ready to hoist the sail. If it is windy, or the forecast is for wind, you should also rig the clew-reef line(s), *before* hoisting the mainsail. This line or lines allows you to shorten sail (see Figure 11.10, page 195).

Rigging the Headsail

Before rigging the headsail, be certain the forward hatch, if your boat has one, is closed. Otherwise, the sail can hide the hatch, making it easy to fall into. Anytime you work on the deck, in fact, make sure all hatches are closed.

Some boats allow a choice of headsails, where a distinguishing feature is size. If your boat allows a choice, you must decide which to use. Simply considered: use a smaller headsail, or jib, if it is windy, a bigger one, or

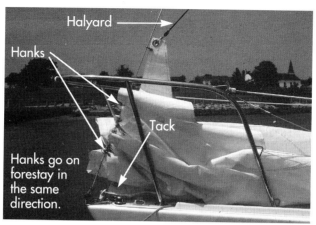

Halyard

Hanks

Tack

Hanks go on forestay in the same direction.

PHOTO 5G *Rigging the headsail.* (Michael Levitt photo)

genoa, if it isn't.* The major difference in rigging the two types of headsails is that with a bigger genoa, the sheets are usually led *outside* the shrouds, or side stays. With a smaller jib, they are usually led *inside*.

To rig the headsail: One, start by putting the tack, or forward-bottom corner, into the tack fitting on the bow of the boat (see Photo 5G). In most cases, the front, or luff, of the sail is fastened to the forestay with hanks, or metal fasteners. Attach the hanks to the forestay starting at the bottom. Make sure the luff isn't twisted. Also, be sure the hanks aren't twisted and that they go on the forestay in the same direction.

Headsails on racing boats often lack hanks; rather, the luff tape of the sail is fed through a prefeeder and then into a grooved foil or forestay device.

Two, stretch the foot out. Then using the bowline knot (see Photo 5E), tie the sheets to the clew or back-bottom corner. Don't tie one sheet to the sail with a bowline and the other sheet through the loop in the first bowline; rather, tie each *separately* to the clew.

Three, if rigging a larger genoa, take each sheet *over* the lifelines—if your boat has them—then *outside* the shrouds. Pass each sheet through a block, or "fairlead", on one side of the boat. Often this line runs through a second turning block. Then lead the line *through* the lifelines and into the cockpit. Finally, tie a figure of 8 knot (Photo 5B) eight inches from the end

*Sometimes headsails are marked with numbers, which appear on the sail bags. To confuse things, larger numbers indicate smaller sails; a number 2, for example, is smaller in size than a number 1.

to keep the sheet from accidentally pulling out of the block. (If a smaller jib, run the sheets *inside* the shrouds. Also the fairlead block for the sheet is usually placed farther forward than for a genoa.)*

And, four, to keep the headsail from blowing overboard, tie it with a slipped-reef knot (Photo 5D) to the lifelines, pulpit, or grab rail with nylon cord or line. As an alternative, take the top hank off the forestay and attach it to the lifelines. (Replace it before hoisting the headsail.)

Hoisting the Mainsail

The mainsail is usually hoisted first, as noted. To hoist the mainsail: One, it is important that the bow of the boat be pointed into the wind. When at a mooring this is usually no problem as the bow of a boat normally swings into the wind.† When launching from a beach, a crew member standing in the water holds the bow into the wind while another crew hoists the mainsail. A wind indicator, like a masthead fly, helps to aim the bow into the wind.

If you keep your boat at a mooring, the "rudder," used for steering, is probably already in place. If you trailer your boat, however, the likelihood is that the rudder isn't fitted to the boat. Don't hoist sails without the rudder being affixed to the boat by way of the gudgeons and pintles. (That's the third time I've used those words.) This way, if the bow of the boat is no longer pointed into the wind, you can steer it so it is.

If your boat has an engine and you are under power, the boat motors slowly into the wind as the mainsail is hoisted. Before turning upwind, make sure that the water is sufficiently deep and that there are no other obstructions. If hoisting a main at a dock, the boat is typically moved around until the bow is facing into the wind. (This as well as engine safety is discussed further in the next chapter.)

Two, the mainsail is controlled by a few lines. There is often a boom vang, or kicking strap, which holds down the boom. (Not every boat has a

---

*To determine the proper lead location, turn to Figure 11.5, page 185.

†One situation at a mooring can complicate hoisting the main; that is, when the boat is facing into the tidal stream rather than into the wind. This can happen when the tidal stream is strong and the wind light. If your moored boat isn't pointing into the wind, the likelihood is that it is pointing into the tidal stream.

    If there isn't too much difference in direction between the wind and tidal stream, normally, the boat will swing into the wind once you begin hoisting the mainsail. However, if the wind and tidal stream are in opposite directions, it can prove troublesome. You can sometimes walk the mooring line to the stern of the boat and cleat it there. Then the stern will face into the tidal stream, and the bow will face into the wind. Sails can then be hoisted in the normal fashion. Don't attempt this, however, if the tidal stream is too strong.

boom vang, however.) There is also the mainsheet, which brings the boom and, thus, the mainsail in and out. Before hoisting the mainsail, these two lines must be slack or eased way out. If the lower mainsheet attachment of the boat you sail has a "traveler"—a movable car that allows the mainsheet to "travel", or move, from side to side—cleat or lock it amidships. You don't want the traveler sliding back and forth when hoisting the sail.

Three, starting with the top of the sail, feed the bolt rope on the front of the mainsail about six inches into the slot on the back of the mast. Then take the halyard off the mast and fasten it to the head of the sail. Be sure the shackle is properly locked.

Sometimes the main halyard supports the boom when not sailing, rather than merely being ended at the mast. If this is the case, undo the main halyard from the end of the boom. Be very careful, however, that the heavy boom doesn't drop on a crew member but is let down under control. A falling boom can be deadly. (A safer arrangement is a "topping lift," a line whose only job is to keep the boom elevated when not sailing. Ease the topping lift *after* hoisting the sail. Remember to tighten it again *before dropping* the sail.)

Four, it is best to hoist a mainsail with three people: One crewmember works the halyard—used to raise the sail—and another feeds the luff, or

PHOTO 5H *Hoisting the mainsail is typically a job for three people. One hoists the halyard; one feeds the luff into the groove; and one steers.* (Michael Levitt photo)

front of the sail, into the groove (see Photo 5H). Also, the helmsperson steers so the boat remains facing into the wind. If the boat needs to be turned into the wind in the midst of hoisting the mainsail, the crew should stop raising the halyard until the boat is again properly oriented. (Steering is discussed in the next chapter.)

Five, take up the tension on the mast end of the halyard to make sure the halyard runs straight and isn't fouled around a spreader or something similar. Then hoist—or pull on the halyard. Another crew should help feed the luff of the mainsail into the groove on the mast. As when loading the mainsail on the boom, make sure that the cloth is smooth without any kinks or overlaps. If it kinks, stop raising the halyard, lower it a few inches until the kink clears, and start again.

Rather than a bolt rope, the luffs on some mains feature cars or slides, which run up in a track, or mast slot, at the back of the mast. Once the cars have been fed onto the track, a "gate" normally keeps them in place. This obviates the need for feeding the luff on the mainsail into the mast each time you raise it, thus making it a two-person job to hoist the mainsail. Make sure when hoisting the mainsail that each car slides up when its turn comes.

Six, in the beginning, it is easy to hoist a mainsail. As more of the sail is raised, however, it gets heavier and harder to do. If this happens, or if the halyard changes from soft line to wire by way of a rope-wire splice— wire is hard on your hands—take a few *clockwise* turns of the halyard around the winch. (Note that winches, whether on the mast or in the cockpit, are always loaded clockwise.) Then you can gain a further mechanical advantage by sticking a winch handle into the winch and turning it. Be certain, however, that the handle positively locks into the winch. Some winches have more than one speed, meaning you can turn the winch in the opposite direction with the handle, for a lower or higher gear.

Seven, raise the mainsail to the top of the mast. Often there is a black band painted on the top, signaling the top or the sail's maximum hoist point. Even then it is not easy to see this from deck level. (Better is a mark on the halyard, at the bottom, signaling that the main is completely up. This is common on many boats.)

And, eight, secure the halyard to its cleat with the cleat hitch (see Photo 5F); however, make the hitch, which secures the line, on the upper horn. If the hitch is made at the bottom, it can slip off. Once the sail is up, slacken the topping lift, supporting the main boom—if you have one. Coil the halyard (see below).

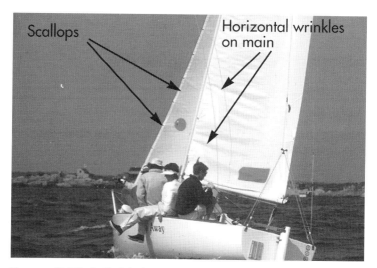

Scallops

Horizontal wrinkles on main

PHOTO 5I *The luff of the headsail should be straight; there shouldn't be scallops as here. The headsail needs more halyard tension and there shouldn't be horizontal wrinkles in the mainsail. The main needs more Cunningham tension or perhaps more halyard tension.* (Photo courtesy J Boats, Inc.)

Hoisting the Headsail

One, put the halyard on the head, or top of the headsail, and positively lock it in place.

Two, make sure the halyard is clear and that it hasn't twisted around the forestay, or a spreader. A halyard is less likely to twist if tension is kept constant.

Three, when hoisting the headsail, there should not be any tension on it from the sheets, so make sure the headsail sheets are free to run.

Four, with the halyard, raise the sail. Stop if you find that there is a twist in the luff or hanks. Correct this by dropping the sail and starting again. If your headsail has a luff tape rather than hanks, a crew member must help to feed the sail into the prefeeder and then into the headfoil.

Five, fully hoist the headsail. Use a winch if necessary and, of course, if you have one. Remember, winches are wound clockwise. The sail should be tight at the luff, or front; there shouldn't be scallops between hanks. (The boat in Photo 5I shows such scallops; they signal that more halyard tension is needed. Also note the horizontal wrinkles in the mainsail that show this sail needs more upward halyard tension, if the sail isn't fully hoisted, or more downward Cunningham tension if it is.)

And, six, cleat the halyard and coil and hang the line (see below).

Coiling Lines

In sailing, neatness counts. Coil halyards and sheets to keep things neat and to keep them from kinking. A kink in a halyard can keep you from dropping a sail. This can be dangerous if a sail has to be dropped in a hurry in a squall, or a sudden storm. Also, lines dragging over the side or left in a mess on a deck look terrible and can be dangerous, as they are slippery and easy to trip over. Trailing lines can foul the propeller.

First, know that there are two types of lines used on sailboats: "braided" and "laid." Braided lines are distinguished by a soft cover that surrounds a hard braided core. While called "braided lines," the braided part is hidden beneath the core. These lines are most often used for sheets, which trim sails, and halyards, which raise and lower them.

Laid lines, while far less common today, are still used as mooring lines and anchor lines. You can see the strands, or braids, in laid line.

It is necessary to know which type of line is used in a particular application, as the coiling methods are slightly different. A major difference is that you twist each coil of a laid line when coiling it (see below) to keep the line from kinking. With the twist, the laid line falls into neat circles. You don't twist the more common braided line, however; allow it to fall naturally into a figure of 8 configuration. Also, braided line can be coiled in a clockwise or counterclockwise direction. Laid line should only be coiled clockwise.

To coil a halyard, which I will assume is a braided line: One, grab the line about six inches from the cleat in your left hand if you're right-handed (see Photo 5J). (We're going to use those six inches shortly.) Then with your right hand make two-foot loops. As described braided lines can be coiled either clockwise or counterclockwise. Remember, don't twist a braided line, let it fall in a figure of 8 pattern.

Two, when fully coiled, reach through the coils and grab the remaining line—those six inches. Pull it through the coils. As such, it is a loop. Twist the loop a few times.

Three, with the twisted loop, hang the halyard on the cleat.

To coil an anchor line or a sheet, for that matter: One, take one end in your left hand. The remainder of the line is in front of you.

Grab line six inches from cleat. Make two-foot coils. Don't twist braided line.

Pull loop (those six inches of line) through the coils and twist a few times.

Hang the halyard on the cleat with twisted loop.

PHOTO 5J *Coiling a halyard and making it fast to a cleat on the mast.* (Michael Levitt photos)

Two, with your right hand make two-foot loops (see Photo 5K). Remember, laid lines should only be coiled clockwise while braided line can be coiled in either direction.

Three, hang each loop over your left hand; however, before hanging a loop give it a quarter-turn clockwise twist if laid line, no twist if braided. If you make a mistake and twist a braided line or don't twist a laid line, the line can kink.* Should the line get too heavy or too thick to hold easily in your left hand, place it on the deck and continue coiling it.

Four, stop coiling when about three feet of line remains. Then, with the free end, make three or four turns around the coils. These turns should be on the top third of the coils.

And, five, make a bight in what little line remains and pass it through the top half of the coils. Pass the free end through the bight. The turns should slide to the top, which helps to hold the coiled line together. The line can be hung on a hook or something similar by tying a knot at the free end.

---

*The remedy for kinked line, be it laid or braided, is to stream it behind a boat. (Make sure it is tied to the boat before throwing it overboard.) This will allow the line to untwist. Don't do this when using your boat's engine as the line can get caught in the prop. Also, make sure other boats don't run over your line for the same reason.

Make two-foot coils. Don't twist braided line, twist laid line.

Stop coiling when three feet of line remains. Take three of four turns around coils with free end.

Make a bight in free end and pass it through coils.

Pass the free end through the bight.

PHOTO 5K *Coiling a sheet or anchor line.* (Michael Levitt photos)

6 | Cutting Loose

L ike a weather vane, a properly balanced sailboat wants to point into the wind. Recall, however, a sailboat can't sail if its bow is closer than about forty-five degrees to the wind. Closer than that, and you've entered the no-sail zone (see Figure 2.9, page 22). Thus, to start to sail, a force must be applied to turn the bow off the wind. That turning force comes largely from the rudder or, in some cases, a shove off the wind, or both.

Steering with a Tiller or Wheel

Sailors control the rudder through the tiller and, sometimes, the tiller extension. Alternatively, they use a wheel.

Steering with a tiller is fairly confusing, at least for the first five minutes. The problem is: If the tiller is moved to the *left* side of the boat, the boat steers *right*. The opposite is true, too: If the tiller is moved to the *right*, the boat steers *left*. Imagine turning a car steering wheel *left*, or counterclockwise, to make the car turn *right*, and you can understand how odd this arrangement is.

Perhaps you've seen pedal cars for children, or a forklift where the back wheels steer rather than the front. If the back wheels go to the left side of the car, the car goes right (see Figure 6.1). And vice versa. That's basically how a boat with a tiller steers.

Fortunately, this action-reaction is more complicated to explain than to perform. In due time, steering with a tiller becomes second nature. Your mind and body quickly grasp the relationship: Tiller left, boat goes right.

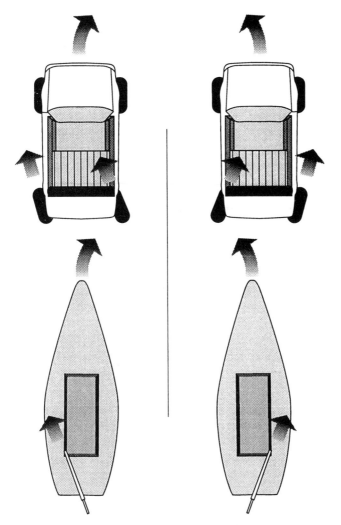

FIGURE 6.1 *Push the tiller left, and the boat steers right and vice versa. This is similar to a child's car or forklift where the back wheels steer rather than the front.*

Tiller right, the boat goes left.

No such complication exists when steering with the wheel, which steers exactly like a car. If you want the bow to go left, turn the wheel left, or counterclockwise. To go right, turn clockwise.

The result of this is that every action in this book that describes the use of the tiller and wheel is opposite. Shortly, for example, we will see that to avoid an accidental gybe you should come up, or sail closer into the wind. To come up when using a tiller, you push it *toward* the mainsail; however, to come up when using a wheel, you turn it *away* from the mainsail. Don't be confused by this.

It is also important to note that as sails need wind, or air, flowing over them to work, the rudder needs water flowing past it to work. Without flow moving past the rudder—if the boat isn't moving through the water or is moving very slowly—the rudder won't be effective in turning the boat. Thus, pay special attention to steering when departing shallow water, a mooring, or a dock. You are often going slowly at such times. In some ways it's like riding a bicycle: it is easier to ride a bicycle at a reasonable clip of speed than when going very slowly.

Steering with the Sails

Note that any time you change the direction of a flow, be it water or air, a turning force results. This means when you change the trim of the sails— bring them in or let them out—there is a change in airflow. The result is a turning force; indeed, the sails are second only to the rudder in steering the boat. (In Chapter 9, we will see how heeling steers a boat, too.)

Sails are effective enough at steering that boats that have lost their rudders have made distant landfalls by steering with the sails alone. It works this way: To come up into the wind, trim the mainsail and ease the headsail. To fall off the wind, ease the mainsail and trim the headsail. With a catboat with one sail, trim or ease the mainsail to make the boat come up or fall off, respectively.

Sail trim, complementing the steering action of the rudder, is an important concept in sailing. This is an idea we will develop in this chapter.

Sound Planning + Skillful Execution + Revision = a Sailor

In sailing, there are a host of maneuvers, such as departing from shallow water or a mooring or tacking, that must be planned as well as executed. A sound plan leads to skillful execution. However, beyond planning and execution, you must expect the unexpected in sailing.

Therefore, this book endeavors to provide you with a fundamental knowledge of boats, wind, and weather so the unexpected won't throw you. It also tries to provide you with the tools so you can revise your plan when necessary.

Cutting Loose

The gear is aboard, the boat is rigged, the sails are hoisted, the halyards are coiled, and the rudder is in place. It's time to cut the ties that bind us to shore. However, before departing, secure all gear properly.

Remember, once sailing, the boat is likely to heel, or lean away from the wind. Any gear not held positively in place will slide downhill. That can be hard on the gear and hard—or worse—on the passengers should a projectile, like a winch handle, strike someone sitting on the low side. Keep winch handles, for example, in their pockets, near the winches. Place other items in "lazarettes," or lockers, if you have them, or down below. Remember, in sailing, neatness counts.

It is strongly recommended not just to have buoyancy aids or lifejackets aboard for each member of the crew but to wear them.

Four descriptions characterize most departures:

One, the departure will be from shallow water, as in sailing off the beach or away from a launching ramp. (Shallow-water departures are usually the sole domain of centerboard boats.)

Two, the departure will be from a mooring—an anchorage, surrounded by navigable water.

Three, the boat is anchored, and the departure will require retrieving an anchor—known as "weighing anchor."

Four, the departure will be from a dock or position—by either sailing or motoring.

Shallow-Water Departures

After launching from a ramp or a beach, walk or paddle the boat into thigh-high water.* The water should be deep enough so that the rudder can be "shipped," or positioned at the back of the boat. Some rudders, as on a Sunfish, for example, will kick up if you hit something. Be sure the rudder is down and locked before departing; otherwise steering will be difficult.

Fundamental to sailing, and to a successful departure, is to study the wind in view of your initial course: normally, that first course is into deeper water. You will recall that there are five sailing angles: close-hauled, close-

---

*The assumptions here are that this is a centerboard, rather than keelboat, as boats with fixed keels aren't normally launched in shallow water; also, that this boat is steered by a tiller—as most centerboard boats are. Further assumed is that this is not a beach with breaking surf or large waves. Such conditions are beyond the skill level of those learning to sail. In other words, avoid them—find another place to launch or don't go sailing this day.

reaching, beam-reaching, broad-reaching, and running (see Figure 2.9, page 22). For simplicity's sake, when planning a departure, we can further reduce that to three angles: close-hauled, reaching, and running.

Ask yourself: To get to where I first want to go, will I be sailing on a close-hauled course, or with the wind in my face; on a reaching course, or with the wind more or less on my side; or on a running course, with the wind behind me? In Figure 6.2, the departure is upwind, which means you will be sailing on a close-hauled course.

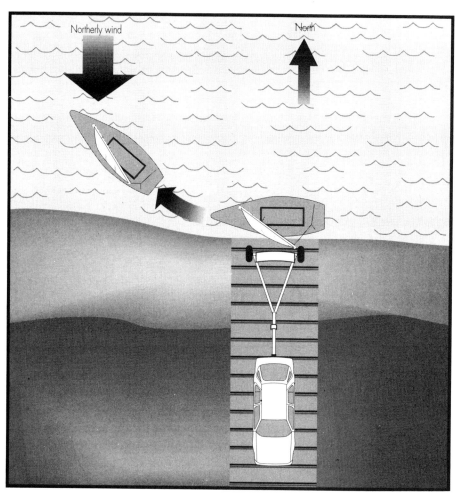

FIGURE 6.2 *An upwind departure on starboard tack. On starboard tack, the wind strikes the starboard, or right, side first.*

STARTING UPWIND

If the wind is in your face, you're going to have to sail on a close-hauled course and likely "beat" upwind to get offshore. Beating, as described in Chapter 2, is the zigzag course that allows a sailboat to reach a point upwind. It requires tacking, or turning, so the bow crosses through the eye of the wind.

The next decision for a departure that requires tacking is: Do I want to start on starboard tack (this is the orientation shown in Figure 6.2), or on port tack, with the wind first striking the port side (see Figure 6.3)?

Usually, one tack will get you into deeper water more directly—a major theme of any departure. Of course, moored and moving boats, swimmers, rocks, or shallows can also make one tack more desirable ("favorable," in the language of sailing) than the other.

It is important that the skipper, or leader, announce to the crew his or her plans for the departure. First, the crew must know what to do and when to do it. Further, the crew may have noticed something that the skipper has missed; for example, a boat passing nearby that is obscured by the sails. Such information can change how or when you will depart.

In the last chapter, in preparation for departure, a crew member was standing in the water, holding the bow of the boat into the wind as the sails were hoisted. However for the departure (see the bottom of Figure 6.3) he holds it at the side by the shrouds, or side stays. Ribbon telltales, masthead fly, or other boats can be helpful in aiming the bow of the boat into the wind.

Suppose the decision is to depart on port tack, as in Figure 6.3. Then the crew member holds the boat by the shrouds on the port, or upwind, side of the boat. (That is easy to remember with the words: *port-port.*) Be sure the centerboard is down as far as it will go—don't allow it to strike the bottom, however. The helmsman holds the tiller and the "mainsheet"— the line that brings the mainsail in and out. The mainsheet isn't trimmed yet, however; the mainsail is allowed to luff, or shake, as is the headsail. That represents a neutral position.

The crew, from the upwind side, shoves the bow of the boat forward and off the wind on port tack. Then he immediately scrambles aboard, using the shrouds, or side stays, to help him aboard. At the same time, the helmsman and any other crew members balance the boat—they likely move to the center of the boat or even the low side. Also, the helmsperson uses the tiller to turn the boat off the wind. To do that, the steerer angles the

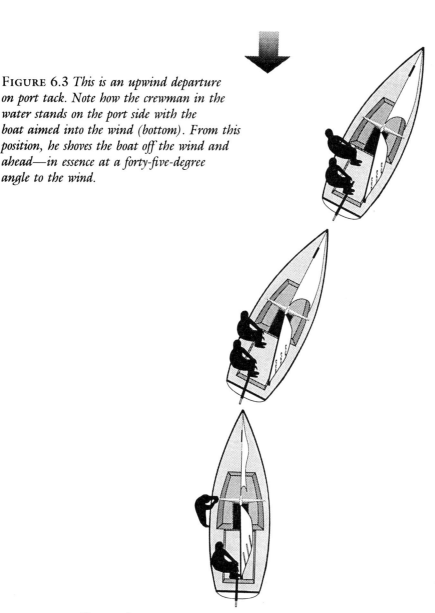

FIGURE 6.3 *This is an upwind departure on port tack. Note how the crewman in the water stands on the port side with the boat aimed into the wind (bottom). From this position, he shoves the boat off the wind and ahead—in essence at a forty-five-degree angle to the wind.*

tiller to the port side of the boat, when on port tack, or away from the sails. (Tiller angles in this and the other illustrations in this book are correct.)

When the bow is turned off the wind and the boat is moving ahead, trim the headsail first and then the mainsail. As we now know, this order will prevent the boat from turning back into the wind and stopping. Note that the headsail sheet typically turns around a block—called a turning block—or fitting before going to a winch or a cleat. That block or fitting can be highly loaded. Never stand or sit in the apex of a turning block or fitting. If it should break, you can be injured. Similarly, to avoid injury, keep your head away from the boom. You need to develop a sense of where the boom is now and where it might be next.

The sails should be trimmed tight when departing upwind or close-hauled. The boom, which controls the mainsail, should be close to the centerline of the boat; the leech, or back edge, of the headsail is trimmed so it is close to but not touching the shrouds or spreader (this is shown later in Figure 7.3, page 106). This is as tight as the sails are trimmed. Also, once the water is sufficiently deep, fully lower the centerboard. (In the next chapter, we will see that trimming the sails in tight and fully lowering the centerboard are the "distinguishing positions" when sailing on a close-hauled course.)

STARTING ON A REACH OR RUN

The technique for starting from shallow water when the first course is a reach or run is much the same. If starting on a reach, or with the wind at your side, the centerboard needs only to be about halfway down. This is the distinguishing position for a reach described in Chapter 8. The crew moves to the upwind side—port if it is a port-tack departure, starboard if it is a starboard-tack departure. From there, the crew shove the boat ahead and scramble aboard, using the shrouds. Those in the boat must balance it while the crew climbs aboard.

On a reach, trim the sails in about halfway—between the (tight-in) beating position and the (perpendicular to the boat) running position, described next.

If the wind is behind you, as it is when running, the centerboard isn't necessary. When running, the sails don't require much trim. Keep the mainsail at a right angle to the wind, which means perpendicular to the boat.* The headsail should be eased well out so it fills. This, as will be described in Chapter 9, is as far as sails are eased.

One caution is necessary when departing on a run, or with the wind behind you. If you turn too far off the wind, the boom of the mainsail can accidentally gybe, or swing rapidly and uncontrollably across the boat to the other side. An "accidental gybe" can capsize the boat; even cause serious head and other injuries.

---

*In Figure 9.5, page 141, the position of the mainsail for a run is more accurately given as ninety degrees to the wind, but eighty degrees to the centerline of the boat. Nevertheless, "perpendicular to the boat" is close enough for departing from shallow water. Don't allow it to chafe on the spreaders, however.

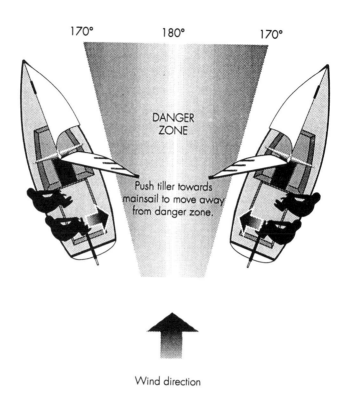

170° 180° 170°

DANGER
ZONE

Push tiller towards
mainsail to move away
from danger zone.

Wind direction

FIGURE 6.4 *To avoid an accidental gybe, push the Tiller Toward the mainsail, or T-T. Turn the Wheel aWay, W-W.*

To avoid an accidental gybe, keep the wind on your weather quarter, not directly on your stern. (See Figure 6.4; this is an illustration we will turn to often.) If, however, the wind vane at the top of the mast points to your transom, or the headsail tries to fill on the opposite side, you are in the danger zone, or close to an accidental gybe. Immediately push the tiller *toward* the mainsail, which will move the wind back to the weather side. You can remember this by the letters "T-T"—*T*iller *T*oward the mainsail.

If you steer with a wheel, rapidly turn it *away* from the mainsail. This can be remembered by "W-W"—*W*heel a*W*ay.

If this turn is done in a timely fashion, you can avoid an accidental gybe. The accidental gybe and how to prevent it are more fully explained in Chapter 9.

Starting from a Mooring

If departing from shallow water is a maneuver reserved for centerboard boats, both keelboats and centerboarders commonly take their leave from moorings. Typically, departing from a mooring requires that a second boat be used as a water taxi. Often that second vessel is a small dinghy, which, due to its size, appears more innocuous than it is.

Don't use such boats in rough water, due to their lack of "freeboard," or low sides. Big waves can swamp a boat with low sides. (That said, this is less of a problem in an inflatable, with its exceptional flotation, than in a dinghy made out of fiberglass with less flotation.) Also, because of their diminutive size, dinghies can be unstable, or "tippy". Before stepping on or off a dinghy be sure it is well tied to a dock or boat. You have to be careful when you board and when you step off. Balance is the watchword in peacefully coexisting with a dinghy. Don't overload with people, gear, or an oversized motor. Always wear a lifejacket, even in calm conditions.

Once the dinghy is unloaded, it is often left tied to the mooring and retrieved when you return. If you are not returning to the same mooring, or you will need the dinghy for some later shore-side errand, tie it to the back of the boat. If towed, keep the dinghy as light as possible—that means remove all gear—to minimize its impact on sailing and to prevent it from capsizing. Keep it close to the boat's stern, or back, until out of a crowded anchorage. When clear, let out the "painter", the name given to the line pulling the dinghy so it rides just in front of the second or third wave following your boat. Adjust the length of the painter to be certain the dinghy is riding comfortably. Check it periodically to be sure it isn't filling with water.

If it's rough or if you're going far, carry the dinghy aboard if possible, as its impact on sailing is considerable.

SAILING AWAY FROM A MOORING

Before departing a mooring, check the "bilge," the lowest area near the keel where the water collects, and pump any water out. As you can learn much about a house you're thinking about buying by checking the basement, you can learn much about your boat by checking its basement—the bilge. (See the section Motoring Away from a Mooring, below.)

The skipper, or leader, must determine whether to depart on starboard or port tack. Again, one tack will usually get you into deeper water more directly—important in any departure. Obviously, moored and moving boats, rocks, shallows, or swimmers can make one tack more favorable than the other. Once you've made the decision, share it with the crew; for example, "We'll depart on port tack."

If keeping the dinghy at the mooring, tie its painter to the mooring buoy loop—with a bowline knot (see Photo 5E, page 61). The dinghy should be kept on what will be upon departure the weather side of the sailboat. So if it's to be port-tack departure, the dinghy will be on the sailboat's port, or left, side. Again, port-port. When tying the dinghy to the mooring buoy loop, don't, however, untie the sailboat from the loop, until you are ready to leave.

When on a mooring, a sailboat—the weather vane that it is—usually points upwind, so departing from a mooring is usually in that direction. (Once sailing, you can turn any way you wish.) Since it is an upwind departure, the centerboard should be down. When the gear is secured and everyone is ready, a crew member goes to the bow and prepares to undo the sailboat's mooring line. As when hoisting the headsail, be certain when going forward that all hatches are properly closed.

After freeing the mooring line—this can be strenuous work in heavy winds or with a bigger boat—the crew member doesn't cast off the line but takes two 360-degree turns, or wraps the free end around the cleat on the bow. This provides a good temporary hold.

The boat should leave from the downwind side of the mooring buoy. To put this another way, the mooring buoy should be upwind of your boat so you don't drift down onto it. If you do, you can tangle your boat in the mooring line—which typically makes a mess of things.

If it is to be a port-tack departure, leave the mooring buoy on your port or left side. (This is the same as a crew member being on the port side before departing on a port tack from shallow water. The mnemonic, port-port, works here, too.) If it is a starboard-tack departure, leave the mooring on your right or starboard side.

If the boat refuses to head off on the proper tack, you can "back" the headsail—in essence, pull it with the windward sheet to the "wrong" (upwind) side. (This is shown later in Figure 6.5, the middle illustration). The wrong or upwind side is on the port, or left, side, if you want to depart on port tack, as in the figure, or to the starboard, or right, side if you want to depart on starboard tack.

Alternatively, or in lighter winds, you can head the boat off in the proper direction by pulling hard on the mooring line on one side of the bow or the other—whichever is appropriate.

If there is sufficient wind, above eight knots or so, a boat on a mooring tends to sail around a little bit: first to one side of the buoy and then to the other. Often, you can time your release of the bow line to when the boat is on the proper side of the buoy, on the proper tack, and moving forward. When the skipper says he is ready, a crew member should wait until the boat is on the correct side of the buoy and moving forward. Then he should quickly unwrap the turns from the cleat, drop the free end overboard while pulling in the other end. Thus the free end passes through the loop on the mooring buoy and ends up on board the boat. As soon as the rope is free of the buoy, the foredeck crew should inform the skipper, "We're off." Trim the headsail first and then, when on course, the mainsail. As noted, trimming the headsail before the mainsail will keep the boat from heading back into the wind and stopping.

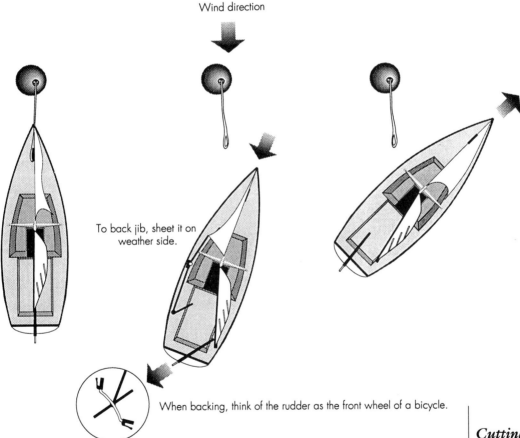

Wind direction

To back jib, sheet it on weather side.

When backing, think of the rudder as the front wheel of a bicycle.

FIGURE 6.5 *If, when departing a mooring, the boat goes backward rather than forward, aim the rudder in the direction you want the stern to turn. (This is opposite to the tiller.) You can also back the headsail to turn off the wind more quickly.*

If in light winds there is not too much strain on the mooring line, you can undo the line from the cleat. Then when the boat is downwind of the buoy, "walk" the boat past the mooring buoy. When the back of the boat is even with the buoy, let the line go. The boat should be moving in the proper direction. Trim the headsail and then the mainsail.

Sometimes, when free of the mooring buoy, the boat won't go forward; rather, it goes backward. If this happens, turn the *rudder* in the direction you want the stern to turn (see Figure 6.5). When *backing* think of the rudder as the front wheel of a bicycle. The boat backs in the direction the rudder points, which is opposite to the tiller. If the tiller is pushed to the right side of the boat (as in the illustration), the boat backs left. Similarly, if a wheel is turned to the left, or counterclockwise, the boat backs left. The opposite is true, too. (This is easy when you can see the rudder, which you usually can in small boats. In larger boats, you often can't see the rudder, which is underwater.)

MOTORING AWAY FROM A MOORING

Departing a mooring with an engine is not much different, except that the sails are rigged but usually not hoisted.* If your boat has a gas (petrol)-inboard engine—run the blower for at least four minutes to get rid of explosive gasoline fumes.

If gasoline is present in the bilge, you can often smell it.† If you do, or see any evidence of spilled gas—you should periodically check for this around fuel hoses and connections—DON'T START THE ENGINE. It isn't even a good idea to run the blower, as a spark from the blower can ignite the gasoline vapors. Find the source of the leak, repair it or have it repaired, clean the bilge, and ventilate.

This is an appropriate place to discuss fueling precautions: You should fill portable fuel tanks, such as for an outboard motor, off the vessel. All hatches and other openings on the boat should be closed before taking on fuel. Smoking material must be extinguished; the engine should be off; as should all electrical equipment, such as radios, and cooking appliances.

Spilled fuel should be wiped up immediately. After fueling, open all hatches to air out the vessel. Again, check the bilges for fuel vapors before starting the engine and don't start the engine or even run the blower if you

---

*Some sailors prefer to hoist the mainsail before leaving the mooring. When free, they trim the main and hoist the headsail.

†Some boats have automatic sniffers that sound an alarm if gasoline, propane, or other heavier-than-air fuels, used in cooking stoves, are detected in the bilge. Don't start an engine if you hear such an alarm.

detect evidence of fuel in the bilge. If all seems in order, run the blower for at least four minutes before starting the engine.

Diesel engines, which burn oil rather than gasoline, aren't normally at risk for such explosions and fires. While the fuel will burn, it requires a very high temperature before it ignites. (Incidentally, boats equipped with inboard gas- or diesel-fired power plants are referred to as "auxiliaries.")

If running an auxiliary of either type, check the engine instruments to make sure oil pressure and water temperature are normal. Check the exhaust, too, to be sure that cooling water is being expelled.

Before shifting into forward gear, check to see that there are no lines in the water that can catch in the spinning prop. To undo the mooring line from the bow when under power, shift the engine into forward gear and then almost immediately shift back to neutral. This brief spurt of power should be sufficient to take the strain off the line. Then, with the mooring buoy upwind, release the line and off you go. Again, the crew on the bow should tell the helmsperson, "We're off." Keep the buoy in view until you're clear.

Hoist sails, beginning at the back of the boat. As noted in the previous chapter, before hoisting the mainsail, turn the boat into the wind. Also, be sure you are clear of obstructions—both above and below the water.

Weighing Anchor

When the boat is anchored, the anchor must be retrieved, or "weighed" as sailors say, before departing. To do this under sail, hoist the mainsail—if it isn't already—but don't trim it. With the anchor line, known formally as the "rode," pull the boat toward the anchor.

When under power, come slowly ahead by shifting between forward and neutral gears. Watch out for anchor lines in the water, however, as you don't want to foul one with your prop. Often, the anchor will break loose from the bottom before the boat is directly over it.

If it does break free, quickly haul the remaining anchor line out of the water. Don't allow the pointed flukes of the anchor to bang into the hull, as damage can result. While keeping the flukes away from the hull, clean off any mud or debris from the anchor before bringing it aboard. Do this by pulling the anchor free of the water and then submerging it again. You may have to repeat this "bath" a few times.

If the anchor doesn't break loose, continue pulling on the rode until you are directly over it. A few strong *vertical* pulls on the rode should break the anchor loose. If it does not break free, give it a few minutes, with the boat directly over the anchor. Then try a few more strong vertical tugs.

A trip line, a light line that attaches to the anchor at its crown, can also be very handy in breaking loose a recalcitrant anchor (see Figure 10.11, page 168). It has its own buoy, a plastic bottle, or cushion, for flotation, making for easy retrieval. By pulling on the trip line, a stuck anchor should come free. Of course, you had to have rigged a trip line *before* lowering the anchor. A trip line is essential when anchoring in a rocky area. Don't forget to allow some extra line for high tide if you sail in a tidal area.

Once the anchor is free, hoist the headsail. Fall off the wind and start sailing by trimming the headsail first. If the boat won't fall off the wind so you can start sailing, the headsail may have to be backed, brought over to the wrong side (see Figure 6.5). If the boat starts drifting backward—making "sternway"—use the rudder as shown in Figure 6.5. Remember that when *backing* think of the rudder as the front wheel of a bicycle. The boat backs in the direction the rudder points, which is opposite to the tiller; once sailing, trim the mainsail. Properly coil the rode (Photo 5K, page 73). Leave it on the deck to dry, and then carefully stow the anchor and its rode so the anchor will be handy the next time you need it.

Departing from a Dock Under Sail

Keeping a boat at a dock or pontoon, which is connected to land, offers many conveniences. For example, you can more easily bring gear aboard the boat and take it off. Also, there is no need to ferry people and equipment in a dinghy. However, departing from a dock—particularly when under sail—is not one of its major conveniences. A key to departing a dock is to use the elements to your advantage—not fight them. That is, in fact, a key to successful sailing.

Again, the most fundamental question is: Which way is the wind blowing? When departing a dock under sail, ideally, you want the dock upwind of your boat, not your boat upwind of the dock. Figure 6.6 shows the desirable orientation. Note how the wind hits the dock *before* it hits the boat. As such, the dock is "upwind" of the boat. Also, if your stay is only to be a short one, such as for fuel or supplies, try to tie up to the dock on its lee, or downwind side. This downwind position will make your departure much easier.

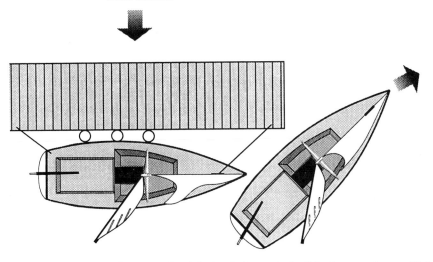

Wind direction

FIGURE 6.6 *The easiest departure is with the dock upwind of the boat as shown. If the wind is on the beam or forward, the sails can be hoisted. Then, if nothing is in your way, the boat is walked along the dock by a shroud or side stay. Once clear, trim the headsail and then the main.*

WHEN THE DOCK IS UPWIND OF THE BOAT

The easiest departure is when the dock is upwind of the boat, as described. When this is the case and the wind is light, hoist the mainsail and the headsail, but don't trim them yet. (If the wind is light and is on the beam [perpendicular to the boat, as shown] or forward of the beam, you should be able to hoist the mainsail by easing the mainsheet [the line used to trim the mainsail in and out]. This can obviate the need to turn the boat into the wind.)

Once the sails are up—again, *not* trimmed—undo the mooring lines. Be sure, however, that there is someone on the dock, holding the boat by a shroud or side stay. Then the boat can be carefully walked with the shroud, while the wind keeps the boat away from the dock. (See Figure 6.6.) The assumption here is that no boat is blocking your way.

When the bow clears the dock, the remaining person can carefully step aboard (assuming he is going with you), using the shrouds to help him get aboard. Then, the headsail is trimmed, which as we now know drives the

Cutting Loose

89

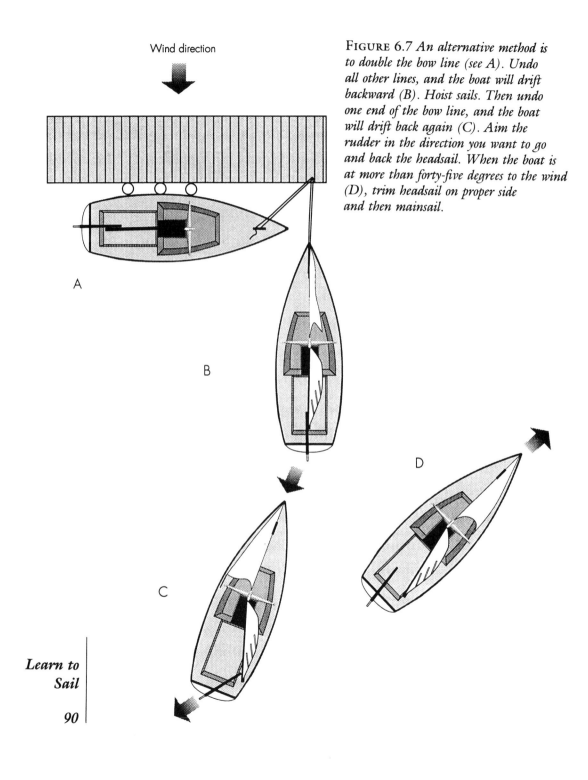

Wind direction

A

B

C

D

FIGURE 6.7 *An alternative method is to double the bow line (see A). Undo all other lines, and the boat will drift backward (B). Hoist sails. Then undo one end of the bow line, and the boat will drift back again (C). Aim the rudder in the direction you want to go and back the headsail. When the boat is at more than forty-five degrees to the wind (D), trim headsail on proper side and then mainsail.*

bow down and starts the boat moving forward. If the main is trimmed, however, the boat will head up, possibly into the dock. When clear and sailing, the main can be trimmed. If it is windy, or the wind is aft of abeam so you can't hoist the mainsail, undo all lines except the bow line (see Figure 6.7, position A). The bow line should be looped, or doubled, around a cleat or piling, so you can easily release it from on board and take it with you.

After the sails are up but untrimmed, one end of the bow line is released. (Of course, before releasing the bow line, be certain that there is nothing behind you, such as a boat about to dock, that is in your way.) The bow line is brought aboard the boat.

The boat, pushed by the wind, is allowed to drift back. The farther the boat is from the dock, the better, because the danger is that when you start sailing, you will head up into the dock again.

While first moving backward, keep the rudder centered, as shown in Figure 6.7B. When far enough from the dock, turn the rudder in the direction you wish to back (C). Remember, it is helpful when backing to think of the rudder as the front wheel of a bicycle. Since, in Figure 6.7, we want to depart on port tack, turn the rudder to the left side. To do this, push the tiller to the right side or turn the wheel to the left, or counterclockwise.

You can back the headsail, too, to help turn the boat off the wind (C). When the boat is at more than forty-five degrees to the eye of the wind (beyond the no-sail zone), trim the headsail (D). If you have backed the jib, ease the sheet on that side and trim it on the correct side using the opposite sheet. Once sailing in the forward direction, turn the rudder in the opposite direction. This will help to resist the boat's natural tendency to turn back into the wind. When the boat has "headway" (is moving forward) and is not in danger of turning upwind and into a dock or other obstructions, trim the mainsail.

WHEN THE BOAT IS UPWIND OF THE DOCK

If you're on the wrong side of a dock, try to walk the boat around it so you're not trapped. If you're lucky, no boats will be blocking your way. Alternatively, you can power off—assuming you have a motor (see below)—or maybe you can find someone to give you a tow.

Another option is to take the anchor in the dinghy and place it upwind as far as you safely can. (Of course, the anchor should be attached to the boat by the rode.) The farther from the dock you can drop the anchor, the better. This is because a boat on a long anchor line is less likely to drag its anchor and drift back.* If you do drift back, place a large "fender," or rubber bumper, between the boat and dock to minimize damage. (Fenders should be kept handy [on deck] for this contingency.) Then, when back aboard the boat, pull the anchor line from the bow—by a winch if you have one—as the dock lines are released.

When clear of the dock, you should be able to hoist the sails without too much difficulty. Watch out that you don't drag anchor and drift backward. You will need to recover the anchor, of course (see above).

The options get worse after that. To try to hoist the sails on the *upwind* side of a dock invites ripped sails, a capsizing, or other assorted indignities. If, however, the dock doesn't present any obstructions to hoisting the mainsail and then traveling parallel to it, and the wind is light, and the boat small, you might try raising the mainsail with the boom *over* the dock. Don't trim it. Be aware that the stack mainsheet can easily snag on a cleat or any other obstruction on the dock. Someone on the dock can push the boat away from the end of the boom. He should walk along the dock with you until you are clear of it, but it will be difficult for him to jump aboard.

Mooring Lines (or "Warps")

"Warps" tie a boat to a dock; they also are helpful when departing under power. Before discussing this, it is important to name each warp.

Figure 6.8 shows a boat tied to a dock. It has bow and stern lines, as labeled. It also has forward and after "springs." (Note the *forward* and *after* designation of spring lines has to do with the line's direction as it *leaves* the boat, not whether it attaches to the forward part of the boat [the bow] or on the after part [the stern].) These four lines are adequate for normal wind and sea conditions. Also note the rubber fenders (circles in the illustration), which help to keep the dock from damaging the boat.

The boat also shows a "breast line," or rope, sometimes secured to another pontoon or attachment point upwind when it is particularly windy, to help keep the boat away from the dock. An anchor, dropped from a dinghy, is sometimes substituted for a breast line. Also, when it is windy, it is possible to double up bow, stern and spring lines. Doubled-up lines

*"Scope," as described in Chapter 10, is the ratio of the length of the anchor line to the depth of the water. Simply considered, the more *horizontal* the anchor line, the better. A five to one scope, if your rode is made of rope, or fifty feet of anchor line in ten feet of water, should provide adequate purchase unless it is particularly windy. Thus, if the water where you're dropping the anchor is ten feet deep, you'd want to paddle upwind at least fifty feet. With a chain rode, a four to one scope should suffice.

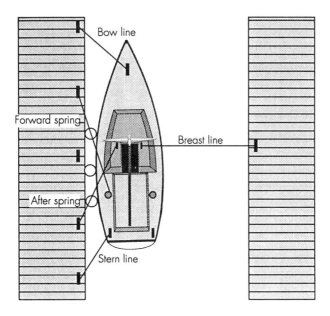

FIGURE 6.8 *Mooring lines and their names. A breast line is a heavy-weather option.*

should be equal in length, otherwise one or the other will do all the work and be more likely to break. The idea is to share the load.

Departing a Dock Under Power

When leaving a dock under power, your first decision is whether you wish to use reverse gear to move away from a dock or forward gear. That decision often depends on the positions of other boats. Once you've made this decision, announce it to the crew.

LEAVING A DOCK IN FORWARD GEAR

If a boat is behind you, you'll likely opt to leave a dock by going forward. To do this, double the forward-spring line around a cleat or piling before releasing the other lines. (Note also that this line will prevent your boat from backing into the other boat [see Figure 6.9, inset A].) Release the other lines. Keep the fenders in place, however.

While this is labeled a forward departure, it begins by shifting into reverse. This causes the boat to back up against the forward-spring line. At the same time, it pivots the back of the boat *toward* the dock; an extra fender

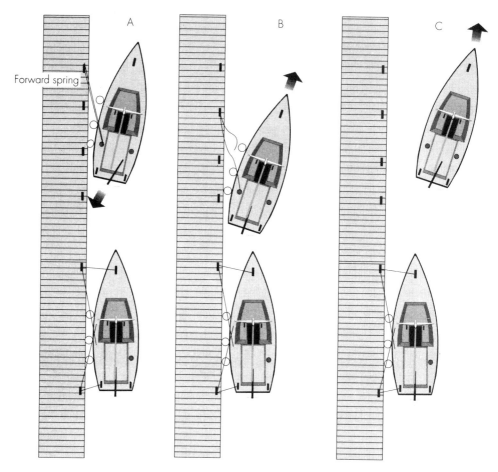

FIGURE 6.9 *Leaving a dock in forward gear: Start by doubling the forward-spring line (left) and back against it. Shift into forward gear and undo one end of forward-spring line (center). Off you go (right).*

might be needed aft when backing up, so keep one handy. At the same time, it pivots the front of the boat *away* from the dock. Note how the rudder angle complements backing against the forward-spring line.

Then shift into forward (see Figure 6.9B) and release the short end of the forward-spring line. Quickly bring it back aboard by pulling the other end, so as to keep it from the spinning prop. Off you go in forward gear.

Pay attention to the tiller angle in Figure 6.9C. Like the child's car, where the back wheels steer (Figure 6.1), this will move the stern of the boat *away* from the dock. A mistake sailors often make is to turn the tiller

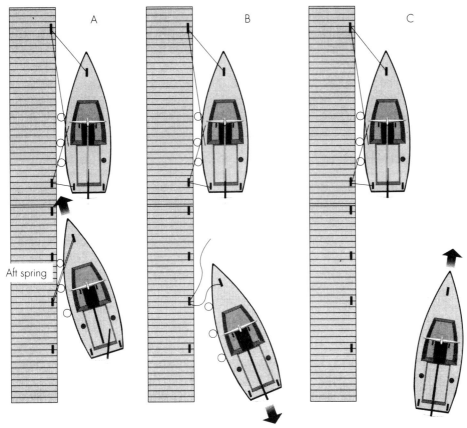

FIGURE 6.10 *Leaving a dock in reverse gear: Start by doubling the aft-spring line (left) and go forward against it. Shift into reverse gear, undo aft-spring line (center), and back away. When clear go forward (right).*

the other way, which moves the stern *toward* the dock—perhaps causing a collision with the dock or another boat.

LEAVING A DOCK IN REVERSE GEAR

If the boat is in front of you, you'll likely opt to back out. To back out, double the after-spring line. Release the other warps and bring them aboard (see Figure 6.10A). Keep the fenders in place.

    While ultimately we will back away from the dock, the maneuver begins by going forward (see Figure 6.10A). Shift into forward gear for a moment.

As the boat strains against the after-spring line, the bow of the boat moves *toward* the dock, and pivoting around the axis, the stern moves *away* from it. Also note the rudder angle; this, too, helps the bow move closer to the dock and the stern away from it. Another fender forward may be necessary, so have one handy.

Once the stern is out (see Figure 6.10B), shift into reverse, and with the rudder centered back out.* Release the short end of the after-spring line and bring it onto the boat by pulling the other end. Once clear, go forward.

Remove Fenders

If your boat was tied to a dock or pier, it likely has fenders over the side to protect the boat from such things as hard pilings. Remove the fenders once free of the dock, even though you will likely need them later.

At the risk of sounding pretentious, a boat displaying fenders at an inappropriate time is a dead giveaway that the people aboard don't know what they're doing. It's the same type of thing as calling lines on a boat ropes.

First Sail

Book work can only take you so far. It's time to take that first sail, to begin to get comfortable with some of the things we've discussed. Of course, the day of your first sail should be suitable for learning—not too much wind, not too little. (See Chapter 4 for more details on the optimum conditions for learning to sail.)

Sailing on a beam reach (see Figure 6.11), or with the wind at a right angle to the boat, is the ideal direction for a maiden voyage. First, the boat doesn't heel as much as when sailing upwind. This lack of heeling when reaching tends to be reassuring. Also, the margin for steering error is greatest when reaching. Then, too, there's nothing more fun than beam-reaching. When sailors have no particular destination in mind, they just beam-reach back and forth.

I certainly don't expect you to solo at this point—I expect you to be with an instructor or experienced sailor. This person should put the boat

---

*When in reverse, the prop in most auxiliary sailboats turns to the left, or counterclockwise. This causes the boat to back slightly to the left. If there were a boat behind the departing boat in Figure 6.10, this natural tendency could be a problem. This is discussed more fully in Chapter 10 in the Docking Under Power section.

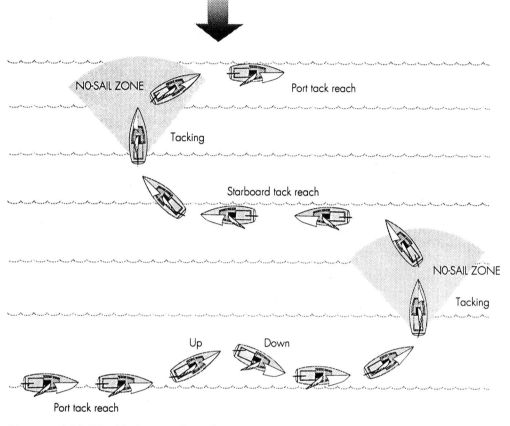

Wind direction

NO-SAIL ZONE

Port tack reach

Tacking

Starboard tack reach

NO-SAIL ZONE

Tacking

Up   Down

Port tack reach

FIGURE 6.11 *The ideal course for a first sail is to beam-reach back and forth. When beam-reaching, the wind is kept at a right angle to the boat.*

on a beam reach. Since you aren't steering yet, study what's happening. Note the wind direction as it registers on the telltales on the shrouds and the angle of the masthead fly. They should be at a right angle to the bow of the boat. Also, note the direction of the waves: usually when beam-reaching the waves run downwind and hit the side of the boat.

Beyond seeing, engage some of the other senses. For example, when beam-reaching, what does the wind feel like on your face?

Watch the positions of the wind indicators as the instructor turns the boat up into the wind; the motion of the boat is usually more spirited. Can you feel it? The boat also heels more, and waves are more likely to splash aboard.

Cutting Loose

97

Conversely, watch the positions of the wind indicators as the instructor turns farther off the wind or down. How does the boat feel then? The boat should be standing taller, and the wind should feel lighter when heading close to the same direction as the wind.

Keep an eye on the telltales as the instructor tacks the boat through the eye of the wind. What are your senses telling you as the boat passes through the no-sail zone? You should feel the boat slowing. What does the wind feel like on your face—is its angle different? Also, watch how the sails swing from one side to the other and how the boat leans in the opposite direction. Be sure to keep your head beneath the boom, however, as it swings across. The sails often make noise when passing through the no-sail zone; did you hear anything? Then watch as the instructor falls off on a beam reach on the other side.

Watch where the instructor sits and how he uses his body—that is assuming he has good form. Body position is important in sailing as it is in most sports. The person steering the boat should sit on the weather, or high side, and—perhaps—at the forward end of the tiller or the tiller extension, if the boat has one. The helmsperson should glance at the headsail and mainsail (see Photo 6A) but through peripheral vision or a quick turn

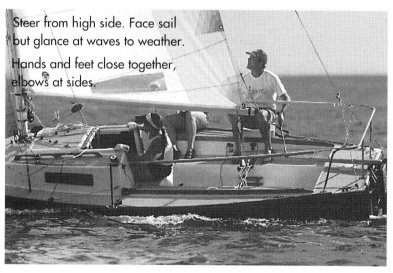

Steer from high side. Face sail but glance at waves to weather.

Hands and feet close together, elbows at sides.

PHOTO 6A *This helmsman shows perfect form. If it were windy, he might hold the mainsheet in his front hand. In a puff when less power is needed, he would ease the mainsheet. In a lull, he would trim it.* (Courtesy J Boats, Inc.)

of the head watch the waves to weather—that is, the waves moving toward the boat. His hands are close together. Elbows are at his sides and feet close together. This is an efficient and comfortable position.

Note how the instructor holds the tiller or tiller extension in his back hand. Good sailors show a light touch on the tiller or wheel. If it is windy, the mainsheet is often held in his front hand. This allows the helmsman to "dump" (ease) the mainsail quickly if the boat becomes overpowered. Easing the main is like hitting the brake on your car. When the boat needs more power, the helmsman may trim it more. That's like the accelerator. With sufficient crew, as is often the case in a bigger boat, another crew member can work the mainsheet.

Now you try it. Take the helm from the instructor. At first, work on body position and try to keep the wind at a right angle to the boat (see Figure 6.11). Remember, to get the boat to turn left, push the tiller right. And vice versa. Get used to it. Try steering up a bit (this is shown in the bottom of the figure): push the tiller toward the sails or turn the wheel away from them. Then try steering off: pull the tiller away from the sails or turn the wheel toward them. Once on course, it can be helpful to aim for a landmark on shore.

From the beginning, it is important to form good habits. When sailing, you should always keep a lookout for other boats or navigational buoys, so as to avoid a collision. This means periodically glance to weather, where visibility is generally good, as well as to leeward, where generally it isn't. Sailboats have a considerable blind spot to leeward under the sails, but that doesn't excuse you from keeping a proper lookout.*

Also, try steering with the sails. When on a beam reach, trim the mainsail and ask a crew member to ease the headsail, and the boat should turn into the wind. Ease the mainsail and have a crew member trim the headsail, and the boat should turn away from the wind.

Prepare to tack, from beam reach to beam reach (Figure 6.11, bottom right). Before tacking, glance directly behind you and check if there is a distinctive landmark, buoy, or boat that can be a helpful reference point. That course is 180 degrees from your present heading. To tack from a beam reach on port tack, to a beam reach on starboard tack, as shown, involves a turn of 180 degrees. Remember, sailing is the sport of geometry. After the tack, you will be aiming at that mark.

---

*Rule five of the "International Regulations for Preventing Collisions at Sea", under which most of us sail, reads, "Every vessel shall at all times maintain a proper look-out by sight and hearing as well as by all means appropriate in the prevailing circumstances and conditions so as to make a full appraisal of the situation and of the risk of collision." See Chapter 13.

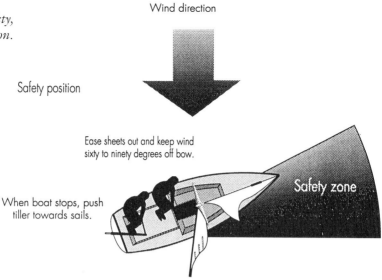

FIGURE 6.12 *The safety, or basic hove-to position.*

Wind direction

Safety position

Ease sheets out and keep wind sixty to ninety degrees off bow.

When boat stops, push tiller towards sails.

Safety zone

The instructor should help in this maneuver. When everyone is ready, push the tiller *toward* the mainsail or turn the wheel *away* from it. Trim the mainsail to facilitate the turn into the wind. The boat will pass through the no-sail zone, and the headsail will be released on one side and trimmed on the other. At the same time, the crew crosses the boat to the new high side. Watch your heads, however, as the boom will be swinging the other way. Ease the main to facilitate the turn off the wind. You're on course again when sailing toward the landmark or buoy you noted earlier. It is a good idea if you do both jobs at different times: steer through a tack and work the sheets. (This important maneuver is shown fully in the next chapter in Figure 7.7, page 116.)

Above all, relax and enjoy yourself. Enjoy the process of becoming a sailor as much as the result.

Basic Hove-to Position

If you get confused, need time to straighten something out, make a repair, or just want a break, you can always stop sailing. There is a proper way to do this, however. With the wind at a right angle to the boat, as it is when beam-reaching, ease the sheets of the mainsail and headsail (if you have one) well out (see Figure 6.12). Once the boat stops, aim the tiller at the sails. (With a wheel, turn it away from the sails.)

This is called the "basic hove-to position." Set up this way, the boat should ride quite comfortably.

To get moving again, center the helm. Then trim the headsail, first, and then the main.

7 | Sailing to Windward

I left you beam-reaching in the last chapter, or with the wind at ninety degrees to the boat. This I described as the ideal direction for a maiden voyage—indeed any voyage. I trust you found it that way. Come up a mere forty-five degrees into the wind, however, and it's another world.

Sailing has an "uphill" and "downhill" direction in the sense of harder and easier. In sailing, this translates directly to upwind and downwind. Upwind, like uphill, is more difficult in practically every respect than sailing downwind, which is loosely defined as reaching and running.

For example, you can't sail directly upwind—the closest a sailboat can sail is about forty-five degrees to the wind—so to reach a point to windward, a sailboat must tack (see Figure 2.10, page 24). If the shortest distance between two points is a straight line, the zigzag course of tacking resembles the route of your laced shoelace. Tacking can easily double the distance you must cover.

Even without tacking, upwind sailing is about the slowest point of sail. This is because, at this wind orientation, more of the wind force goes into heeling the boat than into producing forward motion. (This is shown later in Figure 8.1, page 125.) To be precise, the sideways force (heeling) is four times greater than the forward force when sailing upwind. Not only is excessive heeling slow, but it can be uncomfortable for sailors.

Upwind sailing also feels windier, and it is. It works this way: If your boat is at anchor, or stationary, a 10-knot wind feels and would be measured as a 10-knot wind. If, however, you pulled up the anchor, hoisted sails, and started sailing dead downwind at five knots, that 10-knot wind would be measured as five knots $(10 - 5 = 5)$. If you powered directly into the wind at five knots, that 10-knot wind would feel as if you're sailing in 15 knots $(10 + 5 = 15)$.

Of course, a sailboat can't sail directly into the wind, so maybe that ten-knot wind with five knots of boat speed at a forty-five-degree angle to the wind would be measured as a thirteen-knot breeze. The wind you feel when stationary is called the "true wind." The wind you feel when moving is called the "apparent wind." How fast you move and in what direction relative to the wind affect the apparent wind.

The difference between true and apparent wind is an important distinction in sailing. On the simplest level, it's why you feel cooler when sailing upwind and why the jackets go on; it's why you feel warmer when sailing downwind and why the jackets come off.

With the wind and waves approximately in your face, sailing upwind is often harder on the boat and on the crew. The bow of the boat rises to meet each wave and drops down as it passes. This can be little more than a burble on a lake or a fifteen-foot transition on a stormy ocean. The rising and falling of the bow is formally known as "pitching." Also, when sailing upwind, the waves are more likely to find their way onto the boat and onto those sitting there. This is exacerbated by the fact that optimum crew position when sailing upwind is forward in the boat and on the windward side (more later).

What's in a Name?

It is a direction of many names: Beyond upwind sailing, this orientation of the bow of the boat to the wind is also known as sailing close-hauled, or on a close-hauled course. That is a good descriptive name, as it is as *close* to the wind as a sailboat can sail. As we will see shortly, when sailing on a close-hauled course, the headsail is trimmed *close* to the shrouds, or side stays, and the mainsail is trimmed *close* to the centerline of the boat. Beating is another name for this orientation.

Determining Wind Direction

It is not sufficient to listen to the TV weatherman or the marine forecast and conclude, *OK, it's a west wind. That's that for the day.* Why that isn't sufficient is because the wind is constantly changing in direction and in speed. Watch a weather vane, and you'll see abundant proof of the ever-changing nature of the direction of the wind. Watch an anemometer, a wind-speed indicator, and you'll see a variability in wind speed, too.

This is significant because five degrees difference in wind direction affects how the sails are set and even the course you sail. That is one of the things that makes sailing interesting if challenging.

Monitoring the wind is an ongoing process in sailing. As noted, you can't really see the wind, which is invisible, of course, but you can see and feel abundant evidence of it. The more sensitive you are to the obvious and subtle signs of the wind, the easier learning to sail will be. The better sailor you will become, too.

Centerboard Position

When sailing upwind, where most of the force from the sails is sideways, we need maximum force from the centerboard to help keep the boat from sliding sideways, too. You accomplish this by lowering the centerboard fully—that is, depth of water permitting. While a keel can't normally be raised and lowered, it is noteworthy that the deeper a designer makes a keel, the more resistant the keelboat is to sliding sideways and the faster upwind it is, too.

The centerboard down fully when sailing upwind is the first of what we will term a distinguishing—or characteristic—position. I want you to think, *I'm beating, my centerboard should be down.*

It is helpful, I believe, to think of the centerboard position in the sequence, or continuum, of beating-reaching-running and most-less-least. As will become apparent in this and subsequent chapters, beating-reaching-running and most-less-least tend to go hand in hand.

Leeway

While you can lessen the sideways slipping by fully extending the center-board, you can't eliminate it. This is true for a keelboat, as well. Sailors refer to the inevitable sideways slip of a boat as "leeway."

You've heard the expression about taking one step forward and two steps back. Leeway is analogous to taking five or six steps forward and one to the side.

You will notice leeway—that sideways step—the most when sailing on a close-hauled course. Suppose when sailing in such a direction, you have aimed the bow of the boat at a navigational buoy, familiar cottage, or landmark across a lake. By the time you've reached it, you'll likely have drifted a couple of degrees below it (see Figure 7.1). The lesson of leeway is that given enough time one step off to the side for every five or six steps forward adds up.

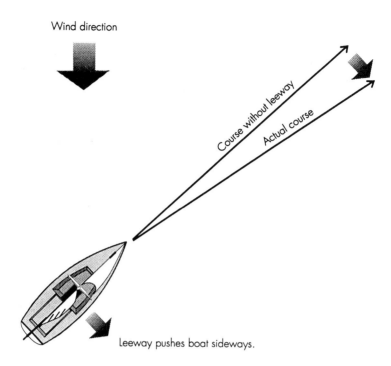

Wind direction

Course without leeway

Actual course

Leeway pushes boat sideways.

FIGURE 7.1 *Leeway—which can be thought of as one step to the side for every five or six steps forward—is most apparent when sailing on a close-hauled course and in light winds. When it is windy, or when sailing on a reach, leeway can be thought of as one step to the side for every seven steps forward.*

Due to the effects of leeway, experienced sailors will try to sail a few degrees high, or above, course to arrive at their upwind destination. This is referred to as "making an allowance for leeway" and is shown later in Figure 10.1, page 152.

Similarly, when sailing upwind, it is often preferable not to pass too close upwind of a moored or moving boat, as you may hit it (see Figure 7.2). It is generally safer to pass such an obstacle to leeward. You can remember this by the words: *leeway, leeward.*

Perhaps, you've noticed, a pattern is beginning to emerge: In the last chapter, we wanted to be on the leeward side of a dock and depart on the leeward side of a mooring. The wind pushing the sailboat away from an obstacle—or a lineup of wind, obstacle, and sailboat—is safest.

Note that a boat going slowly shows more leeway than a boat going fast. When going slowly, it is even more important to avoid passing moored or moving boats too close to weather.

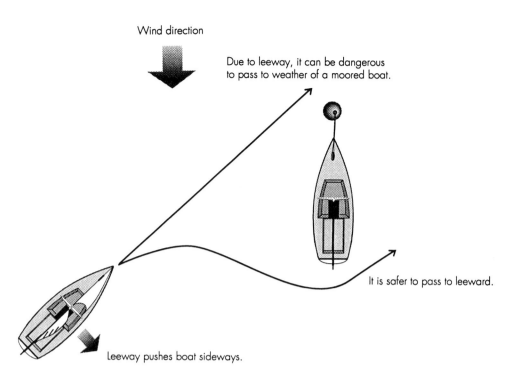

Wind direction

Due to leeway, it can be dangerous
to pass to weather of a moored boat.

It is safer to pass to leeward.

Leeway pushes boat sideways.

FIGURE 7.2 *Due to leeway, it is safer to pass a moored boat, or obstruction, to leeward, or on the downwind side.*

As described, leeway is at its maximum when going slowly and when sailing upwind. To put this in the continuum: It is less when reaching and generally unimportant when running.

Sail Trim

The second characteristic position of upwind sailing, or sailing close-hauled, is to trim the sail(s) in tight. Using the headsail sheet, trim the headsail until it is close to the shrouds, or side stays (see Figure 7.3). If the headsail overlaps the mast—a headsail that overlaps the mast is a genoa—be careful that you don't trim the genoa so much that you put the spreaders, supporting the mast, through it. A nonoverlapping headsail, which is called a jib, is often trimmed inside the shrouds. The crew is responsible for trimming the headsail.

In a small boat that is steered by a tiller, the mainsheet is often the responsibility of the helmsperson: the back hand holds the tiller, the front hand, the mainsheet. With a wheel-steered boat, which generally requires

Sailing to Windward

105

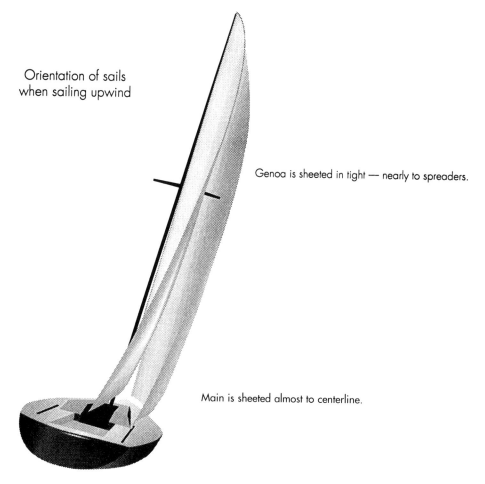

Orientation of sails when sailing upwind

Genoa is sheeted in tight — nearly to spreaders.

Main is sheeted almost to centerline.

FIGURE 7.3 *The sails are trimmed in the most when sailing upwind, or close-hauled.*

two hands for steering, one person steers and often another person tends to mainsail trim.

When sailing upwind, trim the mainsail with the mainsheet until the boom is nearly on the centerline of the boat but not above it (see Figure 7.3). The *close*-in positions of both sails allow the boat to make the best progress when sailing on a *close*-hauled course.

If the sails must be *in* tight, when beating, they also should be *up* tight (see Photo 5I, page 70). Sailing upwind requires relatively flat sails, so when beating make sure the halyards, controlling the headsail and the mainsail, are up tight. Maximum halyard tension will flatten the sails. (Some mainsails use a Cunningham, a block near the bottom-forward corner of the sail [the tack area], to flatten it. How halyard tension and the Cunningham affect sail shape is discussed in Chapter 11.)

Luffing

As mentioned so often, a sailboat can't sail closer to the wind than about forty-five degrees. If, however, you steer it closer to the wind, let's say forty-three degrees—a mere two degrees difference—the sail will start to "luff". Luffing is a bubbling, shaking, or wrinkling of a sail, which begins at the leading edge (see Figure 7.4). (Note that the leading edge of a sail is also called the luff. Later in this chapter, we will see that "luffing up" means altering course toward the wind, or heading up.) Sometimes the entire leading edge (top to bottom) of a sail will luff; other times, luffing is seen at the top, middle, or bottom.

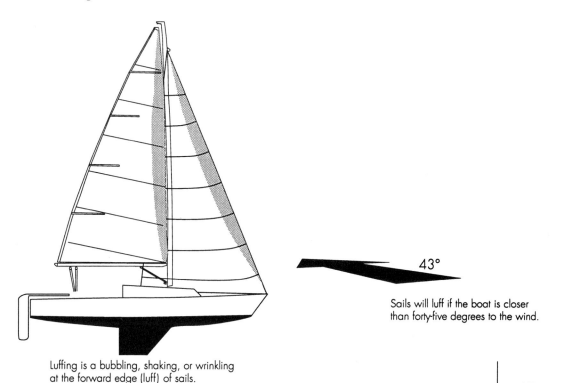

43°

Sails will luff if the boat is closer than forty-five degrees to the wind.

Luffing is a bubbling, shaking, or wrinkling at the forward edge (luff) of sails.

FIGURE 7.4 *If the sails are in tight, as they should be when sailing on a close-hauled course, forty-five degrees to the wind is about as close as a sailboat can sail. Closer than that, forty-three degrees, for example, the sails will luff.*

The Cure for Luffing

Generally, two actions will cure luffing: trimming the sails more or turning farther off the wind, or a little of both. Since, when sailing upwind, the sails should be fully trimmed in—make sure they are—you can't trim them anymore. So when sailing upwind, steering corrections take precedence over sail trim. When reaching, you have a choice (see the next chapter).

When the sails start to luff, turn the bow a few degrees farther from the wind—from forty-three to forty-five degrees, for example. To accomplish this with a tiller, pull the tiller *away* from the sails (see Figure 7.5). With a wheel, turn it *toward* the sails. (You're about to become very familiar with these words.)

In practice, sailors should often glance at the luff of the sails, looking for signs of luffing. It is usually easier to see luffing on the headsail, rather than the mainsail, as the mainsail works in the disturbed flow behind the mast. In other words, the mainsail can give false readings. (Of course, if your boat only has one sail, like a Sunfish, or Laser, you have no choice.)

Notice, we said above that if the sail is luffing, turn the bow *a few degrees* off the wind. You don't want to turn too far off the wind because

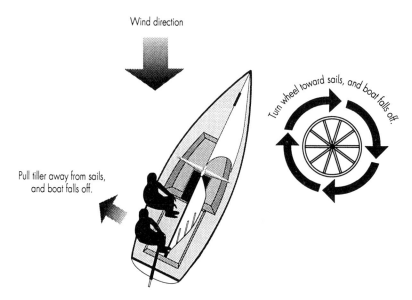

FIGURE 7.5 *The cure for luffing when sailing on a close-hauled course is to turn the bow farther away from the wind—from forty-three to forty-five degrees, for example. When on course, luffing will stop.*

if you do, you could end up reaching rather than beating. If you sail at fifty-two degrees, a close-reaching course, it will take you longer to get to a point upwind than if you sailed at forty-five degrees. To paint this in an extreme manner, if you sailed no closer than ninety degrees to the wind, a beam reach, you'd never get to a point upwind.

Thus, another principle of upwind sailing is that you should try to keep your boat at a forty-five-degree angle to the wind—that will get you upwind most directly.

By the way, sailing consistently high of course is described as "pinching." Sailing consistently low of course is "footing." We will begin to use these terms in this text.

Telltales on the Headsail—Visual Aids

Obviously, when beating, you must steer a fine line. As a steering aid, many headsails have ribbon "telltales" affixed to the front, or luff, of the sail (see Figure 7.6). Often, clear plastic windows frame these telltales, to help you to discern better the windward telltale from the leeward one. (If there isn't a clear plastic window, you can normally see the color of the windward, or front, telltale and the shadow of the leeward, or back, telltale.)

Often, telltales are made of different color yarns: red yarn on the port, or left side, and green yarn on the starboard, or right side. This is to help you better distinguish which is the windward telltale and which the leeward one. (Red, by the way, is the normal color for port—it is seen, for example, on port-side running lights on boats. Green is the color for starboard.) Also, the starboard-side telltales are often slightly higher than those on port.

Three pairs of telltales on a headsail are optimum. One set should be one-quarter of the way down from the top; another should be one-quarter of the way up from the bottom. The third pair—the most important—should be in the middle.

If the headsail is all the way in and its windward and leeward telltales are streaming aft, you're on a proper upwind course: forty-five degrees to the wind. (See the middle boat in Figure 7.6.) If, however, the *windward*—or front—telltale droops (see the left-hand boat), you're too close to the wind, or pinching. The left-hand boat in the figure appears to be sailing at about forty-three degrees to the wind. To correct this pinching, or sailing too high, the helmsperson on this boat should turn the bow a few degrees off, or away, from the wind. Again, if you have a tiller, pull it *away* from the sails. If you have a wheel, turn it *toward* the sails (see Figure 7.5). If this boat fell off two degrees, the windward telltale would stream aft again,

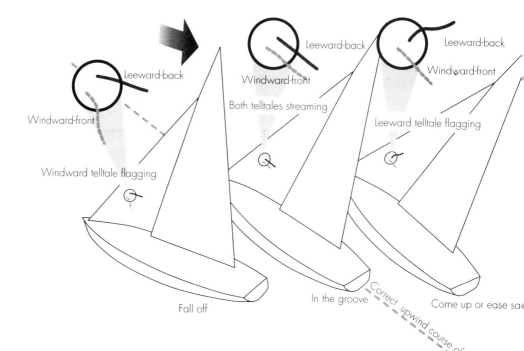

Leeward-back

Windward-front

Both telltales streaming

Leeward-back

Windward-front

Leeward telltale flagging

Leeward-back

Windward-front

Windward telltale flagging

Fall off

In the groove

Correct upwind course of forty-five degrees

Come up or ease sai

FIGURE 7.6 *Once the sails are trimmed fully, you are on course if both telltales are streaming aft as shown on the headsail on the middle boat. Fall off if the* windward *telltale is drooping (left-hand boat), as you are steering too high, or pinching. Come up or ease sails if you are happy with the course if the* leeward *telltale is skying (the right-hand boat), as you are sailing too low, "footing."*

or "reattach." Now the telltales would look like those on the middle boat—the boat that is on course.

If, however, you stray too far off the wind, and the *leeward*—or back—telltale skies (the right-hand boat), you're not sailing as high as you can. You're footing. This boat appears to be sailing at forty-eight degrees to the wind. The helmsman of this boat should turn up again—that is, assuming he wants to make optimum progress upwind (see below). Angle the tiller *toward* the sails, or turn the wheel *away* from them. You're on course when the windward telltale streams aft again or reattaches. Again when on course the telltales will look like those on the middle boat.

Finally, while there is something wrong with steering at forty-three degrees (the left-hand boat has entered the no-sail zone), there's nothing wrong with steering at forty-eight degrees (the right-hand boat). You just won't get upwind as fast. If the helmsperson of the right-hand boat likes this course—if it's taking him where he wants to go—he could ease the sails a little bit. With the ease, the leeward telltale on the headsail would reattach, or flow aft. Then sail trim would be perfect for the close-reaching course, or sailing at forty-eight degrees to the wind.

Obviously, you should have telltales on your headsails.* If you don't have them, you at least have an indicator of when you're pinching, or pointing too high into the wind: the luffing of the headsail. So without telltales steer up until the headsail luffs, and then turn *just enough off* the wind to still the luffing. When the luffing just stops, you're on course: forty-five degrees to the wind. With the changing nature of the wind, you should periodically test this sweet spot to make sure you're on course. It is, obviously, a trial-and-error process. (Other steering aids, such as the compass and a landmark ashore, are discussed in the next chapter.)

Where to Sit

In the last chapter, I wrote that the helmsperson should sit on the weather rail, facing the mainsail. What about the crew and how far forward or back in the boat should they sit? Also, is there a difference in crew position when beating, reaching, or running? Let's get more specific.

Recall that when sailing on a close-hauled course, most of the force is off to the side. This sideways force is reflected in heeling, the natural tendency of a boat to lean away from the wind, and leeway, the inevitable sideways slip. As the boat heels the most when sailing upwind, the placement of crew is most critical at this wind orientation.

When sailing upwind in medium to heavy winds (twelve-plus knots), the crew generally sits on the weather, or high side of the boat along with the helmsman. With a centerboard boat, which doesn't have the weight of the keel to help counterbalance the forces from the sails, the crew might even hike, lean out with their feet under hiking straps, on the high, or weather, side (see Photo 3A, page 36).

Up to twenty degrees or so of heel is normal, but much beyond that and the boat is slow. Also, if sailing a centerboarder, this excessive angle of heel puts you closer to capsizing.

While heeling to leeward—or leaning away from the wind—is normal, you don't want the boat to heel to windward—toward the wind. Thus, in light winds, the crew is often in the center of the boat or even on the low,

---

*If you don't have telltales, and the boat is yours, add them. Red and green yarn should be stuck to the left and right sides of the sail, respectively, with some tape. As noted above, I prefer to see three sets of telltales. Place them on a headsail twelve to twenty-four inches back from the luff; the bigger the boat, the farther back.

or downwind, side. Some leeward heel in very light winds gives the sails some shape, which helps them catch the wind. The crew should be ready to move immediately to the high side in a stronger puff of wind. Similarly, they should be ready to move quickly off the weather rail, or high side, if the wind dies suddenly. Keeping the boat balanced is a mark of a sailor. Failure to do so is the mark of a swimmer.

At the beginning of this chapter, I commented that when sailing upwind, a boat pitches the most. While this rising and falling of the bow with the waves is inevitable, the boat sails better (faster and more comfortably) if the pitching motion is minimized.

A boat pitches around an axis. This axis is perpendicular to a line running from the bow to the stern and is near to the center of the vessel. To decrease pitching, you want to concentrate crew weight at the center of pitching—about the middle of the boat but behind the mast.

This is why when sailing upwind, the crew might sit just behind the mast on the weather rail; the helmsperson might use the tiller extension to sit forward in the cockpit. To put this in the continuum, this is as far forward as the crew generally sits. They move progressively back in the boat when reaching and running.

The problem with this relatively forward position when sailing upwind is that it can be wet—what with waves breaking and wind blowing in your face—especially for the crew. I can tell you, this tends to make them grumpy. Wearing foul-weather gear, or water- and wind-protective clothing, is usually a good idea when sailing, but in particular when sailing upwind. Be smart, put such protective clothing on before you get wet. More to the point, if it's wet forward and you're not racing, or there isn't some other compelling reason to minimize pitching, let the crew move farther back in the boat.

Upwind Sailing Summary

To summarize upwind sailing: One, the centerboard should be fully down if a centerboard boat.

Two, the sails should be trimmed in close when on a close-hauled course.

Three, the sails should be fully hoisted with the halyards or Cunningham in the main to flatten them.

Four, an angle of forty-five degrees to the wind should be maintained if you want to sail to a point upwind most directly. Use the telltales on the headsail or continue to test the luffing point to stay on course.

Five, the helmsperson and crew should be on the weather side, in moderate and windy conditions, even hiking out. In very light winds, one or more of the crew should be on the centerline—even on the low side to give the sails some shape. However, the crew should be ready to move to the high side in a puff of wind. They should be ready to move off the rail if the wind suddenly dies.

And, six, the crew should sit forward in the boat, if it isn't too wet or uncomfortable—at the center of pitching. This helps to minimize the motion. The helmsperson should sit forward, too, using the tiller extension, if there is one.

Steering Up

A boat moves from a run (with the wind at 175 degrees, or on the stern), to a beam reach (90 degrees, or perpendicular), to a beat (45 degrees), by steering the bow of the boat *closer* to the direction of the wind (see Figure 2.9, page 22). This turn toward the eye of the wind is called "steering up", "coming up", "heading up", or "luffing up".

Again, to luff up with a tiller, you push it *toward* the sails (see Figure 6.4, page 82). To luff up with a wheel, you turn the wheel *away* from the sails. (You're going to get familiar with these words, too.)

At the same time as you luff up, trim the sails gradually from a right angle to the boat on a run, to halfway in from there on a reach, to all the way in, on a beat. Depending on the boat's size, this can represent several feet of sheet trimming. This can be a problem when the person steering and trimming the mainsail is one and the same. The problem for the helmsman/mainsheet trimmer is: Without a cleat, or a third hand, what do I do with the extra line I've gained?

Some sailors will trim the mainsheet with their forward hand, then put the line they've gained into their teeth. Then trim the line some more. Frankly, teeth make poor cleats. Having done this, I can tell you the line doesn't taste particularly good. If you sail on the ocean, it tastes salty and dirty. If you sail in freshwater, it's even less appetizing: it just tastes dirty.

I commented in the previous chapter that your hands should be near each other when steering a boat with a tiller. One reason for this is if your hands are close together (see Photo 7A) and you need to trim the mainsheet, you can easily transfer the sheet you've gained to the back, or tiller, hand. It works this way: Trim the mainsheet with the forward hand. Then without losing what you've gained, transfer the mainsheet to your tiller, or back hand. Trap the line between your back hand and the tiller. Reach forward

Trim mainsheet with front hand.
Pass line gained to tiller hand.
Trim mainsheet some more with
front hand.

PHOTO 7A *How to trim the mainsail and steer the boat with only two hands.* (Courtesy Sunfish Laser, Inc.)

and grab more line with your front hand. Then without losing what you've gained, transfer the mainsheet to your tiller, or back hand. And so on.

Recall that both sail trim and the rudder steer sailboats. Trimming the mainsail as you steer up will make the boat turn into the wind more quickly and easily than merely steering up. You should do both when you wish to come up.

Bearing Away

On the other hand, you move from a beat, to a reach, to a run by steering down. This turn away from the eye of the wind is termed "bearing away." To bear away with a tiller, you move it *away* from the sails. With a wheel, you turn it *toward* the sails (see Figure 7.5). When you bear away, it is helpful to watch the telltales on the shrouds or the masthead fly; they should appear to rotate gradually toward the front of the boat. Stop when the masthead fly or telltales are angled off the back. If you continued turning down, you could accidentally gybe, which could be dangerous (see Figure 6.4, page 82).

At the same time as you bear away, ease the sails progressively from all the way in, to halfway, to a right angle to the boat. Easing the mainsail at the same time as you change the angle of the helm will, in fact, cause the boat to fall off the wind more quickly and easily. You should do both when you wish to bear away. This is particularly important when it is windy—when the boat is most resistant to turning off the wind. In fact, there are times it won't turn off the wind until you ease the mainsail.

If the Boat Heels Too Much

Ideally, the crew should anticipate a gust—a sudden increase in wind—and get to the weather rail before the boat heels too much. You can often see a gust moving across the water—it appears darker. You can also see other boats on your weather side, if there are any, suddenly heel. Nevertheless, recognizing a gust is an acquired skill.

If the crew is slow to respond, or even if they are on the weather rail in plenty of time, but you need to flatten the boat more, the helmsman can turn the boat slightly into the wind. To put this another way: pinch when overpowered by a gust. At the same time, you can ease the mainsail to further depower. With a substantial gust, usually all these things happen at the same time: the crew moves to the high side and hikes if necessary, and the helmsman turns the boat into the wind and eases the mainsail.

Sometimes even these three actions are insufficient; in more extreme conditions, ease the headsail as well. (Also see reefing in Chapter 11.)

Be careful, however, about easing the mainsail or headsail too much, especially if you have crew hiking on the weather rail. This is because a sudden loss of power can cause this person to fall overboard, or the boat to capsize to windward.

Tacking

Tacking gets a boat upwind. It is also the simplest and probably safest way to reverse direction. When tacking you pass through that no-sail zone of forty-five degrees on either side of the wind. As such, tacking involves a turn of at least ninety degrees.

Tacking works this way: One, before tacking, the helmsman looks upwind, to make sure there is nothing on that side that will interfere with the ninety-degree turn. (See Figure 7.7. Note the numbers in the text correspond to the numbers in the illustration. The text is more complete, however.) This is analogous to making a turn in your automobile; you wouldn't or shouldn't make a turn without seeing what's on the next street. It is a good idea for the crew to look, too. Remember, keeping a proper lookout is an abiding principle of sailing.

Further, if there is a distinctive landmark, a navigational buoy, or

Wind direction

E

7) Crew trims headsail for new course — all the way in, as shown in E, if continuing to sail upwind.

D

6) When on the new high side, helmsman pivots his body and grabs the tiller with new back hand (right). Sheet is already in that hand. Once seated, helmsperson reclaims the mainsheet with left hand.

C

5) Helmsman follows the crew to the high side (D). Until he pivots (see Step 6), he holds both the tiller and the sheet in the same hands, as in Step 4. Note the rudder angle; the boat is still turning away from the wind.

4) Crew member(s) move first to the opposite side of the boat (C), being careful to avoid the swinging boom. Crew should cross centerline when the boom does. Note in C that the helmsman has the tiller in his left hand and the sheet in his right.

B

3) As the boat swings into the wind, crew releases headsail sheet (on low side) when the headsail starts to luff.

2) Helmsman calls, "Ready about." If ready, crew says so. The helmsman says, "Hard-a-lee," and tiller is pushed toward the sails (B). If a wheel, turn it away from the sails.

A

1) Before tacking, make sure there is nothing in your way. Also, look ninety degrees to the direction of the boat, or at three o'clock, for a distinctive landmark, boat, or buoy. You will be aiming for this after you tack. Keep speed up. Helmsman tells the crew, "Prepare to tack." If using a winch, crew wraps a couple of turns of high-side headsail sheet around it clockwise (Boat A) and checks that low-side sheet is free to run.

Learn to
Sail

FIGURE 7.7 *Tacking: a time-and-motion study. Start at the bottom of the figure.*

another boat at ninety degrees to the boat, or at three o'clock in the illustration (nine o'clock if on other tack), note it. Such things help immeasurably in completing the maneuver—that is, fully crossing the no-sail zone so you can start sailing on the other tack.

The helmsperson also makes sure that the boat has good speed, as a lack of it can ruin the turn. For the full ninety degrees when in the no-sail zone, or one-quarter of a circle, you can't summon extra power. If, before tacking, the boat seems slow for the conditions, head off a few degrees (pull the tiller away from the sails or turn the wheel toward them) to build speed. Also, if the waves are large, don't tack until you are in a smoother patch of water. Waves, like the wind, vary.

If the way is clear and the conditions right, the helmsperson tells the crew, "Prepare to tack."

To do this, the crew makes sure the headsail sheet on the low or leeward side is free to run. On a smaller boat, you can often check and clear this from the high side; on a larger boat, a crew member goes to the low side and checks the sheet.

If this is a bigger boat (i.e., a boat with winches), we'll assume that there are at least two crew, besides the helmsperson, to work the headsail sheets. A smaller boat (without winches) would likely have one person work both sides.

With a larger boat, wrap one or two turns around the winch on the high side—remember winches are wound clockwise—and pull the slack out of the sheet. An unloaded sheet, as this one is for the time being, is a "lazy sheet." If there is only one person tacking the boat, he will shortly move to the new high side, with the lazy sheet in his hand. If there are two people, one stays on what is presently the high side, to trim the lazy sheet once the boat tacks. The other stays on what is presently the low side to ease the sheet and free it from the winch as the tacking maneuver starts.

Two, the helmsperson calls, "Ready about." If the crew is ready, he signals it by saying, "Ready." If not, he communicates that. When everyone is ready, the helmsperson says, "Hard-a-lee," "Hee-ho" or "Helm's a-lee." This means—literally—that the tiller is pushed toward the lee (downwind) side of the boat, or toward the sails. Which way to turn the tiller when tacking is confusing to beginners, so as a memory aid: When *Tacking*, push the *Tiller Toward* the Mainsail. T-T-T (Recall that I used a variation of this when describing how to avoid an accidental gybe [see Figure 6.4, page 82].)

If steering with a wheel, turn the wheel *away* from the sails.

There is a definite rhythm to tacking. Throwing the helm over too quickly is like jamming on the brakes of your car. It can ruin a tack. Not turning quickly enough can ruin a tack, too.

Three, as the helmsperson pushes the tiller, starting the turn into the wind, the crew releases the headsail sheet. The precise time to release the headsail is when it starts to luff (see Figure 7.4)—the front edge breaks.

If the headsail sheet on the low side needs to be unwound from a winch, pull the sheet upward from the winch; be very careful not to get a finger caught under a sheet on a winch or in a block, which can be serious. Make sure the headsail sheet runs smoothly: that it doesn't kink in a block or catch on a shroud. If it does, clear it immediately, but keep your head away from the swinging boom.

Four, as the boat turns into the wind, crew members on the high side— it won't be high for long—duck their heads to avoid the swinging boom. This is very important as serious injury can result should the boom hit someone's head. Then the crew moves to the new high side. They should cross the centerline about the same time as the boom does and they should also always be looking forward, but, again, avoid the boom. (Sometimes the mainsheet is in the way, so look backward.)

If a small boat, the crew member should have the lazy sheet in his hand as he moves to the new high side.

Five, before the boat heels too much, the helmsman should move across the boat with the back hand (left in this case) *still* on the tiller and the front hand (right) on the mainsheet, as these are, in essence, the steering wheel and brake, respectively.

Once across the boat, the helmsperson pivots his body and grabs the tiller with his new back hand (right). The sheet, too, is already in this back hand, and it stays there for a moment trapped between the tiller and hand. The boat is allowed to continue to turn off the wind. (A common mistake is to stop the turn too early; see "caught in irons" below).

Six, after sitting on the new high side, the helmsperson reclaims the mainsheet with his new front hand. He looks at the telltales to make sure he is on course: forty-five degrees to the wind but on the other tack.

Again, a tack involves ninety degrees, to move through the no-sail zone. If you were able to find a reference point, navigational buoy, boat, or landmark at ninety degrees to the boat before tacking, you're through the tack when the bow is aiming at it.

And, seven, the crew member continues trimming the headsail. Before the headsail sheet starts to slip on the winch—if your boat has winches— give the sheet an extra turn or two around the winch. (If a crew member is on the low side, he should do it. If not, a crew member from the high side goes to the low side to perform this duty.)

To add turns to a winch, hold your left hand over the coils (assuming you're right handed) so they don't slip using the flat of your hand and keeping your fingers clear, and carefully take a turn or two of the line with your right hand. Don't allow a finger to become trapped under the line. (The line will have to be cut in a hurry if this happens; this is one reason why sailors keep a sharp knife handy.) Trim the sheet all the way in if the next course is also upwind, as in the illustration.

Getting Out of Irons

As a moored boat automatically turns into the wind, a boat under sail wants to turn into the wind. This is known as "weather helm." Because of this natural tendency of a boat to turn into the wind—and stay there—it is important that the tacking maneuver be done efficiently. If sufficient speed isn't carried through the turn, or if you don't pass completely through the full ninety degrees, the boat can get stuck head to wind—stuck in the no-sail zone. Sailors call this predicament being "caught in irons".

The trap is easy to recognize: When caught in irons, the boat turns back into the wind and stops (see Figure 7.8 top). It doesn't respond to the rudder. (You will recall from the previous chapter, you can't steer a boat if it isn't moving.) Then it begins drifting backward.

The remedy for being caught in irons is to wait until the boat starts drifting backward. Then, turn the rudder to one side and hold it there. If you want the stern to go left and the bow right, as in the figure, push the tiller to the starboard, or right side. Remember, where the back of the rudder points is the direction the back of the boat goes; it is as if the rudder were the front wheel of a bicycle.

Backing the jib, as described in the previous chapter, is also helpful when caught in irons. A backed jib, or mainsail, helps the boat turn more rapidly off the wind. Note in the figure how the backed jib and tiller are on opposite sides. This way, they're working together.

Once the boat has turned sufficiently off the wind, to at least forty-five degrees to the eye of the wind, straighten the rudder. Then tack the headsail (allow the sheet to run) and trim it on the "correct" side. Trim the headsail but not the mainsail. When going forward, you will probably have to pull the tiller or turn the wheel to the opposite side, to help the boat fall farther off the wind. When speed builds, trim the mainsail. If you're going in the wrong direction, don't tack immediately, unless you absolutely have to;

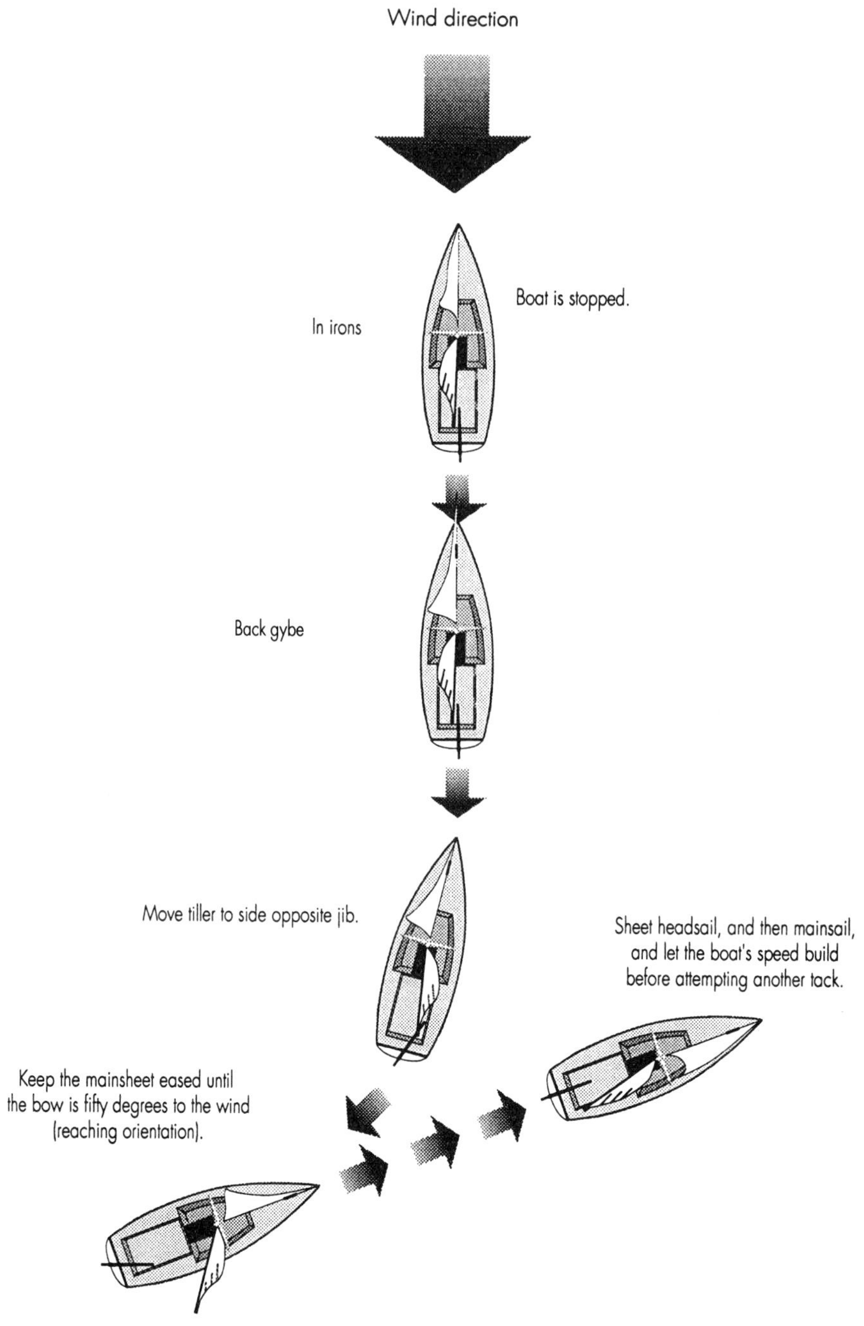

Wind direction

In irons
Boat is stopped.

Back gybe

Move tiller to side opposite jib.

Sheet headsail, and then mainsail, and let the boat's speed build before attempting another tack.

Keep the mainsheet eased until the bow is fifty degrees to the wind (reaching orientation).

Learn to Sail

FIGURE 7.8 *Getting out of irons.*

rather, wait until speed has sufficiently built. Otherwise, you can find yourself caught in irons again.

State of Confusion

If you get confused when learning to sail—and you're going to get confused—the first question to ask yourself is: Where's the wind? The second
question is: What is my angle to the wind? More often than not, you'll find
yourself in the no-sail zone—that is, trying to sail closer than forty-five
degrees into the wind. This is true because of the natural tendency of a
sailboat to turn into the wind.

If you aren't yet caught in irons, fall off a few degrees. Remember, to
accomplish this with a tiller, pull the tiller *away* from the sails (see Figure
7.5). With a wheel, turn it *toward* the sails. (This is the opposite of tacking.)
Due to the natural tendency of a boat to turn into the wind, or weather
helm, you're going to turn off the wind more than anything else. The
quicker you learn how to do that, the quicker you'll become a sailor.

Tacking Geometry

Among other things, sailing, you will recall, is the sport of geometry. The
theory of tacking is relatively straightforward: To reach a point upwind,
you sail at a course of forty-five degrees to the wind on one tack; let's say
starboard. Then you cross the eye of the wind, and sail at forty-five degrees
to the wind on port. Eventually, after two or more tacks, you'll get to a
point upwind. Generally, it is best to make a few shorter tacks, rather than
just two longer ones.

New sailors, as well as seasoned ones, wonder whether one tack is
favored or will help you reach your destination sooner. That is a subject that
people write books about.* A couple of suggestions are helpful, however. If
on one tack the bow of the boat is aimed closer to your destination, sail
more on that tack. If you can't tell the difference, neither tack is favored,
so split your time between the two.

A second suggestion is to sail more on the lifted tack. Earlier, I commented that the wind is always shifting. Note in Figure 7.9 how it can shift
toward the back of the boat, called a lift, or shift toward the bow, called a
"header." A lift will take you closer to your destination, a header farther
away.

---

* See *Sail Like a Champion* (St. Martin's, 1992), by Michael Levitt and me.

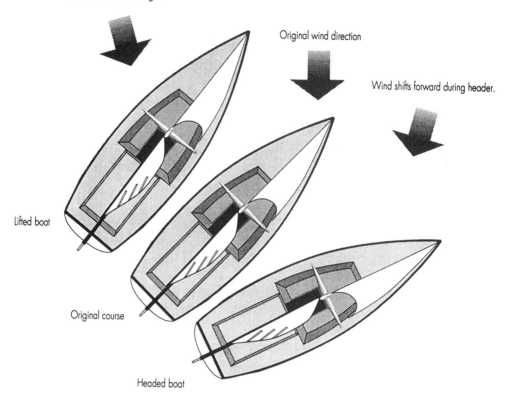

Wind shifts back during lift.

Original wind direction

Wind shifts forward during header.

Lifted boat

Original course

Headed boat

FIGURE 7.9 *An added complication in sailing is that the wind tends to shift in direction. A shift toward the back of the boat (counterclockwise on port tack) is a lift—see the top boat. A shift toward the bow (clockwise on port tack) is a header—the bottom boat.*

If you've been steering fairly straight and the headsail starts to luff (Figure 7.4), or the windward telltale flags (Figure 7.6), you're probably on a header. That might be a good time to tack. If, however, you've been steering fairly straight and leeward telltale flags, you're on a lift. Rather than tacking, come up and sail more directly toward your destination. You'll get there sooner.

Note in Figure 7.10 how you can normally make your final approach to the mark, or a landfall, when it is abeam of your boat, or at ninety degrees, or more, to the boat's centerline. (This number shouldn't surprise you, as the no-sail zone represents an area of ninety degrees.) If this were a clock, you could tack for a mark—or make your final approach—when its bearing was at least nine or three o'clock. Twelve o'clock is represented by the boat's bow.

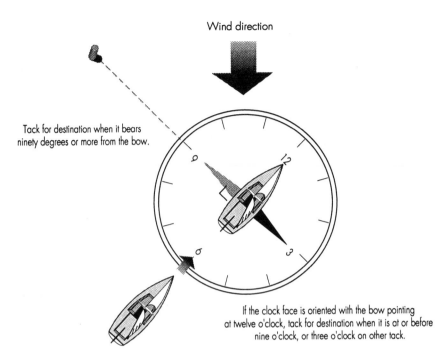

Wind direction

Tack for destination when it bears ninety degrees or more from the bow.

If the clock face is oriented with the bow pointing at twelve o'clock, tack for destination when it is at or before nine o'clock, or three o'clock on other tack.

FIGURE 7.10 *With ninety degrees off limits—the no-sail zone—you can tack for your destination when it is at ninety degrees to your boat, or at nine o'clock, as shown, or three o'clock if on starboard tack.*

Of course, tidal stream can force you to wait a while before making your final tack to a mark as can a shift in the wind. You might want to delay your tack until the mark bears more than ninety degrees to your boat—perhaps half past eight if on port tack, as in the figure, or half past three if on starboard. Another alternative is to take some extra tacks.

Practice!

Learning to sail is both a theory and a practice. Practice sailing upwind: luffing up and bearing away. Watch the telltales and the masthead fly rotate. These things are your reference points; their positions should become as familiar to you as the hands on the face of a watch.

Practice sailing on the fine line of forty-five degrees. To find out how close you are to the wind, use the telltales on the sail or use the luff of the headsail. Practice tacking. When you find yourself in irons—and you will find yourself in irons—practice getting out.

Sailing to Windward

8 | Reaching

It's time to sail downhill. Reaching, the subject of this chapter, is in comparison to beating, or sailing upwind, a walk in the park. It is more like a sprint in the park, as this orientation is the fastest point of sail. And fast, as you will discover quickly, can be great fun in a sailboat.

Why Reaching Is Fast

In Chapter 3, I noted that a soccer ball remains at rest until someone kicks it. Imagine two people kicking one soccer ball at the same instant. An observer would only see the *combined* effect of those two kicks, that is the total force. By constructing a parallelogram, a mathematician could resolve the total-force vector of the soccer ball into the direction and magnitude of the two kicks.

Figure 8.1 shows a boat sailing upwind, or beating, top, and a boat beam-reaching, bottom. Both show a total-force vector.* Note, first, how the total-force vector is more off to the side of the boat that is beating (top) than the total-force vector is when reaching. Simply considered, when reaching, more of the force is in the direction you wish to go: ahead. That's one reason why reaching is faster than beating.

There's another way to look at this. The total-force vector, or the force from the sail, can similarly be resolved into two other vectors: a heeling

*When looking at a vector, always consider its direction and magnitude, or length.

Wind direction

Total force= heeling force + driving force

Upwind orientation

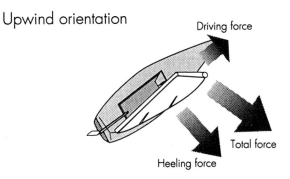

Driving force

Total force

Heeling force

Heeling force is greater in upwind position.

Reaching orientation

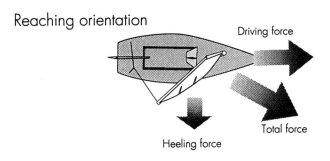

Driving force

Total force

Heeling force

Driving force is greater on reach.

FIGURE 8.1 *Vectors show why reaching is faster than sailing upwind. Most of the force (total-force vector) is off to the side when sailing upwind (top). That translates to increased heeling and decreased driving force. Compare those vectors—their length and direction—to those emanating from the bottom boat, which is reaching.*

force and driving force. Note when beating (top), the heeling force is four times greater than the driving force. When reaching, the heeling force is about one-quarter of the drive force. Thus, a boat heels less on a reach than on a beat, and less heel translates to greater speed. This is because the rig stands taller and the keel, or centerboard, and rudder sit deeper.

Another advantage of heeling less is that bigger sails can be used. They are like having a bigger engine in your car: As a result, you go faster.

A reach is also faster than a run because, when running in the same direction as the wind, a sail is only a wind-blocking device, like a kite. There isn't any pressure differential, or lifting force. Catching the wind is what moves sailboats when running; thus, it isn't possible for a sailboat to go faster than the wind at this orientation. When reaching, a sailboat *can* go faster than the wind. It is noteworthy that boats sail upwind and run at about the same speed.

A keelboat, which is held deep in the water by its heavy keel, is limited in its speed by the waves that form around a hull. The formula that expresses how fast a keelboat can go is: $1.34 \times \sqrt{waterline\ length}$. Waterline, you will recall from Chapter 3, is the horizontal dividing line between the topsides and the underbody.*

A boat with a twenty-five-foot waterline has a top speed of 6.7 knots ($\sqrt{25} = 5 \times 1.34 = 6.7$), or 7.7 mph. This number represents what yacht designers term "hull speed," a true point of diminishing return. For a keelboat to exceed that number requires a huge increase in power, such as the occasional surf down a wave or a tow by the *Queen Elizabeth II*. While keelboats have been known to plane, it is the nautical equivalent of breaking the sound barrier.

Although a keelboat can reach top, or hull, speed at any wind orientation, it is most likely to do so when reaching, specifically with the wind at eighty degrees to the bow. It is least likely to do so when beating, with the wind at forty-five degrees to the bow.

It is the waves forming around a hull that creates this hull-speed limit for a keelboat. When a keelboat is going at half speed, *two* small waves form around a hull (see Figure 8.2, top left). (Note that when talking about waves, it is the horizontal measure from crest to crest [see the figure].) When a boat is going at hull speed, or as fast as it can go, *one* large wave overlaps the hull (see Figure 8.2, top right). The wave pattern looks like a hole and acts like a hole, trapping the boat between the bow (front) wave and stern (back) wave.

Without the downward pull of a keel, a centerboard dinghy, however, can "plane," i.e., rise and ride the forward wave, or bow wave (see the photo in Figure 8.2). At speed, a planing boat has escaped the hole formed

---

*A boat's length of waterline (written as L.W.L.), differs from its length overall (L.O.A). A J/24, for example, is 24 feet overall, which is the distance from the bow to the stern, on deck. Its waterline length is 20 feet.

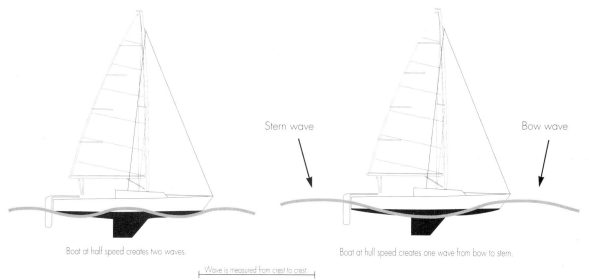

Stern wave

Bow wave

Boat at half speed creates two waves.

Boat at hull speed creates one wave from bow to stern.

Wave is measured from crest to crest.

One wave

A planing boat leaves its stern wave and rides
up its bow wave.

FIGURE 8.2 *At half speed, a keelboat shows two waves (top left-hand boat), measured crest to crest. At hull speed, it shows one (top right-hand boat). At hull speed, which is top speed, a keelboat is trapped by its bow and stern wave. Not burdened by a heavy keel, a centerboard boat can plane—rise out of the water and ride its bow wave (see photo inset), leaving its stern wave behind.*

by the waves. With less of the boat in the water, a planing boat can sail significantly faster than hull speed.

A water-ski boat is a planing boat, too. Apply sufficient power, and the boat leaves its stern wave behind and climbs its bow wave. If you've ever waterskied, perhaps you've noticed the distinctive wave several feet behind

Reaching

127

the boat. That's its stern wave that the boat has left behind. The tow rope is made sufficiently long so the skier doesn't have to contend with it.

The windsurfer, an ultimate planing sailboat, has reached speeds above fifty mph. That is thirteen times hull speed. At such speed, only the skeg (a centerboardlike device at the back of the board) is in the water.

Again, a boat planes easiest when reaching, with the wind at about eighty degrees to the bow. That, as we will see immediately, is near to the beam-reaching orientation.

Close-, Beam-, and Broad-Reaching Angles

Beating represents a very narrow band: the bow of the boat is from 45 to 50 degrees to the direction of the wind. Reaching, by way of contrast, represents a huge slice of the pie: from 50 to 170 degrees. Thus, reaching is conveniently divided into the continuum of a close reach, beam reach, and broad reach (see Figure 8.3).

A boat is close-reaching when the angle of its bow to the wind is from 50 to about 90 degrees; it is beam-reaching when at 90 to 120 degrees to the wind. A boat is broad-reaching when the angle of its bow to the wind is from 120 to 170 degrees. (That said, these are fairly arbitrary numbers, or divisions, that might differ somewhat in other books.)

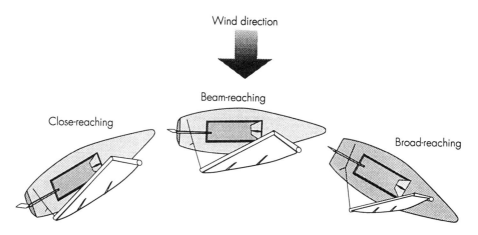

FIGURE 8.3 *Close-, beam-, and broad-reaching angles. Note how the sail is progressively eased when falling farther off the wind.*

Sail Positions

Figure 7.3, page 106, shows the close-in positions of the mainsail and headsail when sailing upwind. To use the continuum idea again: Ease the sails progressively when moving from a beat to a close reach. Ease them farther when moving from a close reach, to a beam reach, to a broad reach, or when bearing away (see Figure 8.3). On the other hand, trim them progressively when moving from a broad reach, to a beam reach, to a close reach, to a beat, or when coming up to wind.

That is too vague, however, to be very helpful. Once on course, or headed in the direction you wish to go, ease the sails until they luff (see Figure 7.4, page 107). Luffing, you will recall from the previous chapter, is the shaking, wrinkling, or bubbling of the luff, or forward edge, of a sail. Once you have established the luffing point by easing the sails, trim them only enough to stop the luffing. Remember, a sail trimmed in too much is slow; so, too, is one let out too much.

Note that when learning, there is a tendency to associate heeling with boat speed. Thus, new sailors often overtrim sails because they think they're going faster and, thus, sailing better. The truth is that when the sails are overtrimmed, you've only increased the heeling force (see Figure 8.1), not speed (the driving force).

Any change in course or change in the direction of the wind will require different trim. The reality of this is that you should test the luffing points of both sails often.

Recall that when beating, sails had maximum halyard tension, which flattens them. Halyard tension can be eased progressively when moving from a beat, to a close reach, to a beam reach, to a broad reach. This is because fuller sails are faster when reaching. When it is windy, however, flatter sails, or more halyard tension, can decrease heeling.

Using Telltales When Reaching

Using the telltales on the luff of the headsail (see Figure 8.4) is a better way to trim the headsail on a reach. First, the helmsman steers the boat in the direction he wishes to go. Then, once on course, if both telltales on the luff of the headsail are streaming aft, this signals proper trim (see the middle boat).

If, however, the windward, or front telltale, is drooping (in Figure 8.4, see left-hand boat), you are sailing too high for the sail trim. You have the options of trimming the headsail more or bearing away—that is, turning

Reaching

129

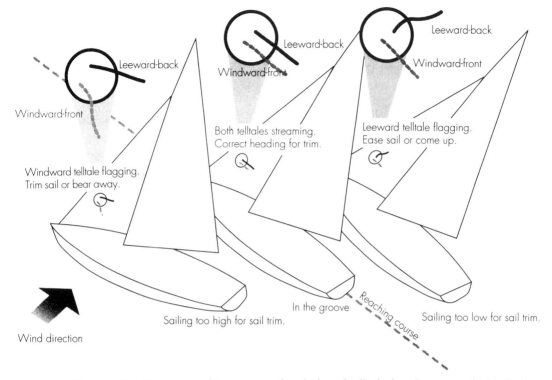

Leeward-back

Windward-front

Leeward-back

Windward-front

Leeward-back

Windward-front

Windward telltale flagging.
Trim sail or bear away.

Both telltales streaming.
Correct heading for trim.

Leeward telltale flagging.
Ease sail or come up.

Wind direction

Sailing too high for sail trim.

In the groove

Reaching course

Sailing too low for sail trim.

FIGURE 8.4 *If, when reaching, you see the windward telltale drooping, as on the headsail on the left-hand boat, you have the options of trimming the headsail, bearing away, or both. If you see the leeward telltale skying, as on the right-hand boat, you have the option of easing the headsail, coming up, or both. You want both telltales streaming aft, as on the middle boat.*

the boat farther off the wind – or doing a little of both.* To bear away, as I've said so often, pull the tiller away from the sails or turn the wheel toward them (see Figure 7.5, page 108). Once you do one or both of these things, the front telltale, like the back telltale, will stream aft. When both telltales stream aft, the sail trim is right for the course.

When the leeward, or back, telltale skies (Figure 8.4, right-hand boat), you are sailing too low for the sail trim. You have the option of easing the

*When reaching, you can stop the sails from luffing by steering off the wind or trimming the sails, or both. Compare this to beating, discussed in the last chapter, where only steering off the wind cures luffing. Why sail trim isn't an appropriate remedy for luffing when beating is because, at this orientation, the sails are all the way in. You can't trim them any more. They aren't, however, fully trimmed when reaching and thus, either action—trimming sails or bearing away—is an appropriate answer to luffing.

sail or turning the boat closer into the wind, or both. To come up, push the tiller toward the sails or turn the wheel away from them (see Figure 6.4, page 82). Once you do one or both of these things, the back telltale will stream aft again. Check the telltales on the headsail often, too, to optimize sail trim.

Generally, there aren't telltales on the luff of the mainsail. As a rule, the main should have a similar angle to the centerline of the boat as does the headsail; to be more precise, trim it a little more than the headsail. A better way to test mainsail trim is to ease it until it luffs (see above) and then trim it back again until the luffing stops.

Other Steering Aids

Luffing and telltales aren't the only steering aids. A compass, for example, a magnetic-north seeking device, can be helpful in steering, whether on a reach, beat, or run. Once on course, look at the numbers on the compass—practically all boats have them. Suppose it says that you are sailing at 090 degrees—note that three numbers are given for courses and bearings to avoid confusion. This means your course is 90 degrees from magnetic north.* If you can keep the bow of the boat at this angle, you'll steer straight. And steering straight is an unequivocal theme of sailing.

That said, it isn't easy to steer straight—particularly when you are learning. Less than attentive steering, or a wave pushing the bow away from the wind, and the compass reads 095 degrees, for example.

When that happens, do you turn the bow of the boat right or left to return to your original course of 090 degrees? That is a more confusing question than you might think.

It is helpful to think of the compass as the face of an analog clock—the old-fashioned kind with hands. As the clock goes clockwise, or right, the numbers get larger. If the clock could go counterclockwise, or left, the numbers would get smaller. If the number on the compass (095°) is larger than the desired course (090°), as in the example, turn the boat left, or

---

*A magnetic compass points to magnetic north, or the location of the earth's magnetic pole. To complicate matters, this magnetic pole is at some distance from the earth's north pole, which is also known as "true north." This is where the meridians, or north-south longitude lines, meet at the north pole. The difference between magnetic north and true north (or the north pole) is known as "variation." Depending on where you are on the earth, variation can be negligible, or close to zero degrees, if you sail on Lake Michigan, or sixty degrees off the west coast of Greenland. On a nautical chart are two compass roses; the inner one shows magnetic north, the outer one, true north. Since magnetic compasses read magnetic courses, sailors are more interested in the inner compass rose.

counterclockwise. The numbers will get smaller. If the number on the compass is smaller than the required course, turn the boat to the right, or clockwise. The number will get larger.

While a compass is a very helpful device—I wouldn't sail without one—it is often easier to stay on course when you aim the headstay at a landmark or buoy, assuming there is one.

Centerboard Positions When Reaching

As the centerboard is fully down when beating, raise it about a quarter of its depth when close-reaching, halfway up when beam-reaching, and three-quarters up when broad-reaching. Again, think of it in the context of a continuum. However, if the boat starts sliding sideways—this is often something you can see by turning around and watching the boat's wake, or trail—put the board down a few inches until the sideways slipping stops. Some centerboards will vibrate in their trunks, or housings, when less board is needed. Remember, in sailing, pay attention to the obvious and subtle clues.

It is a good idea, too, to mark the centerboard positions for the various points of sail. Often, the line or lever that controls the depth can be easily marked.

Where to Sit When Reaching

The crew was forward in the boat when beating. When reaching, they can move progressively back in the boat, as you move from a close reach, to a beam reach, to a broad reach. This is the continuum idea again.

While a boat that is reaching heels less than when beating, and progressively less when moving from a close reach, to a beam reach, to a broad reach, it still heels. Therefore, the side-to-side balance of the boat is still important whether you sail a centerboard boat or keelboat. Generally, when it is moderate to windy, the skipper and crew sit on the high side—even hike out if a centerboard boat.

For the helmsperson, the high side is a better place to see the wind on the water and the waves. As a driver watches the road surface to avoid potholes, a helmsman watches the waves to avoid big ones. If a sizable wave is coming, you turn *slightly* into it and into the wind to meet the wave more squarely on the bow. Once the wave passes, you turn off *slightly* for acceleration. Don't, however, overdo this.

The steerer should be comfortably and securely perched on the weather rail; many boats have angled footrests to help the helmsman when steering—these are particularly useful on a windy reach, where the motion of the boat can be quite spirited.

If, when it is windy, one hand isn't sufficient to hold the tiller, use two. Make sure, however, that a crew member is poised to work the mainsheet if there is a gust that heels the boat excessively. If the boat heels too much, quickly ease ("dump") the mainsail sheet, and even the jib sheet. When reaching in heavy winds, the boom vang, rather than the mainsheet, is used to alleviate excessive heeling (see Chapter 11).

When steering with a wheel on a reach, the helmsperson often stands, using the wheel itself and the angled footrests to stay securely in place. It is then a crew member's responsibility to dump the mainsheet, boom vang, or traveler (the latter two controls are also discussed in Chapter 11). As when sailing close-hauled, watch out for other boats to weather, as well as under your sails.

Reaching Summary

In summary, when sailing on a reach: One, ease the sails progressively when moving from a beat, to a close reach, to a beam reach, to a broad reach, or when bearing away. Use the luff of the sails—or better yet, the telltales on the luff of the headsail—to determine proper sail trim. The sails are progressively trimmed when moving from a broad reach, to a beam reach, to a close reach, to a beat, or when coming up.

Two, don't overtrim the sails when reaching—a common error. While undertrimming is more obvious—due to the luffing of the sails—don't undertrim them either.

Three, ease halyard tension when moving from a beat through a broad reach; full sails are better when reaching. If it is windy and the boat is heeling too much, however, flatter sails, through increased halyard tension or Cunningham tension in the main, can decrease heeling.

Four, sit progressively farther back in the boat as you move from a beat through the three reaching orientations.

And, five, steer from the high side. Watch the waves. Turn the bow up slightly as a big wave approaches, to meet it more squarely. After the wave passes, turn off slightly to accelerate. If necessary, use both hands on the tiller. If using two hands, make sure a crew member is available to dump the mainsheet, the jib sheet, the boom vang, or traveler if the boat suddenly heels too much. With a wheel, it is often appropriate to stand when steering on a reach. Then, too, a second person works the sail controls.

Practice

When sailing, practice the various reaching angles. Experiment with sail trim. (Ease sails progressively as you move farther away from the wind.) Also, adjust the centerboard if your boat has one. (Raise the centerboard progressively, too, as you turn farther away from the wind.) Try easing halyard tension, also, to match sail depth to wind angle. (Ease halyard tension progressively the farther off the wind you sail.)

Practice steering down and up. To turn down, or away from the wind, on a reach is the same as turning away from the wind on a beat. If you use a tiller, pull it *away* from the sails (see Figure 7.5, page 108). If you have a wheel, turn it *toward* the sails. Remember that when falling off the wind, the helmsperson should ease the mainsheet, controlling the mainsail. This way steering with the sail will complement steering with the rudder, and the boat will turn more easily. At the same time, as you bear away, watch the rotation of the telltales or the masthead fly.

Practice associating the angles of these wind indicators with the courses you should be familiar with: beating (45 to 50 degrees to the wind), close-reaching (50 to 90 degrees), beam-reaching (90 to 120 degrees), and broad-reaching (120 to 170 degrees). The sooner you can "read" telltales, or the masthead fly, the better.

The crew should practice using the telltales on the headsail and the luffing of the mainsail to match sail trim to course.

From a broad reach, turn closer to the wind. To do this, push the tiller *toward* the sails, or turn the wheel *away* from them. Trim the mainsheet to facilitate this turn into the wind and practice transferring the line you've gained from your front hand to your back hand. Practice tacking.

Try steering with a compass. Remember, if you turn the boat left, or counterclockwise, the compass numbers get smaller; if you turn it clockwise, the numbers get larger. Steer, also, toward a landmark on shore.

9 | Sailing Downwind and Gybing

R unning, or sailing approximately dead down-wind, can be the nautical equivalent of living on the edge. With the wind at 170 to 180 degrees to the bow of the boat, or on the transom, there isn't much margin for error (see Figure 9.1). If the boat is accidentally steered so the wind shifts much beyond 180 degrees to the bow, the back of the boat has crossed through the eye of the wind (see the right-hand boat in the figure). Often this happens unbeknownst to the sailors. When the stern crosses the eye of the wind, the mainsail can fill on the other side, possibly causing the boom to swing across the boat with alarming and murderous intent. This is descriptively known as an "accidental gybe," or "flying gybe."

Accidents and uncontrolled actions have absolutely no place in sailing. In fact, being competent in sailing means anticipating and preventing accidents. As a chess player tries to stay several moves ahead of an opponent, a sailor tries to stay ahead of the elements. That is the sailing version of defensive driving.

If the boom doesn't get you in a flying gybe, this action can threaten the rig, as all that uncontrolled force smashes to the opposite side. For the same reason—all that uncontrolled force—it is sometimes difficult to balance the boat following an accidental gybe. Given sufficient winds, centerboard boats often capsize after a flying gybe.

It is easy to blame a flying gybe on casual or less skilled steering. However, know that it is difficult to steer a boat when running—particularly in the waves—as there is no consistent feel, or feedback, from the helm.

Wind direction

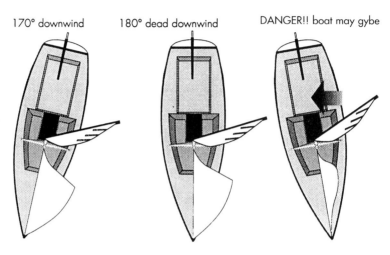

170° downwind   180° dead downwind   DANGER!! boat may gybe

FIGURE 9.1 *When running, a small margin of error—maybe fifteen degrees—can lead to big trouble: the accidental gybe. Since the wind has moved to the lee side on the right-hand boat, the boat "sailing by the lee" may gybe accidentally.*

Then, too, there are other causes, all of which can combine. For example, a wind shift aft, or away from the bow—called a lift—can cause an accidental gybe (see Figure 7.9, page 122). So, too, can the boat heeling too much or too suddenly to windward, or toward the wind. Boats tend to rock from side to side, or oscillate, when running in waves. Should the vessel heel suddenly and precipitously to windward, it will steer down, or away from the wind. Before you can stop it, the boat can steer down sufficiently so the transom has crossed the wind. The result, again, is the accidental gybe.

In Chapter 6, I commented on how the rudder and the sails steer sailboats. So, too, does heeling. If the boat heels to windward, it will turn away from the wind, as just described. This is lee helm. If, however, it heels to leeward, it will turn toward the wind. This is weather helm.

For these reasons, sailing texts are full of warnings about running. After reading them, you might find it surprising that anyone runs downwind and gybes. Without trying to minimize the dangers, boats do run and gybe all the time. There is nothing wrong with running or gybing—gybing is a fundamental maneuver in sailing—there is something wrong with accidental or flying gybes, however.

Broad-Reach, Don't Run

A problem for those who are learning to sail is they understandably aren't that precise about wind orientations. The difference between 170 degrees and 180 degrees or beyond isn't that obvious. The boat feels the same. Also, with the rocking, or oscillating, the masthead fly and telltales move around a lot.

Particularly when running, you have to be most sensitive about wind direction. For example, try to feel its angle on the back of your neck or watch its angle carefully on the masthead fly or the telltales. That isn't a skill that comes quickly, however.

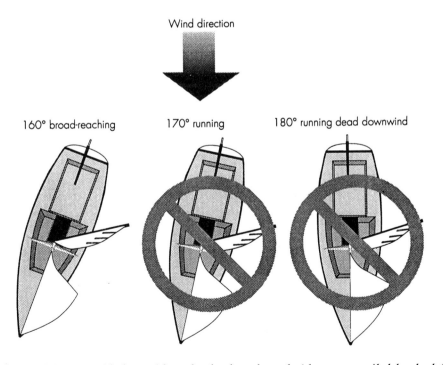

FIGURE 9.2 *To avoid the accidental gybe, broad-reach (the course sailed by the left-hand boat), don't run, and certainly don't sail by the lee. Broad-reaching is safer and usually faster.*

Wind direction

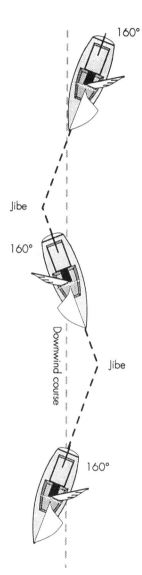

160°

Broad-reaching and gybing are
usually faster and safer than running.

Jibe

160°

Downwind course

Jibe

160°

FIGURE 9.3 *If you sail high of course, or broad-reach, rather than run, you'll have to gybe back and forth downwind in a controlled fashion to reach your destination. The operative word is* controlled. *This downwind course is known as tacking downwind.*

Until you can tell the difference between 170 and 180 degrees, broad-reach with the wind at 160 to 170 degrees to the bow. Don't run. The left-hand boat in Figure 9.2 is broad-reaching.

Broad-reaching is considerably safer than running. Not only is broad-reaching less risky, but as we will see in a moment, it's usually faster. To put this another way: running may be a nice place to visit, a nice place to pass through when gybing, but don't live there.

If you broad-reach in one direction, then gybe properly (see below), and broad-reach in another, eventually you'll get to a point downwind (see Figure 9.3). That is the downwind equivalent of tacking; it is known as "tacking downwind."

Is broad-reaching, not running, a radical idea? The truth is that running is a slow point of sail. When running, the sails don't work that well. If you sail with a headsail, rather than a spinnaker, the mainsail typically blocks the headsail—starving it of wind. You'll have trouble keeping it filled no matter what you do (see Sailing Wing-on-Wing below).

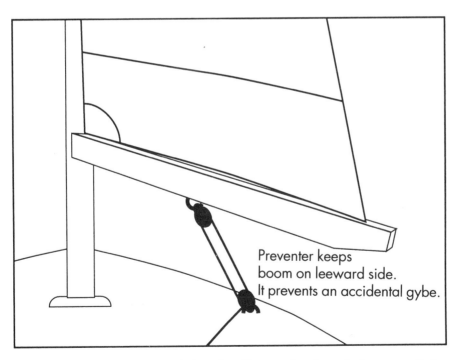

Preventer keeps boom on leeward side. It prevents an accidental gybe.

FIGURE 9.4 *A preventer is a block and tackle, running from the boom to a fitting on the leeward side and into the cockpit that mechanically prevents the accidental gybe.*

More to the point, it is usually faster to broad-reach and gybe back and forth than to run. While you cover more distance, you typically sail fast enough to more than compensate for the added distance. Racing boats almost never run, or sail dead downwind. Rather, they broad-reach and gybe back and forth. Only when the wind is particularly strong do racing boats run.

Finally, if you're determined to run, use a "preventer," a block and tackle that goes from the boom to the leeward side (see Figure 9.4), to prevent mechanically the accidental gybe. It's a good idea to use a preventer when broad-reaching as well. The preventer must be undone before gybing (see below) or adjusted along with sail trim. If you want to trim the mainsail, ease the preventer first, trim the mainsail, and retighten the preventer. If you want to ease the mainsail, ease it first and then retighten the preventer.

Preventing an Accidental Gybe

Beyond using a preventer, attentive steering is key to averting the accidental gybe. Simply considered, this means keeping the wind on the stern quarter (at 170 degrees or less).

If the masthead fly moves so it points directly on the transom or worse, so it moves to the *lee*ward side, or the same side as the mainsail—called "sailing by the lee"—you have to correct it immediately to prevent the gybe. Promptly, turn the boat upwind by moving the tiller *toward* the mainsail (see Figure 6.4, page 82). Recall that you can remember this by the letters T-T—*Tiller Toward* the mainsail. If you steer with a wheel, rapidly turn it *away* from the mainsail. This can be remembered by W-W—*Wheel aWay*.

If you have turned upwind in time to avoid the accidental gybe, don't however, allow the boat to continue turning any closer to the wind than a broad reach—particularly if it is windy. The boat will accelerate when moving from a run to a reach, and too rapid a turn into the wind can cause a boat to capsize as a result of centrifugal force. It's like taking a turn too fast in your automobile; you can skid off the road.

There are warning signs when nearing the danger zone, which are useful but not infallible: One, the headsail starts collapsing behind the mainsail, indicating that it wants to be shifted to the other side (see Sailing Wing-on-Wing below). Two, the back, or leech, of the mainsail crumples, or starts to flag. And, three, the luff of the mainsail shakes or luffs (see Figure 7.4, page 107). When one, two, or all of these things are seen, you're on the edge—very close to gybing.

Sail Positions When Running

If running isn't generally the best long-term solution, it is often done in the short term. Thus, as when sailing close-hauled and reaching, there are distinguishing positions for the sails, centerboard, and the location of the crew.

As we now know, the sails are progressively eased when moving farther away from the wind (see Figure 2.9, page 22). Again, this is the continuum

Wind direction

One hundred and seventy degrees downwind

Wind direction

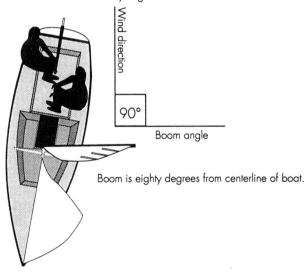

90°

Boom angle

Boom is eighty degrees from centerline of boat.

FIGURE 9.5 *When running, the mainsail should be at ninety degrees to the wind or eighty degrees to the centerline of the boat. Ease the headsail well out until it fills. It is difficult, however, to fill the headsail when running, as it is blanketed by the mainsail. It is sometimes dropped.*

idea. When running, try to keep the mainsail at a right angle to the wind. To do this, look at the masthead fly, or the telltales on the shrouds. Then set the mainsail at a right angle to them—that is, a right angle to the wind (see Figure 9.5).* In practice, the mainsail ends up at about eighty degrees to the centerline of the boat.

Don't allow the mainsail to rest on the shrouds (side stays) or spreaders. Such chafing between the sails and rigging can damage sails. Chafe isn't the only concern about overeasing the mainsail when running. If the mainsail is eased too much, the boat will try to steer into the wind. Particularly when it is windy, this can overwhelm the rudder's ability to correct it. This out-of-control windward turn is formally known as "broaching."

Ease the headsail enough until it fills. Know that filling the genoa or jib when running isn't easy, as it is blanketed by the main. If filling the headsail gets to be too much trouble, try sailing wing-on-wing (discussed in the next paragraph) or alternatively drop it entirely. Another alternative, not discussed in this book as it is a more advanced technique, is using a spinnaker.†

Sailing Wing-on-Wing (or Goosewinged)

The headsail, as noted, is fairly ineffectual at this wind orientation. Thus, when running, you can often pull the headsail over to the windward side, with the windward sheet (see Figure 9.6). (This is similar to backing the headsail, to help you depart a mooring [see Figure 6.5, page 85], or to help you get out of irons [Figure 7.8, page 120].) Once the sail is on the windward side, ease it well out, however, as is appropriate to a run. This orientation, known as sailing "wing-on-wing," or goosewinged, can improve speed when running, as it more fully exposes the headsail to the wind.

While sailing wing-on-wing can be faster and, certainly, looks impressive, it isn't an easy orientation to maintain. There is a tendency when running to sail a little high of course—probably to avoid the accidental jibe. As you favor a slightly high course, the headsail won't want to fill on the windward side. It will collapse. You can sail a lower angle to the wind, which will help to fill the sail, but then you must be wary of the accidental gybe.

---

*Note that when running—even broad-reaching—telltales *on sails* don't work. For telltales to work, sails need high pressure on one side, low pressure on the other. When running, sails merely block the wind. Luffing isn't a very reliable guide either.
† Spinnakers, both symmetrical "racing spinnakers" and asymmetrical "cruising spinnakers," are discussed in my book *Sail Like a Champion*.

Wind direction

Headsail is gybed to windward ("wrong") side of boat.

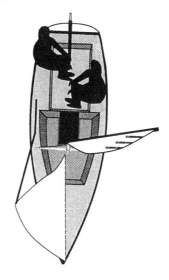

FIGURE 9.6 *An alternative solution for the headsail when running is to pull it over to the windward side and then ease it out. This is known as sailing wing-on-wing. A spinnaker pole or whisker pole can make this more stable.*

Using a lightweight whisker pole, or spinnaker pole, can help keep the headsail filled—particularly if the crew is up to the task. The pole, typically with a jaw at each end, is held aloft by the topping lift or an extra halyard. Attach the pole's inboard end to an appropriate fitting a few feet up the front part of the mast.

After the boat is sailing wing-on-wing—with the headsail on the "wrong" side—place the *windward* genoa sheet through the outboard jaw and trim it. With the windward headsail sheet, keep the headsail at an angle of roughly forty-five degrees to the centerline of the boat. Adjust the pole height with the topping lift so the back, or leech of the sail, is nearly straight. Obviously, remove all this gear before gybing or when altering course to windward.

Centerboard Position

As the centerboard can be progressively raised when moving off the wind, it can be all the way up, or in the centerboard trunk, when running. There is friction between the water and the hull and its underwater appendages: the centerboard, keel, and rudder. Since a boat has little or no sideways force when running, raise the centerboard. Speed will increase as a result of this decrease in wetted surface and, thus, friction. If, however, steering becomes difficult, because of such things as waves, a few inches of centerboard can help steering.

As noted, boats tend to oscillate, rock from the windward to leeward side, when sailing downwind in waves. If this rocking gets too pronounced—when, for example, it is windy and/or the seas are lumpy—the boat can even capsize. Also, while heeling to leeward—the normal direction—will help to steer the boat closer into the wind and away from a gybe, heeling to windward can force the boat farther off the wind. This can lead to an accidental gybe. A little bit of centerboard in the water can dampen rolling somewhat and improve steering.

Not to be minimized is that should the boat capsize, the easiest way to right it is to stand on the centerboard. This obviously isn't possible if the centerboard is fully raised. (See Chapter 12 for a discussion on capsizing.)

Crew Position

The crew typically sits toward the back of the boat when running. This helps steering by keeping the rudder in the water and improves speed.

Obviously, in small boats, there isn't much difference between the crew's positions when moving from a reach, to a run, because there isn't much boat.

As there is not much sideways force when running, there isn't much heel. Thus both the helmsperson and crew may not need to sit on the high side in a small boat. However, rather than stating inalterable rules, balance the vessel according to the requirements of the wind and seas. The salient point is that when running, you *don't* want to heel the boat to windward.

The tiller extension is rarely used when running. With a wheel, the helmsperson often stands directly behind it at this wind orientation and steers with both hands. As always, watch out for other boats.

Controlled Gybe

If running is optional, gybing is more of a requirement, however. Here, I am talking about a "controlled gybe," not an accidental, or flying gybe. Obviously, the operative word is *controlled*. In a controlled gybe, the sailors are in control; the gybe happens when, where, and how they choose. In a flying gybe, the elements are in control and what happens isn't always predictable.

The first thing to know about gybing is that there is an alternative. If it's windy, or rough, or beyond your abilities, don't turn by gybing: tack. Tacking, described in Chapter 8, requires less skill. This is because when you turn the bow of the boat into the wind to begin tacking, the sails lose power for a full ninety degrees. It's like stepping on the brakes. In gybing power is always on.

Beyond deciding *whether* to gybe, you should decide *when* to gybe. For example, if hit by a gust, or you find yourself in a patch of rough water, delay the gybe if you can do so safely until the conditions ease. Wind strength varies as does the height of waves.

Speaking of when, ideally, you want to start practicing gybing when it isn't windy, a day without whitecaps, for example.

For purposes of illustration (Figure 9.7), the boat is gybing from a broad reach to a broad reach, or with the wind at 160 degrees to the boat on starboard tack (at the top) to 160 degrees on port tack (at the bottom). You can, of course, gybe from a beam reach, or even from a beat by turning farther off the wind. As mentioned, if your boat resists such a downwind turn—this often happens when its windy—ease the mainsail. Don't allow the mainsail to get beyond 80 degrees to the centerline of the boat, however.

A successful gybe works this way: One, gybing begins with the helmsperson announcing, "Prepare to gybe." (See Figure 9.7. The paragraph numbers here correspond to the numbers in the illustration. The body text is more complete than the call-outs in the illustration.)

Two, the preventer (see Figure 9.4) is undone—if using one—and the course to leeward (under the sails) is checked for other boats or obstacles that can interfere with the downwind turn. Also, a crew member checks that the centerboard is no more than a quarter of the way down.

Three, if your boat is big enough to warrant winches, a crew member goes to the weather side and wraps the headsail's windward sheet clockwise around a winch (always wrap winches clockwise). After doing this, he likely returns to the leeward side with the sheet. Whether your boat uses winches or not, a crew member makes sure that the headsail's leeward sheet is ready to be cast off and is free to run.

Wind direction

A

1) Helmsman calls, "Prepare to gybe."

2) Preventer is undone and course to leeward is checked as is centerboard position.

3) Headsail sheets are prepared for gybe.

4) Crew replies, "Ready."

B

5) Helmsman initiates turn downwind by pulling tiller away from mainsail.

6) Crew has windward jib sheet ready.

7) When dead downwind helmsman says, "Gybe-ho."

C

8) In light air, or on smaller boats, crew pulls boom across deck by grabbing vang or mainsheet.

9) In heavy air or on larger boats, sheet the mainsail to centerline prior to gybe.

10) Avoid swinging boom.

D

11) Back of the boat crosses the wind.

12) Helmsman shifts sides while crew sheets jib on new leeward side.

13) If gybing with the mainsheet, ease it well out after boom swings to absorb shock.

14) Both crew should be on windward side to prevent capsizing to leeward.

15) Steer new downwind course.

16) Once the boat is balanced, crew can move to low side if appropriate.

FIGURE 9.7 *Gybing: a time-and-motion study. Start at the top of the figure.*

Four, once everything is in order, the crew replies "Ready."

Five, the helmsperson *slowly* turns the boat farther off the wind. If you have a tiller, pull it *away* from the sails; if you steer with a wheel, turn it *toward* the sails.

Six, the crew has the windward jib sheet in his hand, in preparation for the gybe. Often, the headsail is trimmed on the new side at this point. By gybing the headsail first and cleating it on the new side, you can forget about it and concentrate on gybing the boom, steering, and balancing the boat. (Alternatively, see step 12 below.)

Seven, when dead downwind, the helmsperson announces "Gybe-ho."

Eight, if the wind is light or the boat is small, it is relatively easy to gybe the mainsail by grabbing the mainsheet or the boom vang. Using either one, haul the boom across the boat. All crew should keep head(s) well under the swinging boom. (Note: the boat must be dead downwind before this is done. Also, tension the boom vang before the gybe, provided that doing this won't prevent the boom from swinging across the centerline of the boat.)

Nine, if, however, it is windy or you sail a larger boat, trim the main all the way in with the mainsheet, as if for a beat. Don't allow the boat to turn into the wind, however, as the mainsail is trimmed. By trimming the mainsail, you keep it on a short leash and, at the same time, decrease its power. This keeps the sail under control and helps to diminish its momentum as it swings across the deck.

Timing is critical when gybing: the mainsail should be fully in by the time you are running, or with the wind at 180 degrees to the boat. If the sail isn't in, stop the turn by centering the helm or even head up a few degrees.

In a small singlehander or two-person boat, this trimming of the mainsail is another job for the helmsperson. Obviously, this person has his hands full. In larger boats, or boats with more crew, another crew member may tend to the mainsheet.

Some mainsheets control the boom from the center; others attach at the back end. The helmsperson should face *forward* during the gybe if trimming a mainsheet that affixes to the *center* of a boom. This is the best orientation to see the boom swing across as well as to avoid it. From this orientation, it is also possible to see better the telltales on the shrouds, to judge where the wind is. The helmsperson should face *aft* if trimming a mainsheet that affixes to the *back* of the boom. This makes seeing the boom more difficult, so be extra careful of the boom when facing aft.

Ten, for safety reasons, it is most important that the helmsman and crew avoid the swinging boom.

Eleven, if your downwind turn was smooth and continuous, the back of the boat should now cross the eye of the wind.

Twelve, the helmsman shifts sides, being careful to avoid the boom. The crew releases the former leeward jib sheet (on the port, or left, side in this figure) and trims the new leeward sheet (on the starboard side). (This is assuming you haven't gybed the headsail earlier in step 6.) Trim the headsail sheet very little, if the next course is a broad reach, as illustrated. Trim it progressively more if the boat will be sailing on a beam or close reach, or close-hauled course.

Thirteen, if gybing by *trimming* the mainsheet, rather than merely grabbing the mainsheet or vang and throwing the boom across, ease the mainsheet out quickly and substantially as the boom moves to the new side. (Be careful, however, to avoid a rope burn. Wear sailing gloves or let the mainsheet out hand over hand.) This quick and aggressive easing of the mainsheet and, thus, the boom acts as a shock absorber. Walk a strong dog on a short leash, and you'll get yanked here and there. Walk him on a long leash or, better yet, one that can be extended, and you'll have an easier time. Easing the main after the boom swings across the boat is even more important when it is windy.*

Fourteen, as the mainsail switches sides, the crew and helmsperson should concentrate on balancing the boat to avoid capsizing.

Fifteen, next straighten the helm. If the helm isn't straightened immediately after the gybe, the boat can continue up into the wind, with what is often sufficient speed and centrifugal force to broach, or capsize the boat.

And, sixteen, the crew member often moves to the low side once balance is established, and the boat is steering straight.

Gybing is one of the most complicated maneuvers in sailing. Obviously, it requires practice. It is much easier to learn with an instructor present. Again, try it first in light air. As your ability improves, you can gybe in bigger winds. Remember, when in doubt, don't gybe. Tack.

* Some boats, particularly racing boats, have running backstays, which strengthen and straighten a mast. If your boat has them, a crew member must tension the new windward runner after the main swings across. Then the leeward runner is eased.

10 | Day's End

It has been a busy day: You've figured out the wind direction and strength, packed the boat, and launched it in Chapter 4. You have rigged the boat in Chapter 5. You departed from a beach, mooring, dock, or anchorage in Chapter 6. You sailed upwind and tacked in Chapter 7; reached in Chapter 8; and ran—more likely broad-reached—and jibed in Chapter 9.

You didn't think we were going to leave you stranded out there, did you? It's time to return to land—to refasten the ties that bind.

Striking Sails

Returning to land often requires lowering one or both sails. It works this way: The headsail is usually lowered first. As always, remember to close hatches, if you have them, before working on the deck. Ease the headsail's sheet slightly to take pressure off the sail and then drop the halyard. Pull the sail down at the luff, or front.

If your headsail doesn't have hanks (fasteners at the luff), it is particularly important that you keep the headsail out of the water. You can temporarily tie it to the forestay or lifelines with long nylon straps, called "gaskets" or "sail ties"—use the slipped-reef knot (Photo 5D, page 59)—or remove the sail entirely to clear the foredeck.

Take the halyard off the head of the sail, and after checking that the halyard isn't twisted or fouled, clip it forward on the pulpit or back on the mast. Take up the tension as you don't want loose halyards beating 149 on the rigging. Not only can loose halyards damage things but their tattoo, or noise, can damage your relationship with neighbors.

Roller-furling headsails are common these days. With such systems, the sail is wound as if a window shade. If your boat has roller-furling, it is best to operate it when sailing on a reach. Ease the headsail's sheet as the sail is rolled; however, you want gentle tension on the sheet to resist the winding of the sail at the luff. This creates a tight furl, which is desirable. Even with the sail completely furled, continue winding it so the headsail sheets wind a few extra turns around the headstay and the sail. This helps to hold the furl together.

When the headsail is completely furled, ease its halyard, as you don't want to stretch the sail when not sailing. When sailing again, tighten the halyard. (Halyard tension is discussed in the next chapter.) Most headsails designed for roller-furling have a special material at the leech, or back end, to protect the furled sail from the elements—especially the sun. Often, the protective material is a different color from the sail. Such sails need not be covered.

Lowering the mainsail is the reverse of hoisting it, as discussed in Chapter 6. Before dropping the mainsail, be certain that the boom is supported by a topping lift or some other device. If not, warn crew members before dropping the halyard. Also, for safety's sake, make sure the hatches, including the main hatch, are closed. Dropped sails can obscure an open hatch, making it a booby trap.

To lower the mainsail, turn into the wind. If under power, motor slowly into the wind. Drop the halyard and pull the sail down at the luff, or front. (Furling, or folding of sails, is discussed below.)

Landings

Landings are the flip side of departures, as discussed in Chapter 6. Identical to departures, the descriptions that characterize most landings are:

One, that the return will be in shallow water, as when coming back to a beach or a launching ramp. (Shallow-water landings are usually the sole domain of small centerboard boats.)

Two, that the arrival will be at a mooring, which is surrounded by navigable water.

Three, that the return will be to a dock or enclosed slip.

And four, that the arrival will require that you drop anchor.

How to Control Your Speed

No matter what the circumstance, the overriding question is: How will I handle my speed? A sailboat doesn't have very effective brakes, and it doesn't have an instant-on, instant-off throttle like a car. Also, ninety degrees of the circle—or a full one quarter—are off limits.

If you are going too fast, you can miss a mooring—or more seriously, damage a boat or injure a crew member. If you're going too slowly, you can miss a mooring and, perhaps, lose steerageway. Then where you go, no one knows. You have to use the wind to stop and use the wind to start.

A sailboat's lack of maneuverability demands sound planning, plus the ability to revise, revise, revise. As I've said, good planning and revision are the keys to sailing.

Returning to a Launching Ramp or Beach

You can beat, or sail upwind, to a launching ramp or beach; run, with the wind behind you; or reach, with the wind at your side. Each orientation requires a different technique when landing.

We start with the upwind or beating approach. Important in this is sailing to a precise point: a launching ramp or a beach. You will recall that forty-five degrees on either side of the wind is about as close as a sailboat can sail. That, to point out the obvious, is an area of ninety degrees. As mentioned, you can tack for a specific point, when it is at, or better yet, slightly behind, a right angle to the boat, or ninety degrees (see Figure 7.10, page 123). That is straightforward math. Another way to think of it, as noted, is you can tack for a point if it is at three o'clock or nine o'clock.

Of course, the wind can change, or there may be tidal stream that you haven't noticed, or the boat may make more leeway (the inevitable sideways slip) than you figured on. But these rules are extremely useful in determining when to tack for a point.

If you've judged the tacking angle correctly, you should be able to sail directly for your destination. If, however, it is still a good distance away, it is better that you sail "high" of the spot you are aiming for than "low."

You are high of a point if it is downwind or obscured by your sails (see the right-hand boat in Figure 10.1). You are low if the destination is on your weather side or not obscured by your sails (see the left-hand boat). By sailing high, or slightly upwind, of your destination, you put a few degrees in the bank, as sailors say. When closer to the landing spot, it is an easy matter to turn the bow down (off the wind) a few degrees, and sail

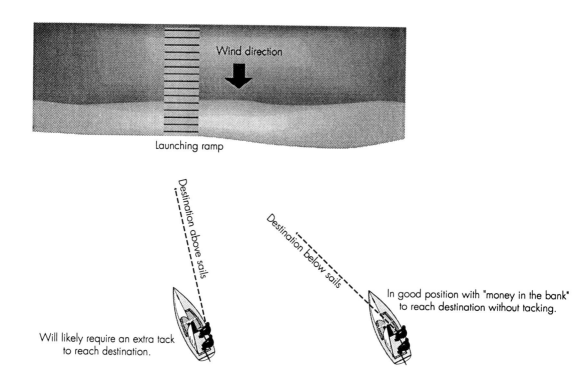

Will likely require an extra tack to reach destination.

In good position with "money in the bank" to reach destination without tacking.

FIGURE 10.1 *When sailing upwind to a launching ramp—indeed to any upwind destination—it is better to sail slightly high of course (the right-hand boat), than low.*

directly for your destination. It is normally impossible to head up to your destination when below it, since a sailboat can't sail closer to the wind than about forty-five degrees. To put this another way: What goes up can usually come down. But what goes down can't normally go up when sailing as close to the wind as possible.

Until the water gets too shallow, your centerboard should be down—the characteristic position when sailing upwind. Remember, though, you don't want it to strike the bottom. Obviously, the distance from the waterline to the tip of the centerboard is important to know. This measurement is referred to as "draft." If, for example, this distance, or draft, is two and a half feet, you want to lift the board *before* you are in two-and-one-half feet of water. Otherwise you can damage the board and, perhaps, the boat. In practice, many centerboards are designed to pivot up and out of harm's way if they strike something, but don't count on it. Daggerboards (see Figure 2.2, page 12) don't pivot, so be more careful when landing a daggerboard vessel.

A primary question on your final approach is: Am I too fast or too slow? You can slow your boat when on a close-hauled course by easing the sheets and/or turning closer into the wind. If you need more speed, retrim the sheets and head off a bit. The problem with heading off, or bearing away, is that you might not be able to head up sufficiently to reach a point upwind. Again, this speaks for putting some money in the bank—staying on the high side.

Turn into the wind at the appropriate depth: not so shallow that the centerboard hits bottom and not so deep that a crew member can't comfortably stand. As the boat slows to a stop, a crew member jumps over the side, while holding on to a shroud or the bow line. (Of course, the bow line should be connected to the boat.) The expression, Look before you leap, is appropriate here, as it is in any shallow-water landing. It is also necessary that you wear shoes to protect your feet when jumping out.

Using the bow line or a shroud, the person in the water holds the bow of the boat into the wind. The sails are lowered and at least lashed so they don't blow out of control. The centerboard is pulled completely up, and the rudder is removed before walking the boat to shore.

When running, or sailing downwind, to a beach or launch ramp, the centerboard is probably up. If the wind is light and the seas calm, you can often sail directly for your destination. If not, put it at least halfway down in preparation for a turn into the wind. Remember, however, that you don't want to strike the bottom with the centerboard or rudder.

A few boat lengths before reaching the spot you've selected, tighten the topping lift of the main boom—if you use it or something similar—to keep the boom from landing on someone when you release the halyard. If you don't have a topping lift, or some other device to support the boom, the crew should be warned before dropping the halyard so as to keep heads and bodies out of harm's way.

Turn into the wind and drop the mainsail (see "heading up" in Figure 10.2). (You may have to drop the centerboard somewhat if the boat refuses to head into the wind.) Once the mainsail is down and out of the way, turn downwind again. If you need more speed to get to shore, trim the headsail, or jib in about halfway. (Raise the centerboard if it is down.) When the water is shallow enough, ease the headsail. A crew member next jumps overboard, from the weather side, holding on to a shroud or the bow line, and keeps the boat oriented into the wind. The headsail is dropped, and the rudder removed before walking the boat ashore.

Lastly, if the wind is in line with the shore, you will reach in with the board about halfway up. You should be slightly downwind of the spot you

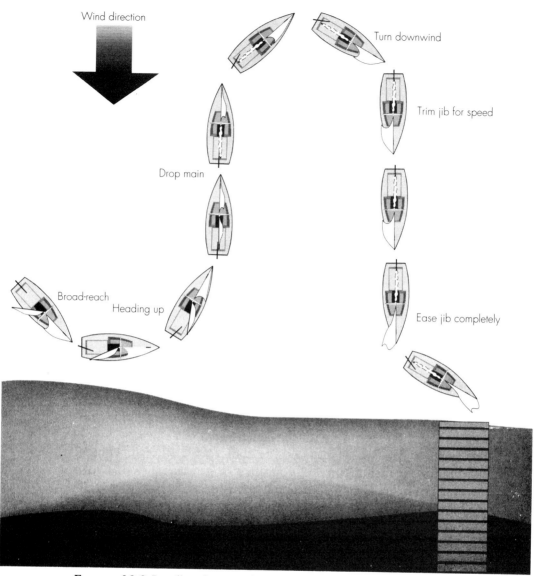

Figure 10.2 *Landing downwind under sail when it is windy at a launching ramp or beach.*

are aiming for which should be on your weather side. Allow the sails to luff if you're going too fast. When the water is shallow enough, turn the boat about ninety degrees into the wind and let the sails luff. As the boat stops, the crew jumps overboard from the weather side, holding on to a shroud or bow line, and holds the bow of the boat into the wind. The centerboard is fully pulled up, sails are dropped, and the rudder is removed.

Removing the Boat from the Water

Most boats are taken from the water by either a trailer or a launching trolley. As a crew member holds the boat, the vehicle and trailer, or trolley, are backed down the ramp (see Figure 4.3, page 52) or down a beach. Again, if the trailer has a tongue, extend it to keep the car's wheels out of the water. Maneuver the boat over the trailer or trolley and float the vessel on it. Often, trailers have winches to help accomplish this.

Be certain that the boat is centered, or balanced, in the correct position fore and aft and side to side. Then, pull the trailer or trolley with the boat on it up out of the way. Make sure there are no power lines that you might hit with the mast. Sails are packed away (see below), the mast is dropped, and the boat is properly secured to the trailer.*

If you must lift the boat out of the water, remember thirty-five pounds per person is about the limit (see Chapter 4).

Returning to a Mooring

Approach a mooring in the upwind direction as that is the best way—often the only way—to stop. Before we get into specifics of boat handling, some general remarks are helpful. It is a good idea to drop the headsail early. (Remember, before working on the foredeck, close all hatches.) Keep the headsail under control, but don't take it off the forestay because if you miss the pickup buoy, which connects to the mooring buoy, you may need the headsail again in a hurry.

If you are towing a dinghy—remember, we left it riding three or four waves behind the back of the boat (see Chapter 6)—when landing, bring it close to the boat again. Otherwise, you might find it trolling for other boats or mooring lines. Should it catch one, that's a mess.

As the buoy may be hard to see, and speed is hard to control, a crew member on the bow can help steering with hand signals. Pointing to the right means, of course, you need to come right; pointing to the left means go left. Pointing ahead means you're on course. Holding your palm up, like a traffic-crossing guard who is stopping traffic, means you're going too fast. Shaking your head no means you're not going to make it—at least that's one man's or woman's opinion. (These aren't official hand signals, they are just obvious, and what I sometimes use.) If you aren't going to

*Stepping a mast on a small boat is described in Chapter 6. Unstepping a mast is the reverse procedure.

FIGURE 10.3 *Unless current is more important than wind, always approach a mooring buoy into the wind, as this is the best way to stop. The upwind turn for the buoy starts when about three or four boat lengths below it. If going too fast, push the boom against the wind to help you slow.*

Wind direction

Pickup buoy

If going too fast, push boom out to backwind main.

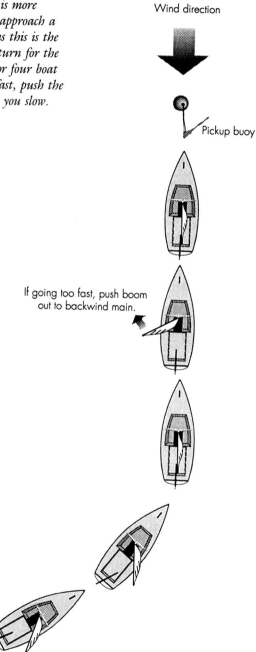

make it, usually, the best action is to bail out early, while you still have some speed, rather than late, when you don't.

The person on the bow must try to keep out of the helmsman's line of sight. Also, when approaching a mooring, or dock for that matter, the boat hook should be on deck ready for use. A boat hook, which can extend your reach significantly, can sometimes make up for a poor aim or a lack of boat speed.

Don't permit the end of the boat hook to point at your body, rather hold it off to the side. If the boat doesn't stop and if the boat hook is aimed at your body, you could be on the receiving end of what amounts to an eight-foot arrow. As Sir Isaac Newton said, For every action there is an equal and opposite reaction. That reaction can hurt.

To be more specific: Plan the maneuver to a mooring so you will close-reach toward the pickup buoy (see Figure 10.3, bottom), and then turn up into the wind and to the buoy when about four boat lengths downwind, or below, your mooring. With the turn into the wind—known as "shooting the wind"—and with the mainsail eased so it is luffing, you should coast to a stop at the mooring. For want of better words, you want to kiss the pickup buoy, not mug it. And not miss it.

While a sailboat doesn't have good brakes, it does have some brakes. If you're sailing too fast when heading up from a close reach, ease the mainsail. When sailing into the wind and at the mark, a crew member can also push the mainsail's boom out toward the bow of the boat (see Figure 10.3). This is a push *against* the wind, which slows the boat. Also, rapidly swinging the rudder from side to side will cause the boat to lose speed; however, it can drive the boat off course, too, if not done carefully.

Landing at a mooring is simple in theory. In practice, you have to skillfully judge the boat's speed and the distance needed to stop in different wind and sea conditions. In this, there is no substitute for practice. Thus, repeat this maneuver and the ones below in a variety of conditions, particularly at an uncrowded anchorage.

Some guidelines are helpful: for example, a heavy keelboat has more momentum than a light centerboard boat. Thus, if you sail a heavy vessel, start your turn up for the buoy farther back, maybe when five or six boat lengths away. Also, a boat carries less upwind when it is windy; similarly, it drifts less upwind when the seas are rough and on the bow. Therefore, when it is windy and/or rough, start your turn closer to the buoy, maybe three boat lengths away, for example.

If the approach to the mooring is downwind, sail *below*, or beyond, the pickup buoy on a broad reach, or run (see Figure 10.4, top left). Turn up

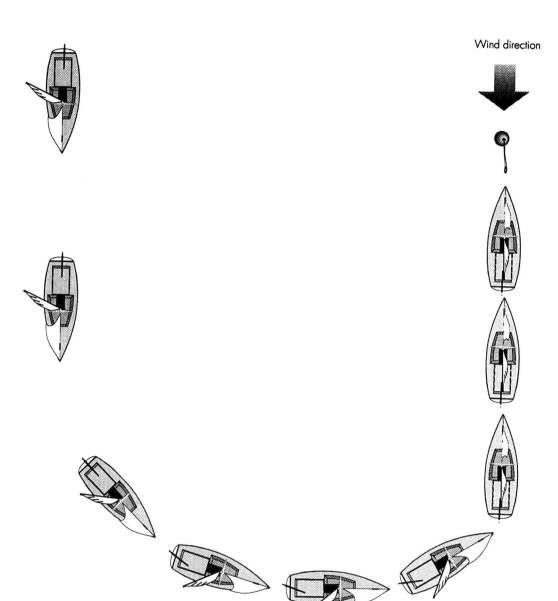

Wind direction

FIGURE 10.4 *If the mooring buoy is downwind, sail below it, then come up until you are aiming at it. Again, allow about three or four boat lengths to stop.*

to a beam reach, and then to a close-hauled course. Finally, head up into the wind. Don't make a quick and tight semicircular turn, but a slower and wider one, as shown. You'll have better control.

An engine can help landing at a mooring, as it has a throttle and a better, if hardly perfect, brake: reverse gear. Engine or not, the maneuver is the same: you should head upwind to the buoy. With an engine, however, you can control your speed a little better by shifting from forward, to neutral, to reverse, as is appropriate, and using the throttle. Be warned, however, sailboats—particularly those with low-drag props—have almost no interest in going backward under power.

A caution with an engine, however, is that you can run over mooring lines and foul them in the prop. Thus, always be aware of the propeller and your mooring lines and those of others.

Docking Under Sail

As a matter of course, only small boats—those under twenty feet—make a practice of sailing to a dock. Any boat that has an engine should use it when docking. That said, sometimes, when an engine fails, big-boat sailors have no choice.

It is best to approach a dock or slip (a slip is a dock partially enclosed by fingerlike piers) by sailing upwind to it. Ideally, you want to be sailing *into* the tidal stream as well, as both the wind and tide will help to slow your boat. If the tide and wind aren't in the same direction, you have to judge which is most significant: With a robust fifteen-knot breeze and a one-knot tidal stream, the wind is probably more important, so plan your landing so you finish into the wind. However, with a five-knot breeze, in which you will have trouble sailing at all, and a two-knot tide, the latter is more important.* So plan your landing into the tidal stream.

You should have warps ready (typically there are four of them: a bow line, stern line, forward spring, and after spring [see Figure 6.8, page 93].†

These lines should be on the cleats and led through the appropriate fairleads. They should be also be neatly coiled and oriented in such a way

---

*If moored sailboats (as opposed to powerboats) are not facing into the wind, the likelihood is that they are facing into a tidal stream. In such a case, the tide would likely be more important than the wind, so land into the tide. Powerboats, particularly those with high superstructures, are less reliable indicators of wind direction and tide. This is due to the high superstructures that can catch the wind in odd ways.

†Smaller boats (i.e., twenty feet and under) can often be moored for a short time in benign conditions with just a bow line and stern line.

that they don't foul when you need them. Also, rig the fenders.* Position one fender at the widest part of the boat, on the side you are tying up to. The other two should be forward and aft of the center fender—in essence, they should be at the pivot points. All fenders must also be at the height of the dock. If they are too high or too low, they won't work, which can be very costly. If unfamiliar with a dock, make a slow pass by it—without stopping, however—to ascertain relative heights and how you might tie up. Use this sail-by to formulate a plan.

Marina design is one of my businesses these days. If possible, when designing a marina, you try to orient the pontoons into the prevailing (most common) winds to make stopping easier. Nevertheless, the prevailing winds don't always prevail. Also, there are any number of dock, wind, and tide orientations, and while I describe several maneuvers below, I can't cover all contingencies. That's why this course of instruction is based on planning—providing you with the tools to make your own decisions. And, of course, the ability to revise, revise, revise.

Landing at a dock under sail is the same maneuver that one uses to approach a mooring. Note, a hard, immovable dock can be less forgiving of errors, however, than a buoy. You approach the dock on a beam reach (see Figure 10.5, bottom). After all hatches are closed, the headsail should be down and out of the way. Then, when four or five boat lengths below the dock—the distance corresponds to how far you think your boat will carry—you turn into the wind. At the same time, ease the mainsail until it luffs. Just before reaching the dock, most of your speed should be gone. Then turn so you are paralleling it.

At this point, a crew member jumps onto the dock, when it is safe, and if it is safe, from a position just forward of the mast. This man should take the after-spring line with him, being careful, however, that there is sufficient slack in the line so as not to interfere with the jump.† Once the spring line is made fast, the bow line is affixed. An alternative is to throw the spring line to a person on the dock—assuming there is a person on the dock and he's in a helpful mood.

If you are going too slowly when you approach the dock, keep the mainsail trimmed in longer or bail out. Sometimes, you can toss a bow line

---

* Use a clove-hitch (see Figure 5.1, Page 60) to tie a fender to a stanchion, supporting a lifeline, or a bowline (Photo 5E, page 61) to tie it to the bottom of the stanchion.

† As mentioned, the *after* and *forward* designation of spring lines has to do with the line's direction as it leaves the boat, not whether it attaches to the after part, or stern, or the forward part of the boat, the bow.

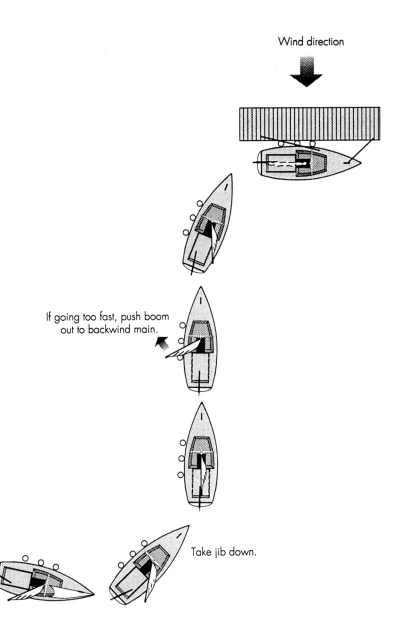

Wind direction

If going too fast, push boom
out to backwind main.

Take jib down.

FIGURE 10.5 *If landing at a dock under sail, with the dock upwind of the boat, treat it as a mooring. At the last instant, however, turn so you are paralleling it.*

to someone on a dock. After this person cleats it, use the line to pull your boat in. A winch is helpful in this regard. Another alternative is to use a boat hook, which can allow you to take a line from someone on a dock, or catch a cleat on the dock and pull the boat in. As when approaching a mooring, the boat hook should be on deck and ready for action before starting the docking maneuver.

If you are going too fast when approaching the dock, beyond letting the mainsail luff, you can push its boom forward against the wind (see Figure 10.5). Alternatively, or at the same time, you can swing the rudder back and forth, which acts as a brake. As noted, this sawing action of the rudder can have an impact on steering, however, so do it very carefully, if at all.

If the boat is still going too fast and will likely hit the dock or pier, place another fender between the boat and dock. Keep an extra fender handy for that purpose. While it may be tempting to fend off with your

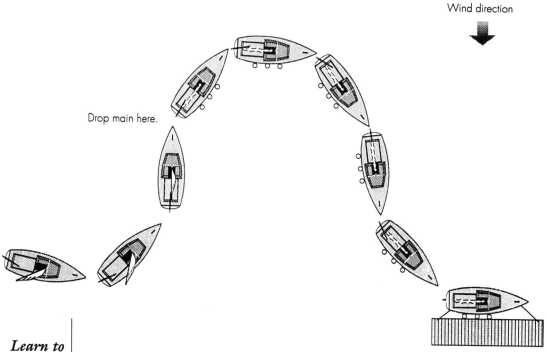

Wind direction

Drop main here.

FIGURE 10.6 *If landing at a dock under sail, and the dock will be downwind of you, try to sail around to the other side of it. If that is impossible, maneuver as shown. Don't try this if it is windy, or if you sail a big boat.*

feet, don't do it, particularly in a larger boat. Larger keelboats have a great deal of momentum, and you might injure yourself if you try to stop such a boat with your body.

If the wind is behind you, docking is more complicated. With a dock, it is often possible to sail around it to the leeward side, and make your approach into the wind from there.

Otherwise, you should approach the dock or slip on a beam reach (see Figure 10.6, left), under mainsail only. Before reaching it, turn up into the wind. After having tightened the topping lift or readying some other boom-support device, drop the mainsail. Finally, turn back off the wind and drift or paddle into the space. Just before reaching the dock, turn so you are almost paralleling it. Don't try this if it is windy or with a big boat.*

Docking Under Power

By any measure, sailboats make poor powerboats. They are slow to accelerate and don't back straight, but rather off to the side. As bad as a sailboat is under power, even worse is a sailboat without any auxiliary or outboard power.

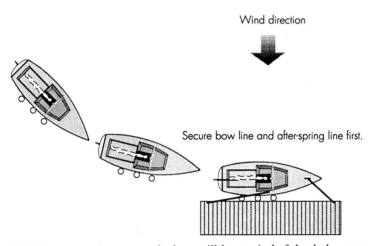

Wind direction

Secure bow line and after-spring line first.

FIGURE 10.7 *If, when under power, the boat will be upwind of the dock, approach it at the angle shown with just enough speed to maintain steerageway. The wind should blow you down to it. Obviously, fenders and minimum speed are crucial to the success of this maneuver.*

*It is also possible to drop an anchor upwind of a dock, and after setting it—see Anchoring later in this chapter—drift downwind to the dock, using the anchor line to control your speed.

If, when under power, the boat will end up upwind of the dock, as in Figure 10.7, approach it at the angle shown, with just enough speed to maintain steerageway. Make sure the fenders are in place. Before reaching the dock, turn so you are just about parallel to it. The wind will blow the boat down onto the dock.

Secure the bow line and after-spring line first. Once these lines are secured, you can power slowly ahead against the after-spring to keep the stern against the dock while the stern line is being secured. Run the forward-spring last.

If the boat will be downwind of the dock, as in Figure 10.8, approach it by turning into the wind. This will help you slow down. (Again, make sure the fenders are rigged.) Before reaching the dock, turn sharply so you are paralleling it. A common error is to be either too far off the dock or, of course, too close to it that you hit.

Propellers on auxiliaries almost always turn clockwise when going forward; they turn counterclockwise when going backward. If your propeller backs with a counterclockwise motion—most do—the stern of your boat walks left—in the direction the prop turns—and the bow pivots right. The sideways force is formally known as "torque," or "prop walk," and depending on the orientation of the boat to a dock, it can help or hurt you. With the approach to a dock as shown in Figure 10.8, reverse gear will help you maneuver the stern in. If, however, your right, or starboard side, will be against the dock, reverse gear would hurt you.

A person on the dock to whom you can toss a line simplifies this approach. The alternative is to have a crew member jump from a position just forward of the mast, when and if it is safe, with the after-spring line. Again, before jumping, make sure there is sufficient slack in the line. Secure the bow line after fastening the after-spring line.

Docking at a partially enclosed slip depends on the orientation of the slip and the wind or the tide. An upwind or uptide approach (if tide is dominant) isn't difficult, as the wind or moving water will help to slow the boat (see Figure 10.9, top). Secure the bow line and after-spring line first. (These are the operative lines in all of these landings. Also, note that appropriate fenders are rigged *before* reaching the dock.) The wind and reverse gear will also help to slow the boat.

With the port side of the boat to the dock, as in Figure 10.9 top, the normal tendency of the vessel to back left could facilitate this landing. If the boat were on the other side of the dock, however, reverse gear would hurt you, so use it more judiciously.

A downwind approach can be managed, too, under normal conditions

Wind direction

Secure bow line and after-spring line first.

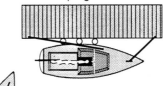

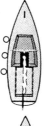

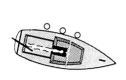

FIGURE 10.8 *If, when under power, the boat will be downwind of the dock, maneuver as shown. With the natural tendency of the boat to back to the left, reverse gear will help you when landing with your port side to the dock. If possible, plan your approach with this backing-left tendency—or port side to the dock—in mind.*

Wind direction

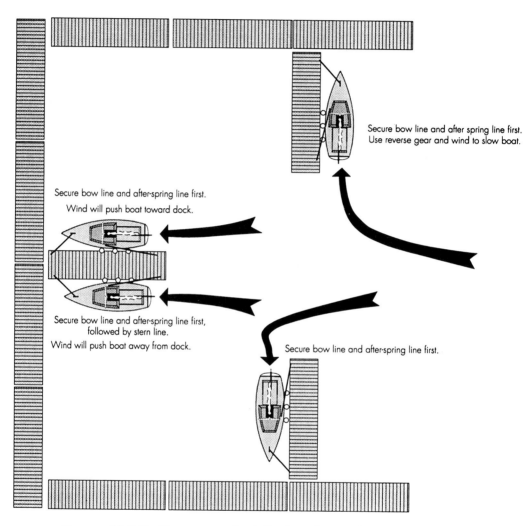

Secure bow line and after spring line first.
Use reverse gear and wind to slow boat.

Secure bow line and after-spring line first.
Wind will push boat toward dock.

Secure bow line and after-spring line first,
followed by stern line.
Wind will push boat away from dock.

Secure bow line and after-spring line first.

FIGURE 10.9 *Docking at an enclosed slip. In each case, the most important lines are the bow and after-spring.*

by entering a slip slowly and shifting into reverse and using the throttle to control speed (Figure 10.9, bottom). (Again, with the port side of the boat to the dock, reverse gear will facilitate this landing; if the boat were on the other side, however, using reverse gear too much could complicate it.) Secure the bow line and after-spring line first.

If the wind is on your side (see Figure 10.9, left) again secure the bow line and after-spring line first.

Anchoring

Anchoring is both a theory and a practice. Theory first: some sea or lake bottoms are better for anchoring than others. For example, the best bottom to hold an anchor—and holding is the absolute theme of anchoring—is hard sand. Next comes soft sand. Then is soft mud, followed by coral and rock.

Charts of an area typically show the makeup of the bottom. Common abbreviations are S for sand; M for mud; Co for coral; and Rk or rky for rocks or rocky.

Similarly, some types of anchors work better in some types of bottoms. Figure 10.10 shows the anchors commonly used on sailboats and the types of bottoms in which they work best.

Beyond a good bottom, you normally want shelter from the wind and waves. Simply considered, this means you want land intervening between you and the wind and wave direction. Land tends to stop, or retard, the wind and flatten the seas.

To find the most appropriate place to anchor, look at the wind direction: What is it now and what is it predicted to be later? To answer the

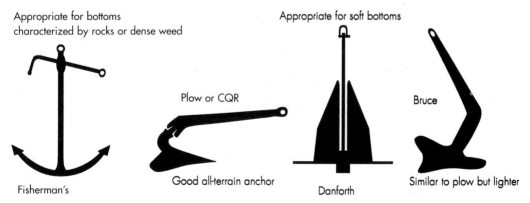

Appropriate for bottoms characterized by rocks or dense weed

Fisherman's

Plow or CQR

Good all-terrain anchor

Appropriate for soft bottoms

Danforth

Bruce

Similar to plow but lighter

FIGURE 10.10 *Anchors and the bottoms where they work best.*

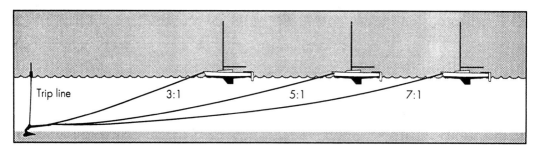

FIGURE 10.11 *For maximum hold when anchoring, you want the anchor line as horizontal as you can get it. This shows the importance of scope—the ratio between the depth of the water and the length of the anchor line, or rode.*

latter question, listen to your marine-weather radio. (The waves usually—but not always—follow the wind.) Then pick an area that offers shelter. For example, an area closed off to the northwest would likely provide good shelter from a northwest wind; however, it might not offer the same protection from a southeast wind. Obviously, unless it is an emergency, you don't want to anchor in a channel or other place exposed to heavy traffic.

At night sailboats at anchor must display a white light (not a strobe light, however) at the top of their mast, which is visible from 360 degrees. A torch hung from the forestay is also acceptable. In daylight hours, a black ball shape should be hung in the rigging where it can best be seen from all directions.

Another concern is the depth of water. You want an area that is deep enough so you won't touch bottom at low tide. However, a key to anchoring is "scope," the ratio between the depth of the water and the length of the anchor rode. Simply considered, you want the pull on the anchor line as *horizontal* as you can get it (see Figure 10.11). That means a high ratio of anchor line to depth. While a 3 to 1 scope (30 feet of anchor line in 10 feet of water) may hold in very light winds, 7 to 1 (or 70 feet of anchor line in 10 feet of water) may be necessary when it is windy or rough. Obviously, if you have a choice between safely anchoring in 10 feet of water or in 100 feet, you'll opt for the former. With scope being so critical, mark your anchor line at, perhaps, 20-foot intervals or purchase one that is already marked.

Also, you want an anchorage that isn't too crowded, so you have room to swing, without hitting or being hit by another boat, should the wind change direction or the tide turn.

If, as usually happens, an anchorage is too crowded to use seven to one

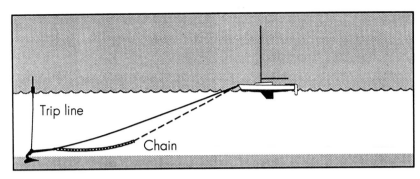

FIGURE 10.12 *Ten feet of chain can substitute, in part, for limited scope. The chain's weight helps to keep the anchor line horizontal. (This drawing is for purposes of comparison; in practice, you'd have one or the other—not both.) Also, note the trip line, which can help free a stuck anchor from the bottom. Obviously, the trip line must be rigged when dropping anchor.*

scope, you can opt to use a heavier anchor. The weight of the anchor is another important variable in whether you do or do not stay put. The more a boat weighs, or the more the wind blows, the heavier the anchor should be. (For the proper size of anchor, talk to your dealer or marine-supply store.)

Also, if more hold is necessary, such as when it is windy, you can set two anchors, at sixty degrees to one another. Do this by setting one anchor in the normal fashion—see below—and use the dinghy to set the second one.

When scope is limited, a second anchor, tied at least one third the distance back (or closer to the boat), can help. This second anchor acts as a shock absorber and helps to keep the anchor line horizontal. As such, it is a good substitute for scope.

If the primary anchor is connected to ten feet of chain, and then the chain to a nylon line, the effect will be the same as a second anchor (see Figure 10.12). The weight of the chain helps to keep the anchor line more horizontal. With a second anchor or chain, scope can be reduced perhaps to five to one—except, of course, when it is very windy.

To anchor, bring the anchor and anchor rode (line) on deck. If the anchor and rode aren't attached, attach them. A shackle or a bowline (see Photo 5E, page 61) can be used to make the connection. (If using a chain, it should be attached, as should a second anchor, if using one.) Before dropping the anchor overboard make certain you have tied the "bitter," or back, end to a cleat or the mast. Put the anchor line through the bow roller, or chocks, which act as a fairlead and help to protect the anchor line and the boat from chafe. (Additional protection might be necessary.*) Be sure the line is carefully coiled on deck so it will run smoothly. Also, keep your feet, in particular, out of the coils.

If you are anchoring in any place that can snag an anchor, such as a rocky bottom, or any place that has a bottom with which you aren't familiar, rig a trip line (see Figure 10.12). Recall from Chapter 7 that this is an extra light line that attaches to the anchor at its crown or opposite end. (Better anchors have attachments for trip lines.) For easy retrieval, this line should be rigged with a buoy, flotation cushion, or a five-gallon plastic jug (with a tightly sealed lid). By pulling on the trip line, a stuck anchor should break free more easily.

The practice of anchoring works this way: select your spot from the perspective of shelter, lack of traffic, bottom type, depth, and room to swing. Then lower the headsail.

Remember, due to the importance of scope, you must drop your anchor considerably upwind or uptide—if tide is dominant (see above)—of where you want to end up. Also, consider where you'll swing if the wind switches direction.

After selecting your spot, round up into the wind as if picking up a mooring. Indeed, treat it as if approaching a mooring. Leave the mainsail luffing. (If under power, all sails should be down, and you should motor upwind or uptide to the spot you choose.) After the boat stops, it should start drifting backward. If motoring, shift into reverse. When the boat starts to drift back, the skipper will call for the anchor to be lowered. Note that is *lowered*—not tossed. Not only is lowering the anchor much safer than tossing it, but this measured action helps you to judge the water's depth. If you use a trip line, it should go over at the same time as the anchor, don't allow the two lines to twist, however.

Slowly pay the anchor line out as the boat drifts or powers backward. The idea is to exert a slight tug on the anchor, which helps to bury, or set it in the bottom.

When you have paid out an amount of line equal to three times the depth, snub the anchor by taking its line around a cleat. If the anchor is now properly set, the bow of the boat will turn into the wind. If it does, let out the remaining scope. Cleat it securely to a cleat on the foredeck.

*Leather, canvas, plastic, or even a short piece of rubber hose of a diameter similar to the anchor line can be used for chafe protection. With a sturdy needle and a sailmaker's palm, sew the material to the line so it doesn't shift. The protected part of the line should be at the chocks or where the line is likely to abrade.

Learn to Sail

170

If, however, the boat doesn't face into the wind when you snub the anchor, continue to pay out enough line equal to five times the depth. Try snubbing it again. If this doesn't set the anchor, power ahead or trim the mainsail, so you start sailing forward again slowly. Then bring the anchor back aboard and check it for weeds or shells that may have fouled it. Remove any obstructions. Try again, or try another place with a better bottom, or use a different type of anchor.

Anchor Watch

There are no guarantees in life or in anchoring. Even after dropping the proper anchor in hard sand, and using scrupulous technique, you can "drag anchor," as it is called when it doesn't hold but moves along the bottom. Thus, it is important when anchored that you be able to raise sails quickly. For example, the headsail should be kept on the headstay, although tied down. Also the sheets should be run and the halyard clipped to the bow pulpit, where it can quickly be affixed to the head of the sail.

With the possibility of dragging anchor, it is important to establish reference points to make sure you aren't drifting. For example, select landmarks on shore (see Figure 10.13). Take compass bearings on them and write them down. (A handbearing compass, sold inexpensively at marine-supply stores, is excellent in this regard.) Let's say one of the landmarks bears ninety degrees, as in Figure 10.13. You aren't drifting if the bearing is unchanged. You are drifting if your reference point suddenly bears seventy-five degrees, though.

The first hour after your anchor, check reference points several times. Check them periodically after that. Also, check them should the wind or tide change. Boats with sophisticated electronics, such as Loran, can electronically sense drift and sound an alarm.

It is a good idea to write down a safe course, or exit route, to a channel or open water, should you have to move quickly. A look at the chart can help establish a safe escape route.

At night, take a bearing on a light, or better yet on more than one light. Write the bearing(s) down. You need to check them from time to time, even in the evening, so set an alarm clock if your boat doesn't have Loran, or something similar that can sound a warning. (Waking to an alarm is better than the rude awakening likely if you unknowingly drag anchor.) Keep a flashlight handy to check the anchor line, as well.

If you are drifting, you must move quickly. Turn on the engine and reset the anchor. Or else hoist sails. Even if you have an engine, remember,

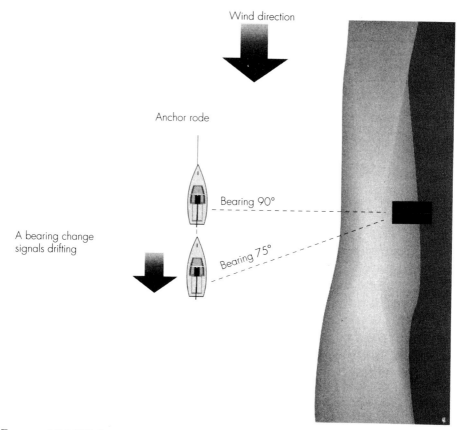

Wind direction

Anchor rode

Bearing 90°

A bearing change
signals drifting

Bearing 75°

FIGURE 10.13 *To be sure you aren't dragging anchor, take bearings with a handbearing compass on distinctive landmarks, buoys, or lights. Write them down. If the bearings stay the same, you aren't dragging anchor. If they change, you are.*

it doesn't always start, and it could be dangerous to start a gas engine without running the blower for at least four minutes.

Flaking and Furling Sails

A dinghy's sails are normally removed and folded or rolled and put away into bags. When not sailing, don't expose sails to direct sunlight, as the sun's ultraviolet rays will degrade the cloth.

If you sail in saltwater, hose the sails down with freshwater and dry them before folding them and packing them away. That is admittedly one of those do-as-I-say, not-as-I-always-do rules, as often it is impossible to wash and dry sails before folding them. Sails made of modern materials, like polyester, are fairly resistant to mildew.

If you fold a sail on board, close all hatches. Before folding a mainsail or a headsail if it happens to have battens, remove them.* To fold, or flake, a sail, start at the foot or bottom (see Photo 10A). With two people working, stretch the foot. The rest of the sail should be over on the opposite side. Then one grabs the sail at the luff (front) and one grabs it at the leech (back). Each person takes the same amount, and the sail is progressively folded into accordion folds. The size of the folds should be slightly smaller than the size of the sail bag. (It is a good idea not to make the folds in the same place every time.) The sail is then rolled or folded from either the front or the back (see Photo 10A, right) and placed in a bag. Often sails are left aboard. If you take them ashore, never store sails in a hot place.

If your boat has a mainsail cover, the mainsail is normally furled on the boom. Battens remain in the sail, but remember to release outhaul tension. Also, have several long gaskets, or sail ties, handy. To fold a mainsail:

One, bring the entire sail over to one side, preferably the downwind side (see Photo 10B), if the boat isn't facing into the wind.

Two, with two people working, grab the sail at the bottom, at its front and back.

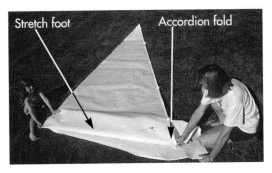 

PHOTO 10A *To flake a sail, stretch the foot (left photo). The rest of the sail is kept on the opposite side. Then, working from the luff and leech, each person takes the same amount of sail and folds it into accordion folds. Lastly, the sail is folded up (right photo) or alternatively rolled.* (Michael Levitt photos)

* Some boats with mainsails with full battens, such as catamarans and windsurfers, don't require that the battens be removed. Rather, the sails are rolled, beginning at the head. When fully rolled, the sails are placed in sausagelike bags.

Three, then, as if folding a headsail, have each person take the same amount. The sail is progressively flaked, into accordion folds that rest on the boom. Be certain that the battens stay parallel to the boom.

Four, to prevent the sail from slipping off the boom, tie it with sail ties starting at the back. (Don't wait until the entire sail is flaked before doing this, however; otherwise the sail is likely to slip off the boom.) Use a slipped-reef knot (see Photo 5D, page 59) to hold the folds together. Flaking a mainsail on a boom is almost identical to folding a sail on deck or on the grass as just described. The main difference is that the sail lies rather precariously on the boom in folds rather than on the deck or grass.

And, five, when you get to the top of the sail, take its head around the boom—this helps to hold it together. Tie the main with more sail ties and cover it to protect it from the elements.

Putting the Boat to Bed

If leaving your boat in the water, tension all halyards, so they don't flap around. Then tie a piece of shock cord to a shroud and pass the other end between the halyards and the mast, and then back to another shroud. This will pull the halyards away from the mast, preventing them from bumping against the mast and disturbing your neighbors. Coil the jib sheets and any other extraneous lines (see Photo 5K, page 73), then place the lines below decks, or remove them from the boat. The sails should be bagged and stowed below. This does not include the mainsail if it is covered or a roller-furling headsail that offers protection on the back or leech. Coil the mainsheet and hang it from the boom or other convenient spot.

If appropriate, the centerboard should be raised. With some boats, the rudder is removed entirely, but more likely the rudder's tiller is lashed in place with a line to keep the rudder and tiller from flapping back and forth in the waves. If your boat has a steering wheel, it can typically be locked in place.

Check the bilge, the lowest point of the boat, for water and bail or pump it out if necessary. Turn off the electricity, remove all gear that is to go ashore, and close any ports and lock up the cabin. Don't forget to lock the hatches, too. Check that the mainsail is properly covered, and that the headsail is furled tightly around the headstay if you use roller-furling. Often, when it is very windy, you see one or both of these sails unrolled by the wind and flogging about. Flogging like that will ruin a sail in short order.

If bad weather, such as a gale, is predicted, it is safer to remove such sails—even remove the boat from the water.

Sail is on downwind side. Each person takes the same amount of sail.

To prevent the sail from slipping off the boom, stop furling and tie it with sail ties.

When done furling, take the head around the boom—this helps to hold it together.

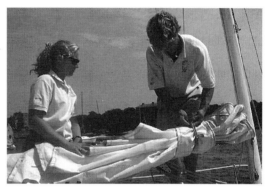

Tie the head around the sail, and then cover the sail to protect it from the elements.

PHOTO 10B *Flaking the mainsail on the boom.* (Michael Levitt photos)

11 | The Other Controls

A sail is not a bedroom sheet. That statement is less obvious than it seems.

A bedroom sheet is a two-dimensional object, or flat, while a sail has a curved (three-dimensional) airfoil shape, like an airplane wing. A bedroom sheet can lie perfectly flat on the floor. A sail cannot; its added shape would cause it to drape, or fold over itself. See for yourself by placing a sail on the ground.

The shape the sailmaker puts into a sail is critical. So, too, is the shape sailors put in when sailing. Sail formation can and should be adjusted when under way, according to the wind angle, wind speed, and how much power is needed. In some ways, sailing is unceasing wing design.

More shape—or the fuller a sail is—the more power. Less shape—the flatter the sail is—the less power. Full sails are appropriate when the wind is moderate; flat sails are desirable when the wind is heavy or—oddly enough—very light. Similarly, sails are flatter when sailing upwind, fuller when sailing downwind.

It's the same in aviation. Next time you fly, watch the wings of your plane before landing. When an airplane is going slowly, it needs all the lift, or power, it can get. You'll see the wings show maximum curvature with the extension of the flaps. When an airplane is at cruising speed, however, the wings are flattened with the retraction of the flaps, to lessen drag.

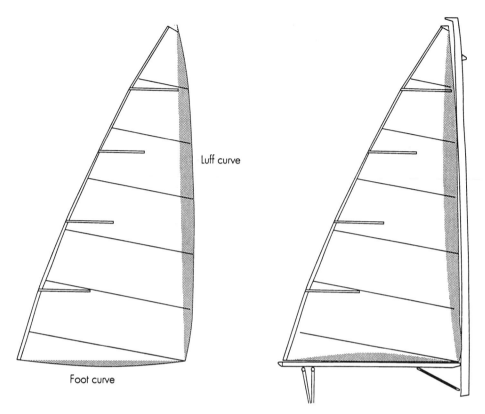

Luff curve

Foot curve

FIGURE 11.1 *The luff and foot of the sail are curved rather than straight. When these two curved edges are affixed to a straight mast and boom, a three-dimensional shape is the result.*

How Sailmakers Shape Sails

There are three common techniques that a sailmaker uses to shape sails three-dimensionally. For example, rather than the front, or luff, of a sail being a straight line, it is curved (see Figure 11.1). This is called "luff curve." Similarly, rather than the bottom, or foot, of the mainsail being a straight line, it is curved. This is "foot curve." When these two *curved* edges are fed into a *straight* mast and boom, shape is forced into the sail.

Broadseaming is similar if more sophisticated. Rather than a sail being one piece of cloth (a bedroom sheet), it is made of several pieces that are sewn together with seams (see Figure 11.2). Most often, the seams run horizontally (as in the illustration); alternatively, they can run vertically, or

The Other
Controls

177

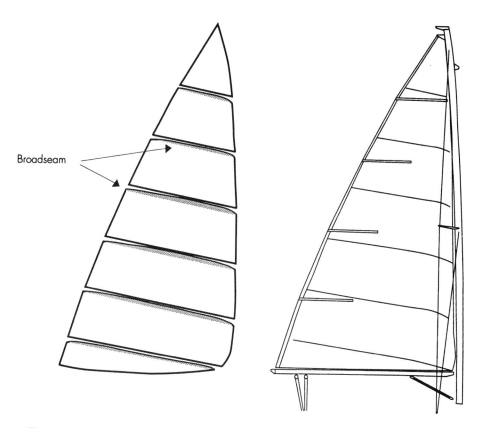

FIGURE 11.2 *In broadseaming, one edge is straight, the other is curved. When curved edges meet straight edges, shape is the result.*

else radially, that is, radiate from the corners. If you were to rip these seams apart, you would find that one edge is *straight* and the other is *curved*. As we now know, when a straight seam, or edge, meets a curved seam, or edge, shape is forced into the sail. A beach ball is a familiar example of how broadseaming gives an object a three-dimensional shape.

How Sailors Shape Sails

While the sailmaker has the major say on sail shape and size, he doesn't have the only word. Nor does the sailmaker have the final word. The sailor does.

In the sailor's tool kit are such things as halyard tension, the outhaul, Cunningham, mast bend, boom vang, traveler, and the position of the

headsail sheet lead (i.e., both fore and aft and inboard and outboard).*
These other controls haven't been discussed or have been mentioned
merely in passing. Like luff curve, foot curve, and broadseaming, these
devices affect the three-dimensional shape of sails.

Further, a sailor is also often able to select the proper size sail for the
conditions and change it or "reef" it (make it smaller) as conditions dictate.
That addresses the size, or two-dimensional shape, of a sail. Shortening sails
and reefing techniques are described later in the chapter.

Halyard, Outhaul, and Cunningham

Four controls on a sailboat affect the drafts of headsails and mainsails: the
halyard, outhaul, Cunningham, and mast bend. Let's begin by focusing on
the first three: halyard, outhaul, and Cunningham. If you tighten any of
them (see Figure 11.3, left), one or both sails grow flatter. If, however, you
loosen any of them (Figure 11.3, right), one or both sails grow fuller.

It works this way: Have three people lift a triangular sail at each corner.
Hold it fairly tight, but not so taut that most of its three-dimensional shape
is removed. Note its depth. Then pull on one, or better yet, all three corners
and note how shape is removed. The sail has grown flatter. That's what the
halyard, outhaul, and Cunningham do; they pull a corner. Any time you
tension one or all of these controls, shape is removed. The sail grows flatter.
The opposite is true, too; any time you loosen one or all of them, the sail
grows fuller.

As noted, the deeper a sail is, the more powerful it is. A sail with a
deep shape helps a boat to accelerate in light winds and helps it to power
through choppy seas. At the other extreme, the flatter a sail is, the less the
boat heels. This is desirable when it is windy.

It is helpful to know that the three-dimensional shape, or "depth," of
a sail can be measured, compared, and repeated. Start by drawing an imagi-
nary horizontal line on a sail that is hoisted and properly trimmed. (If your
sails have horizontal seams, just focus on a seam.) This horizontal line is
the sail's "chord," or the distance from luff to leech (see Figure 11.4, top).
Let's say you measure it, and it is ten feet. Then, on this horizontal line,
find the deepest point. That is the sail's draft. Measure that, too. Let's say
it is one foot. Sail depth is then draft divided by chord length, expressed as
a percentage.

---

*Not all boats have all of these controls, however.

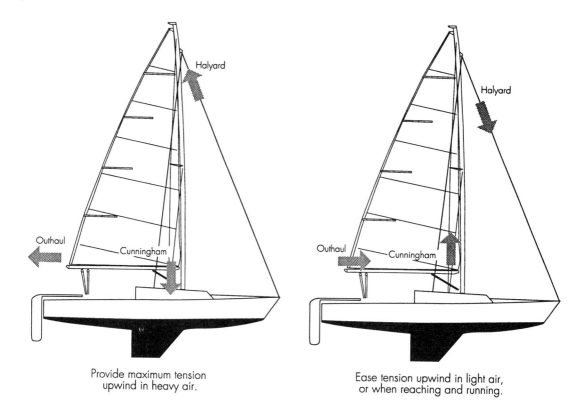

Provide maximum tension
upwind in heavy air.

Ease tension upwind in light air,
or when reaching and running.

FIGURE 11.3 *If you tighten the outhaul, Cunningham, and/or halyard, sails get flatter (left). If you loosen one or all of them, sails get fuller (right).*

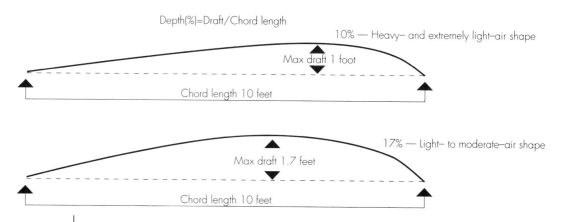

Depth(%)=Draft/Chord length

10% — Heavy- and extremely light-air shape

Max draft 1 foot

Chord length 10 feet

17% — Light- to moderate-air shape

Max draft 1.7 feet

Chord length 10 feet

FIGURE 11.4 *How sail depth is figured. Measure the chord, or the horizontal distance from luff to leech. On that chord locate the deepest point and measure it, too. Depth is then draft/chord length expressed as a percentage. A flat sail (10 percent, top) is good when sailing upwind in heavy and very light winds. A full sail (17 percent, bottom) is good in light to moderate winds, and when reaching and running.*

Learn to Sail

A sail that is 10 feet across (its luff-to-leech measurement), and has a draft of one foot, has a depth of 10 percent.* A sail with that percentage is flat. It would be an appropriate choice for sailing upwind when it is windy (above fifteen knots). If that same size sail had a draft of 1.7 feet (see Figure 11.4, bottom), its depth would be 17 percent. A 17 percent sail is full. It would be a good choice when sailing upwind in light to moderate winds (three to twelve knots), and if the seas were choppy.

The only exception to that rule is very light winds, zero to two knots (see Figure 11.4, top). At such slow velocity, the wind doesn't have sufficient speed or energy to make it all the way around a deeply curved sail. So in very light winds, the sail should be flatter.

Similarly, when sailing upwind in little or no wind, the headsail is not trimmed all the way in with the sheet—rather it is eased a couple of inches from the optimum. Again, this is because the wind doesn't have the energy to make sharp curves. With the headsail out farther, the upwind course steered is also a little lower: maybe forty-eight degrees to the eye of the wind, rather than forty-five degrees. Note the preceding focuses on sailing upwind. At this point of sail, sails show the least curvature. As we now know, they show progressively more shape when reaching and running. This is the continuum idea again.

Halyard tension is very important in shaping a polyester headsail—the material is also called Dacron, which is Du Pont's trademarked name. (The majority of sails are made of polyester or Dacron.) As noted, in Chapter 6, when hoisting the headsail, it should be tight at the luff, or front; there shouldn't be scallops between hanks, or the metal fasteners, if you have them (see Photo 5I, page 70).

That's the starting position. From there, a polyester sail can be adjusted up to 2 percent. This means if the luff length of the headsail is 35 feet, the sail can be adjusted up to 8.4 inches (35 × 12 = 420 inches × 2% = 8.4 inches).

You might crank the halyard of a polyester sail an extra eight inches when sailing upwind in breezy conditions, e.g., fifteen knots of wind and above.† Note, however, you don't want a vertical wrinkle behind the luff of a headsail; if you have one, the halyard is too tight. Moreover, you don't

---

*For those who are interested, the shape of a sail is not consistent from top to bottom. Generally, a sail is flatter at the bottom and deeper at the top.

†Headsails made of low-stretch materials—Mylar, Kevlar, and Spectra—shouldn't be stretched more than .5 percent of luff length. When a Mylar, Kevlar, or Spectra sail requires more than 1 percent halyard adjustment, it is usually a sign of old age or poor design. Unlike polyester, Mylar, Kevlar, and Spectra sails set correctly without all the horizontal wrinkles removed from the luff.

want the sail to rip or the mast to break, so use discretion when doing tensioning.

Returning to the continuum, you would ease halyard tension from there if the wind grows lighter and/or the course you sail is farther off the wind.

While the headsail halyard can be easily eased when sailing, to provide more shape, it is harder to tighten it, to remove shape. To facilitate this, you can ease the headsail sheet until the sail luffs, tighten the halyard, and then retrim the sheet. Alternatively, you can tighten the halyard in the midst of a tack, when the sail is unloaded.

In a mainsail, the Cunningham (see Figure 11.3) substitutes for halyard tension in the headsail. You will recall from Chapter 5 that when hoisted, the mainsail is raised to the very top of the mast. If you were to haul the halyard up farther, to flatten the mainsail, you might damage the head (top) of the sail by pulling it into the pulley, or sheave, at the masthead. It can even get stuck there. To avoid that, rather than pulling the sail *up* with the halyard, the mainsail is normally pulled *down* with the Cunningham. By tensioning the Cunningham, the sail will grow flatter.

Similarly, the outhaul is at its maximum when sailing upwind and it is a breezy fifteen knots or more. It is eased progressively when the wind speed drops or when falling farther off the wind.

Mast Bend

The fourth control that affects sail depth, or shape, is mast bend. The mast is designed to be bent in most boats.* This is because mast bend is a powerful way to shape sails.

Earlier, we noted that a sail is designed with luff curve, and if the *curved* luff of a mainsail, for example, meets a *straight* mast, shape, or extra depth, is forced into the sail. Those emphasized words are important. What would happen if we bent the mast, using the backstay or mainsheet, for example, so the mast's curve matches the mainsail's luff curve? The result would be the removal of shape, or a flat sail (see Photo 11A). That's exactly how mast bend works. If you bend the mast so its curve matches the mainsail's luff curve, shape is removed from the mainsail. The sail grows flatter.

*Sailors of small simple boats, older boats, or those in poor shape may not bend their masts at all, for fear that something might break—the mast, for example. Obviously, when in doubt don't bend your mast.

Mast bend makes for flat sail.

PHOTO 11A *Bend the mast with the mainsheet as here, or with the backstay in a bigger boat, and the mainsail gets flatter. Straighten the mast, and it gets fuller.* (Courtesy Daniel Forster)

Returning to the continuum: the mast is bent the most when sailing upwind in a good breeze.* It is bent progressively less when reaching and running or when the wind grows lighter.

Mast bend affects the headsail, too, and in the same way: Bend the mast more and the genoa grows flatter; bend it less, and it gets fuller.

For those who are interested, the fullness of the genoa is a function of the sag in the forestay (as well as halyard tension, broadseaming, and the luff curve of the sail). Forestay sag is controlled by backstay tension. The more backstay tension, the straighter the forestay, and the flatter the headsail. And vice versa.

When sailing in conditions where more power is needed—e.g., light air, choppy seas—a deep genoa is best. Sag the forestay by easing backstay tension and/or easing the halyard. (Of course, that is what the main would want, too: decreased backstay tension giving rise to a fuller mainsail.) When the wind increases, tighten the backstay to reduce forestay sag. This flattens

---

*Normally, small boats equipped with bendable masts and with hulls robust enough to handle the loads will bend their masts a few inches, while eighty-foot racing boats, with specially designed masts and hulls, will bend their masts up to four feet. To determine maximum bend, sail upwind in about twelve knots of wind. Have one person gradually tension the backstay if you have a masthead rig— that is, the forestay goes to the top of the mast—or the runner if you have a nonmasthead rig while a second person sights up the forestay. When increased tension no longer reduces forestay sag, you've reached the maximum point. Record this number and don't exceed it. This number can be estimated in inches, feet, a mark on the backstay, or even hydraulic pressure if you bend your rig hydraulically.

the headsail. At the same time, you can tighten the halyard. (Again, the main wants the same thing.) Flattening both sails will reduce heeling forces and make your boat perform better, as well as sail more comfortably.

There are many ways to bend masts. It is beyond the scope of this book to examine all of them.* Usually, however, the mast is bent with the backstay. The backstay, in turn, is tensioned by a crank or a split backstay. On small boats, with nonmasthead rigs, the mainsheet is often sufficient to bend the mast when sailing upwind.

Boom Vang (or Kicking Strap)

When sailing upwind, or beating, the mainsheet is the most important sail control. In summary, when you need more power, trim the mainsheet; when you need less power, such as when the boat heels too much, ease it.

However, as soon as you bear away from the wind and start to reach or run, and ease the mainsheet (as is appropriate), the mainsheet loses its effectiveness at controlling the boom. Watch how, when you fall off the wind and ease the mainsheet, the boom skies and the mainsail's leech, or back , twists (or sags) off. This is particularly apparent when it is windy. Thus when reaching and running, the boom vang (see Figure 2.8, page 21), rather than the mainsheet, is used to control the attitude of the boom and the back edge of the mainsail.

For the proper amount of vang tension when reaching or running, tension the vang to keep the boom parallel to the water, or alternatively, the top two battens on the mainsail parallel with the boom. (To best determine this, crouch under the boom and sight upward, lining up the top two battens with the boom.)

Using the vang is more important when it is windy, when the boom skies the most, than when the wind is light. In light winds, the weight of the boom is often sufficient to keep the boom parallel to the water.

When reaching and running in heavy winds, the vang is more important in maintaining control of the boat than is easing the mainsheet. You tension the boom vang when more power is needed. You ease it quickly when the boat heels too much, when the steering starts to get overpowered (see Weather Helm below), or if the boom ends up in the water. The boom vang is often used when beating in heavier winds on small boats. At such times, boom-vang tension can limit the pumping of the mast, which helps to protect it.

---

*A more complete description of mast bend can be found in my book *Sail Like a Champion*.

Headsail's Lead: Fore and Aft

In many boats, the headsail's lead, turning block, or genoa car, can be moved along a track similar to a boom vang in the mainsail. For a rough approximation of the lead's fore and aft location, extend a line from midluff, through the clew, to the deck (see Figure 11.5). Place the lead block there.

A more precise way to locate the headsail's lead is to use the telltales on the headsail. Recall from Chapter 7 that three pairs of telltales on a headsail are optimum. One set should be one-quarter down from the top; another should be one-quarter up from the bottom, and the third pair in the middle. Slowly turn the boat into the wind and watch the three sets of telltales. The idea is to get all three windward telltales breaking at the same time. If the *top*-windward telltale breaks first, move the lead *forward*. If the *bottom*-windward telltale breaks first, move the lead *back*. You can remember this with the expression: Bottom back.

From there, if you want more power, move the lead of the headsail slightly forward. If you want less power, move it aft. The simplest way to move the lead, if your boat allows this, is to slack off sheet tension, move the car forward or back, properly resecure the car, and tension the sheet again.

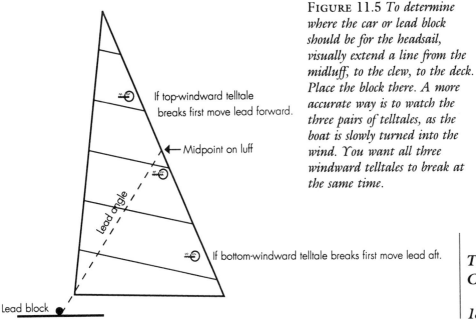

If top-windward telltale breaks first move lead forward.

Midpoint on luff

Lead angle

If bottom-windward telltale breaks first move lead aft.

Lead block

FIGURE 11.5 *To determine where the car or lead block should be for the headsail, visually extend a line from the midluff, to the clew, to the deck. Place the block there. A more accurate way is to watch the three pairs of telltales, as the boat is slowly turned into the wind. You want all three windward telltales to break at the same time.*

The Other Controls

Weather Helm and the Traveler

A sailboat should automatically turn into the wind. Normally, if you take your hands off the tiller or wheel, the boat will steer itself into the wind. This automatic turn is weather helm, and within limits it is desirable.

The optimum amount of weather helm when sailing upwind is three to five degrees. This means that to steer straight, the tiller will not be on the centerline; rather, it will be from three to five degrees *above* the centerline (see Figure 11.6) to compensate for weather helm. While a tiller is turned three to five degrees *away* from the mainsail, a wheel is turned the same amount *toward* the mainsail.

A manageable amount of weather helm is desirable for a number of reasons. If you want to sail closer to the wind (i.e., "up," see Figure 2.9, page 22) simply release pressure on the wheel or tiller, and due to weather helm, the boat automatically turns into the wind. Of course, you still have to turn the wheel or tiller to force the boat off the wind. So steering up is automatic, while steering down is manual. That is better than having to steer manually in both directions.

Also, trimming the rudder slightly—three to five degrees—makes the underbody of a sailboat more efficient. With that amount of trim, the rudder helps the keel. It's analogous to trimming sails: Trim sails properly, and they do plenty of work. Trim them too much or too little, and they do little usable work.

The lower end of the mainsheet assembly, where it attaches to the boat, is often mounted on a traveler, a device that enables the assembly to be moved athwartships, or from side to side. "Raising" the traveler means moving the mainsheet assembly to the "uphill", or weather side. "Easing" the traveler means moving it to the "downhill" or leeward side. The mainsail traveler is used to increase or decrease weather helm (see Figure 11.7). If, for example, you have more than five degrees of weather helm, when sailing upwind, you're overpowered, so drop the traveler. Should more power be needed (if the boat lacks sufficient weather helm or feedback or "feel"), raise the traveler. (Note that while the *traveler's car* can be above the centerline, don't allow the *boom* to be above it.) Raising the traveler is often necessary in light winds.

When reaching in heavy winds, you can ease the traveler when the boat heels too much or if the helmsman feels he is about to lose control.

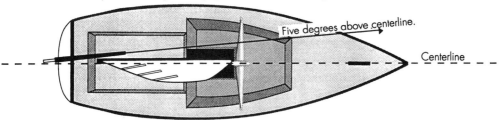

Optimal tiller angle sailing upwind is three to five degrees above centerline.

Five degrees above centerline.

Centerline

FIGURE 11.6 *A manageable amount of weather helm—three to five degrees—is desirable. To counteract weather helm and to allow this boat to steer straight, the tiller and, thus, the rudder is angled five degrees to weather. With this amount of trim, the rudder works like a sail that is trimmed. Its lift complements keel or centerboard lift, so the boat's underbody works harder.*

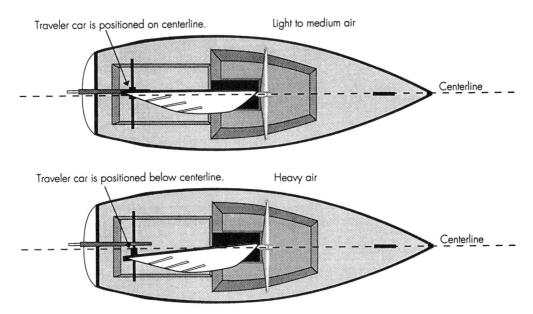

Traveler car is positioned on centerline.

Light to medium air

Centerline

Traveler car is positioned below centerline.

Heavy air

Centerline

FIGURE 11.7 *Traveler position and weather helm go hand in hand. Ease the traveler to leeward (bottom) if, to steer straight when sailing upwind, the boat requires more than five degrees of weather helm or steering is unmanageable. This typically happens in heavy winds. Trim it (top) if more power is needed. Note that while the traveler can be above the center of the boat, the boom shouldn't be. When reaching, eight or even ten degrees of weather helm is acceptable.*

The Other Controls

The formal name for how much a sail is trimmed is "angle of attack." The *more* a mainsail is trimmed by moving its traveler toward the center of the boat (see Figure 11.8)—even above the centerline—the *greater* its angle of attack. Similarly, when you trim the headsail or mainsail with their sheets, you increase their angle of attack.

Overtrimming a sail *slightly,* or increasing its angle of attack, can increase its power. For example, if the sailors of a planing boat want to start planing, they will pump or overtrim the sails for a moment (see Figure 8.2,

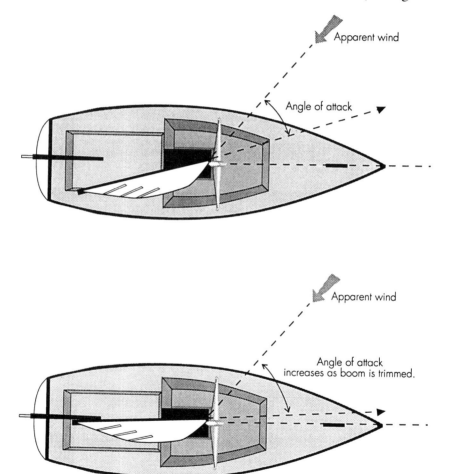

FIGURE 11.8 *The more a sail is trimmed, the greater its angle of attack. Note a slight amount of overtrim—or increased angle of attack—can make a sail more powerful. Easing a sail—decreasing its angle of attack—can make it less powerful. In a mainsail, the mainsheet and traveler control angle of attack.*

page 127).* Undertrimming a sail or easing it temporarily in a puff (both of which decrease its angle of attack) can decrease its power. This, you will recall, is the normal technique when overpowered.

You should start to feel weather helm when there is about five knots of wind. If you take your hand off the tiller or wheel, the boat should turn into the wind. At ten or twelve knots, the boat should require three or four degrees of helm to steer straight, and at fourteen or fifteen knots, five degrees (see Figure 11.6).

When sailing in winds of twelve to fifteen knots, weather helm can get out of control. To steer straight then, the tiller or wheel must be angled eight or even ten degrees off center. At that point, you have to start thinking about decreasing weather helm. This can be accomplished most easily by dropping the traveler, easing the genoa sheet, and/or easing the mainsheet, or boom vang. A more complicated but, perhaps, better solution is changing to a smaller headsail, if you have one, or reefing the headsail or the mainsail, if your boat allows this (see below).

When reaching, you can live with eight to ten degrees of weather helm. When running, there is no consistent weather helm, however, or lee helm (discussed next).

Lee Helm

What happens, however, if there is no weather helm at five knots, or—less desirable still—lee helm (i.e., the tendency of the boat to turn *down* or away from the wind)? A simple solution is to move the boom of the mainsail closer to the center of the boat with the traveler.

Sometimes that works. Two other solutions to lee helm are to move the entire mast aft in a boat or else rake (lean) it aft by easing the forestay and tensioning the backstay. Most people starting out in the sport will probably require help to properly tune the mast.

Inboard and Outboard Tracks for the Headsail

Some boats have an outboard as well as inboard track for the headsail's lead location, or turning block, and other boats allow you to snap a block to the boat's rail. Moving the headsail's lead out or in is similar to the use of the traveler on the mainsail: It changes the angle of attack of the headsail (see

---

*Note that racing rules place limits on how often racing sailors can pump sails. That, of course, has no relevance to recreational sailors.

Figure 11.8). If your boat allows this adjustment, when beating, the lead of the headsail should be inboard. When reaching or running, it should be outboard.

Sail Size

Lay one sail on top of another, and the bigger sail is more powerful than the smaller one. Thus, larger sails are more desirable in light winds, as extra power is needed at such times. Smaller sails are more desirable in heavy winds, as minimizing the heel of the boat is more important than maximizing sail power.

A sailmaker matches sail size to wind speed. For example, he designs smaller sails for heavy winds, larger sails for lighter winds. When sailing,

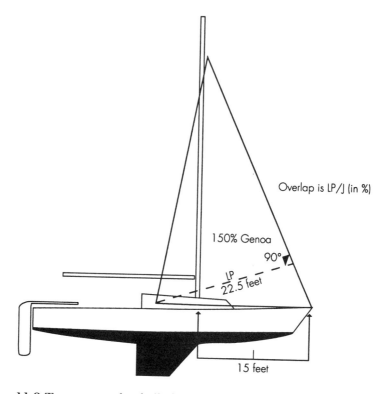

Overlap is LP/J (in %)

150% Genoa

90°

LP ——
22.5 feet

15 feet

FIGURE 11.9 *To measure a headsail, draw a line perpendicular to the luff through the clew. This is LP, or luff perpendicular. Then compare that to the boat's J measurement— the distance from the front of the mast to the forestay. Finally, use the formula in the illustration.*

sailors, too, have a say about sail area. Many boats, for example, allow a choice of headsails distinguished by their size or allow the mainsail or headsail to be reefed (shortened). Affected is sail size and profile, or two-dimensional shape.

Incidentally, there is a formal way to measure a headsail. Headsails on cruising boats are measured most often with the concept of "overlap." It works this way: A line is drawn perpendicular to the luff, through the headsail's clew (see Figure 11.9). This line, called "luff perpendicular" (LP), is then compared to the boat's J measurement—the distance from the forestay to the mast. If, for example, LP is 22.5 feet and J is 15 feet, then the headsail, expressed as a percentage, has an overlap of 150 percent.

On cruising boats, a 150 percent genoa is, by convention, called a Number 1. A *smaller* Number 2 is about 130 to 135 percent. A Number 3, used when it is very windy, has an overlap of about 98 percent, or less. A sail with a number less than 100 percent doesn't overlap the mast and is more correctly termed a jib. Many boats also have a Number 4, or storm jib.

Reefing and Shortening the Headsail

The performance of a sailboat suffers beyond twenty or thirty degrees of heel (see Figure 3.6, page 35). So, too, might one's peace of mind. Thus, many recreational sailors prefer less heel.

Changing to a smaller headsail, or reefing a headsail or mainsail, are all answers to too much wind or too much sail. They require, however, a significant amount of work. Thus, before shortening sail, try adjusting sail trim as follows: The headsail and main should be flattened as much as possible by tensioning the halyard, Cunningham, outhaul, and bending the mast. Also, move the headsail's lead to an outboard setting, ease the traveler, hike harder, or put more weight (more people) on the rail. All of these things can reduce heeling and make the motion of the boat more pleasant.

At some point, however, reducing sail area becomes necessary. Should you first reef or change the headsail or reef the mainsail? The correct answer is usually to start with the headsail. A reef in the main not only reduces sail area, but it means that more of the boat's sail area is located forward. This can upset the balance of the sail plan to the point where the wind can blow the bow to leeward (lee helm). It might even be impossible to sail to weather.

Which sail to make smaller first is also a function of rig type. Typically, a fractionally rigged boat—that is, a boat with a forestay that doesn't go to the top of the mast—might have its bigger main reefed sooner than later.

A masthead boat might have its smaller main reefed somewhat later than earlier.

With most boats, you don't reef the headsail; rather, you change it. While this is a complicated maneuver when racing, as you don't want to sail without a headsail—called sailing "bareheaded"—it isn't complex at other times. Just drop the headsail as described in Chapter 10, sail bareheaded, and raise one of the appropriate size, as described in Chapter 5. (Note, however, that it is typically windy and rough when shortening sail, so take appropriate precautions. Wear a harness, for example [see Chapter 12], and a lifejacket [see Chapter 4].)

Another alternative is a roller-reefing, roller-furling headsail. Here, the headsail rolls up, as if a horizontal window shade. Recall that flat sails are desirable when it is windy, so it is important that the genoa furls around the forestay as tightly as possible when roller-reefing it. If you have the equipment, roller-reefing of the headsail works this way:

One, before reefing, tighten the forestay by tightening the backstay adjuster—if your boat allows this—to flatten the headsail. With the sheet eased, but the sail not quite luffing, roll it to the desired size (see Step 2). Keep slight tension on the sheet, although ease it as the sail grows smaller. The sheet tension plus the wind pressure on the sail will help to flatten the sail and reduce luff wrinkles. For an even smoother shape, try reefing the sail on a broad reach.

Two, reef the sail the appropriate amount. It is easy to overreef a sail with roller-reefing as sail area is removed from the foot, leech, and luff. To avoid this, have your sailmaker put a mark on the foot of the sail when it becomes a Number 2 (135 percent), for example. Reef to this mark. Too much sail exposed to the wind, and the boat heels excessively, is uncomfortable, and is difficult to steer. Too little sail, and a boat can be sluggish at the helm and likewise uncomfortable. That a boat can be uncomfortable with too little sail area is surprising to many.

Three, adjust lead position. In general, move the headsail's block forward when the sail is made smaller, or reefed. Move the lead back when the headsail is unreefed (see Figure 11.5 for a more complete description of the proper forward and aft lead position).

Jiffy- or Slab-reefing the Mainsail

Eventually, however, the mainsail has to be reefed. When that occurs depends on the design of your boat, but you should reef if down to your smallest headsail, if the heel angle is more than twenty or thirty degrees.

Also, reef the mainsail if the helm becomes unmanageable or the boat tries to round up (weather helm), even when it is at an acceptable angle of heel.

Then, too, you should reef when you've tried everything else, and the only way to control the boat is to flog (luff) the main regularly. Or you should reef for safety reasons—such as the approach of a storm or squall. (When a storm or squall is approaching it is better to reef early rather than late. See the lightning discussion at the end of the next chapter.) A mistake sailors often make is to fail to have the reef line run ahead of time; it is awkward and can be dangerous to lead it when conditions turn nasty.

Jiffy-reefing of the mainsail is the most common method of shortening this sail. For an overview of jiffy-reefing, you use an alternative tack (forward-attachment point) and outhaul (back-attachment point on the luff of the mainsail) *higher* up in the sail. Obviously, the sail has to have these alternative rings on the leech built in. Some boats will have one extra tack and outhaul fitting, while some boats have two or three. You can shorten a mainsail that has two or three reef points more than one with one.

The maneuver begins with the main's halyard being eased. Then, the new tack ring is typically placed over a horn near the gooseneck, which traps it once the halyard is retensioned. Then the back of the sail is wound down with a reef line that runs from one side of the boom, through the reef cringle, back to a fairlead, or block, on the other side of the boom, and then to a winch. Again when it is windy, you want the sail to be flat, so make sure the halyard is up tight and the foot well stretched.

For a more detailed view of jiffy-reefing:

One, check the reef line and the main halyard aren't tangled. Tension the topping lift, which supports the boom. (If your boat has a boom vang that holds the boom *up*—most of them merely pull the boom down—you can skip this.) If the vang doesn't support the boom, ease it.

Two, ease the mainsheet and sufficiently lower the halyard, so the reef cringle (see Figure 11.10A) can easily slip over the "tack horn"—hook. (Rather than a tack horn, some boats use a block and tackle. After dropping the halyard, place the hook from the block and tackle into the forward tack cringle.) If reefing when sailing downwind, follow the same procedure. However, rather than easing the mainsheet, trim it almost to the centerline.

Three, have the crew strongly retension the halyard when the new tack is secured.

Four, trim the clew-reef line (see 11.10B) once finished with the tack, or luff of the sail. Pull it harder than normal to overstretch the foot of the sail. If it seems too difficult to tension the clew-reef line, make sure the line isn't pulling part of the sail into the block. Also, check that the vang and mainsheet are well eased.

Five, trim the mainsheet when done with the back of the sail. The boat should be balanced and easier to steer.

Six, check sail depth. A reefed main should be very flat (e.g., 10 percent, see Figure 11.4). If the sail is too full, ease the sheet and increase luff and/or foot tension.

Seven, glance up the mast and make sure that mast bend isn't extreme, and it isn't flexing or pumping. In big seas, it is often a good idea to set up an intermediate forestay or ease backstay tension slightly to reduce mast bend or compression.

Eight, perform general housekeeping last. This means coiling loose lines and readjusting the topping lift or vang, if necessary. Also, neatly tie the reefed part of the sail to the boom (see Figure 11.10C). Mainsails made for jiffy-reefing typically have smaller reef cringles, which allow nylon lines to pass through them and then around the folded part of the sail and the boom. Use a slipped-reef knot (Photo 5D, page 59) to secure the extra sail.

You can reach or run without a headsail. To make progress against the wind, you will likely need a headsail, however. Never drop the mainsail and sail with a headsail only. A mainsail helps to support the rig. In severe conditions, boats rig a storm trysail.*

Trim Guides

What follows are trim guides for sailing in different wind conditions and wind orientations. This guide can be considered a good review of what has come before in this and other chapters. Also provided, in some cases, are the illustration numbers for reference or review.

UPWIND IN LIGHT AIR (ZERO TO SIX KNOTS)

One, keep the centerboard down, to resist the side forces.

Two, trim the main fully in. However, if the wind is under three knots, the headsail should be eased slightly with the sheet. (Remember, in very

---

*A storm trysail is a much diminished mainsail found on some boats that venture offshore. The sail typically has its own track on the back of the mast, and its foot doesn't feed into the boom. Being loose footed, it is trimmed like a headsail.

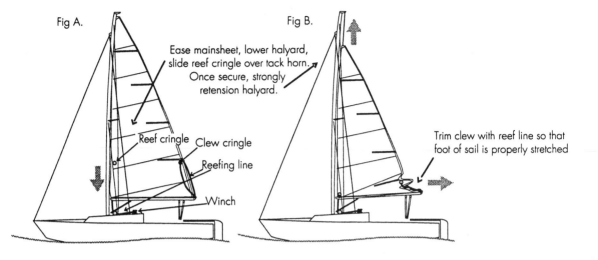

Fig A.

Ease mainsheet, lower halyard, slide reef cringle over tack horn. Once secure, strongly retension halyard.

Fig B.

Reef cringle Clew cringle

Reefing line

Winch

Trim clew with reef line so that foot of sail is properly stretched

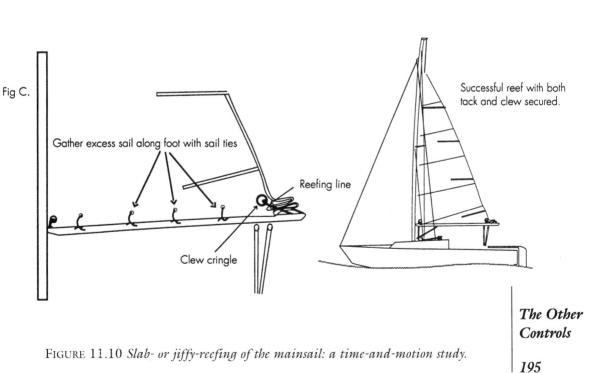

Fig C.

Gather excess sail along foot with sail ties

Reefing line

Clew cringle

Successful reef with both tack and clew secured.

FIGURE 11.10 *Slab- or jiffy-reefing of the mainsail: a time-and-motion study.*

light winds, the wind lacks sufficient energy to turn sharp corners.) Also, steer a slightly lower course.

Three, keep the boom in the center of the boat with traveler (Figure 11.7), but ease mainsheet slightly.

Four, ease the outhaul on the mainsail about one inch from its maximum setting (see Figure 11.3), which will increase sail depth.

Five, bend the mast slightly, if at all.

Six, tension the halyard on the headsail lightly to keep the sail full (Figure 11.3); however, there shouldn't be scallops between hanks.

UPWIND IN MEDIUM AIR (SEVEN TO FOURTEEN KNOTS)

One, keep the centerboard down.

Two, trim the sails tightly, making them more powerful.

Three, tension the boom vang so the boom is parallel to the water, or so the top two battens on the mainsail are parallel to the boom.

Four, tension the Cunningham only enough to take the wrinkles out of the mainsail (see Photo 5I, page 70). This maximizes power by keeping the sail full.

Five, tension the outhaul to flatten the mainsail at the bottom (Figure 11.3).

Six, the mast should be bent about halfway to flatten the mainsail.

Seven, with the traveler, keep the boom centered until the boat heels beyond twenty-five degrees or the angle of heel is uncomfortable (Figure 11.7). Then drop the traveler.

Eight, the genoa halyard should be tighter than in very light winds.

Nine, if boat begins to get overpowered, change to a smaller headsail or reef the mainsail or headsail (if the latter is roller-reefing).

Ten, crew weight should be on the weather rail; hiking may become necessary if sailing a centerboard boat.

UPWIND IN HEAVY AIR (FIFTEEN KNOTS AND ABOVE)

One, keep the board down.

Two, trim the sails tightly. However, they should be eased in gusts. It also helps if you turn the boat upwind at the same time.

Three, bend mast fully (assuming your mast is designed to be bent) and use boom-vang tension on smaller boats. Boom-vang tension has the added advantage of preventing the pumping of the mast.

Four, hike or put all crew not otherwise engaged on the weather rail.

Five, increase Cunningham tension, as heeling increases.

Six, to prevent the boat from heeling beyond twenty or thirty degrees, which is about the maximum, ease traveler to leeward (Figure 11.7), ease mainsheet slightly, or reef main or reef or change headsail if necessary.

SAILING DOWNWIND

As should be obvious, upwind sailing requires precise sail trim and technique. Reaching and running, which we will group together as sailing downwind, are less demanding, however.

One, tension the boom vang to keep the boom parallel to the water or alternatively, the top two battens on the mainsail parallel to the boom. Don't, however, overvang the mainsail in light winds. When it gets windy, tension the vang further to reduce the rolling of the boat in seas. If, however, the boat heels too much, the vang must be eased immediately. In heavy winds, a crew member should be poised to do this.

Two, when reaching, ease the sails until they luff and then trim them just enough to stop the luffing (see Figure 7.4, page 107). An alternative is to trim the headsail with the telltales (see Figure 8.4, page 130); when both the windward and leeward telltales stream aft, the sail is properly trimmed. A sail doesn't luff, however, when running, so at this wind orientation ease the mainsail until it is at a right angle to the wind, which is about eighty degrees to the boat (see Figure 9.5, page 141). Unless sailing wing-on-wing (or goosewinged) (see Figure 9.6, page 143), the headsail is fairly ineffective when running.

Three, when sailing downwind, the mainsail should show increased depth. This can be accomplished by easing the outhaul, backstay, and Cunningham (Figure 11.3, right), and straightening the mast by easing the backstay. If, however, when overpowered on a windy reach—or close to it—the mainsail should be made flatter, which will make the boat easier to steer.

Four, to increase depth in the headsail, the halyard should be eased slightly from the upwind position, and the mast straightened by easing the backstay. If your boat allows the headsail's lead to be moved outboard, this should be done when reaching and running. Often a snatch block can be placed on the rail to accept an outboard jib sheet. This affects the sail's angle of attack. Remember to bring the lead back inboard when sailing upwind again.

12 | Emergencies

In the 1988 America's Cup, I sailed a catamaran, a two-hulled boat, against a huge monohull from New Zealand. A catamaran—or a cat, as it is called—is a different breed of cat than a monohull. Just how different was the subject of a bitter two-year court battle that the San Diego Yacht Club, which I represented, eventually won.

The boat we ultimately sailed was a sixty-foot catamaran with a solid-wing mast. However, before launching this boat, we trained in a similar forty-foot catamaran.

I capsized this boat in four knots of wind, when not paying attention to what I was doing. Yes, an insignificant four knots of wind. It took us five and a half hours to right this wrong and clean up the mess. Other than feeling silly, it didn't bother me. There was no harm done; it didn't cost us any money. In many ways it was good for the program, because we learned what to do when you capsize one of these extreme boats.* I tell this story for several reasons. At any level, mistakes happen. Boats capsize and run aground. People fall overboard. Knowing what to do in an emergency can

---

*In Chapter 2, we divided boats into keelboats and centerboard boats. Obviously, another way to divide them is into monohull boats (i.e., those with one hull) and multihull boats (boats with more than one hull). In the latter category are catamarans with two hulls and trimarans with three. From sailing multihull boats to righting them in the event of a capsize, the technique is very different than with monohulls. This book hasn't and won't address multihull technique, however, because very few people learn to sail on them. In some ways, learning to sail on a multihull is like learning to drive with a Ferrari. In other ways, it is like learning to drive with an eighteen-wheel truck.

spell the difference between an inconvenience—an embarrassment—and disaster.

This chapter addresses what to do in an emergency. The maneuvers that follow should be learned under the supervision of someone who has experience with them. Once learned, they should be practiced so everyone knows what to do.

Capsizing

A centerboard boat, which depends on human reactions to keep it upright, is more prone to capsizing than is a keelboat. It's not that keelboats can't capsize, they are just much less likely to do so, as the keel works along with the crew to keep the boat upright. Finally, if a keelboat should capsize, the keel is normally of a size and weight to right the boat quickly.

By the way, when sailing a keelboat in rough weather, keep the hatches, ports, and companionway doors closed. This will help to keep water from entering the below-decks area. Should too much water enter this area, the boat can sink. That's a bigger problem than a capsized but floating centerboarder.

While a centerboard boat will capsize, most modern boats are designed with flotation (foam), and attention paid to rig size and centerboard length to make righting them relatively easy—if you know what to do. Remember that a modern boat in good condition will stay afloat indefinitely.

When sailing a boat that can capsize, you absolutely must wear a buoyancy aid or lifejacket. If you aren't wearing one, don it immediately after you go over. Putting a lifejacket on when in the water is fairly easy. The way to do it so as not to fight the flotation is similar to how a child is taught to put on a coat. You start with the lifejacket upside down and inside out as you face it (see Photo 12A). Place your arms into the arm holes, and then raise your arms so that the lifejacket goes over and then behind your head. Finally, float on your back and fasten it, so it can't ride up.

If your boat isn't self-bailing, you will need something to bail it once it is upright. A bucket, of course, is very handy in this regard; however, if the bucket is floating fifty feet from the boat, it has lost its utility. This means securing the bucket to the boat. *Never* leave a floating craft, unless it is on fire, no matter how good a swimmer you are or how close the shore appears. Remaining with a floating boat is an abiding principle of sailing.

As you face it, the lifejacket is upside down and inside out. Place arms in arm holes.

Raise your arms so the lifejacket goes over and behind head.

Float on your back to work fasteners, either zipper or ties.

PHOTO 12A *Putting on a lifejacket when in the wat* (Michael Levitt photos)

RECOVERING FROM A LEEWARD CAPSIZE

A boat most often capsizes to leeward. What happens is that a sudden gust of wind heels a centerboard boat too much and too suddenly for the crew to react. (As we now know, the correct responses to an overpowering gust of wind are to put weight on the high side, hike out, ease the sheets, and/ or turn the boat into the wind.) The boat capsizes to leeward, meaning the rig points downwind (see Figure 12.1).

Righting a boat after a leeward capsize works this way:

One, immediately following a capsize, all crew members should swim for the boat. Don't panic and don't struggle to remove clothes or shoes. The truth is that air trapped in your clothes provides considerable flotation. Further, trying to disrobe will quickly exhaust you. Float on your back with your knees bent and paddle with your arms to the boat. Hold on to the boat for support, and to prevent anyone from drifting away.

Make sure that everyone is present. Render assistance to anyone who needs help; don't, however, risk your own life to do so.

While you should use the boat for support, don't allow your weight, if possible, to cause the vessel to turn over so the mast points down. This is because a boat that has "turned turtle," as sailors term this orientation (see Figure 12.3), is considerably harder to right. To prevent this state, don't try to avoid the water by sitting on an overturned boat. This is almost instinctive, but it can quickly make matters worse. It is also a good idea for a crew member, wearing a lifejacket, to move the mast and push it up at the "gooseneck," where the mast and boom meet (see Figure 12.1A).

(Recall from Chapter 4, that hypothermia—a lowering of the body's core temperature—can occur in water that is seventy degrees or warmer. If there is a danger of hypothermia, or you suspect someone is hypothermic, get in or on the overturned boat. The more of your body that is out of the water, the better.)

Two, a crew member—typically the stronger and heavier one—uncleats the boom vang (if the boat has one) and the mainsheet if it is cleated. Then using the mainsheet as a tether, this person makes his way to the centerboard at the bottom of the boat. (To avoid confusion we'll refer to this person as the "heavier one," or words to that effect; the second crew member, presently holding up the mainsail, at the gooseneck is the "lighter one.")

The heavier person should take hold of the centerboard but not climb it yet. However, this person should monitor the attitude of the boat through

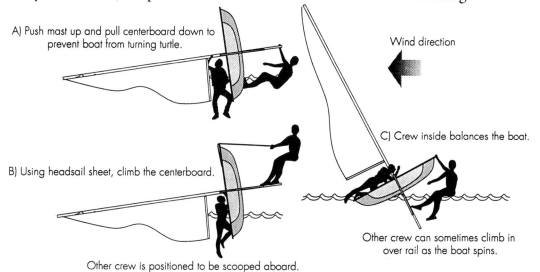

A) Push mast up and pull centerboard down to prevent boat from turning turtle.

Wind direction

C) Crew inside balances the boat.

B) Using headsail sheet, climb the centerboard.

Other crew can sometimes climb in over rail as the boat spins.

Other crew is positioned to be scooped aboard.

FIGURE 12.1 *Righting the boat after a leeward capsize.*

the centerboard: If the boat feels as if it is about to turn turtle—if the centerboard wants to twist up—he should pull down on the board, even climb it (see Figure 12.1A).

It is important that the centerboard be completely extended. If it isn't, this is done from inside the boat by the lighter person.

Three, the lighter person should try to throw the *windward* (high side) headsail sheet up and over the windward rail. This crew member next places himself between the boom and the boat, so as to be *scooped* back aboard when the boat turns upright. This method, incidentally, is known as a "scooped recovery." To ensure he comes aboard, the lighter crew member should hold on to the centerboard trunk, a hiking strap, the boom, boom vang, or mainsheet (see Figure 12.1B). When both people are ready, they should communicate that.

Four, the heavier person climbs the centerboard with the help of the windward genoa sheet.* Then by pulling on the sheet and placing his full weight on the *end* of the centerboard and leaning back, the boat turns upright.

With the turn of the boat, the lighter person should have been scooped aboard. This person's first job is to balance the boat (see Figure 12.1C). This is important because at the same time that the boat spins upright, the person standing on the centerboard is often able to scramble from the centerboard, over the rail, and into the boat, too, using the headsail sheet as an added assist. If the boat isn't balanced, it can capsize again, however. It can even capsize to windward, which is even less fun (see below).

Five, bail the boat if it isn't self-bailing.† Then, one or both of the crew members help others, if there are any others, over the low point of the *windward* rail. Why the windward rail? Because the sails, mast, and boom will likely be leaning to leeward. This leeward heel will help to counterbalance someone climbing over the *windward* rail.

To get subsequent people aboard a centerboard boat, carefully rock the windward rail down, which effectively lowers the freeboard of the boat.

---

*Some old but still popular training boats float "high" when capsized, meaning the centerboard may be too high to climb easily. Similarly, some people lack the size or upper body strength to climb the centerboard easily. If the heavier person can't climb the centerboard, the lighter one might be better for the job. Alternatively, if you tie a bowline (see Photo 5E, page 61) at an appropriate position at the end of the headsail sheet, you can use it as a step to help climb onto the centerboard.

†Note that some self-bailing boats, with the bottom of the cockpit sufficiently higher than the bottom of the boat, will bail themselves automatically; and some boats will bail themselves once the bailers are opened and the boat starts moving. Obviously, if you have a self-bailing boat, it is important to know how the bailers work.

When the windward rail goes down, a person in the water can often get the top part of his body aboard. When it rocks back another time or two, he can often get his feet in. With an assist from those already in the boat, this should be fairly easy.

If a person is unable to help himself in, tie him to the boat. This way he won't be able to drift away. Then have the person float on his back, with his head just behind the shrouds (side stays) and his feet pointed aft. He should wrap his arm closest to the boat around a shroud. Again, carefully rock the boat to windward. Those already on board should be able to grab the victim by the lifejacket or belt, turn him over and roll him into the boat.

RIGHTING A SINGLEHANDER

If alone in a small singlehanded boat that has capsized to leeward, uncleat the boom vang and the mainsheet. Then climb the centerboard, stand on its end, and lean back while holding on to the rail. As the boat spins upright, climb from the board, over the rail, and in. Quickly get off the rail, to ensure that the craft doesn't continue to spin over on top of you.

If unable to climb back aboard when it spins, once the boat is upright, climb into the cockpit on the windward stern-quarter.

RECOVERING FROM
A WINDWARD CAPSIZE

There are two problems that distinguish recovering from a windward capsize and recovering from a leeward one. For example, following a windward capsize, once the boat starts to stand up, the wind can get under the sail. The boat then can right with such speed, it can capsize again—this time to leeward. The other problem with a windward capsize is that when the mainsail fills, it can whip across the boat to the downwind (leeward) side. So—as always—watch your head. Again, having a sense of the boom is a lifesaver in sailing. This is particularly important because a windward capsize generally happens when it is blowing.

If the boat capsizes to windward (the mast points into the wind), first, try to swim the bow into the wind. Do this by holding on to it and kicking with your feet. If a second crew member kicks from the stern, in the opposite direction, it is easier to orient the bow into the wind. An alternative is to drop your feet, while holding on to the bow, so your body is vertical. This turns your body into what is termed a "sea anchor," and you might now offer sufficient drag to move the bow into the wind. If successful in moving

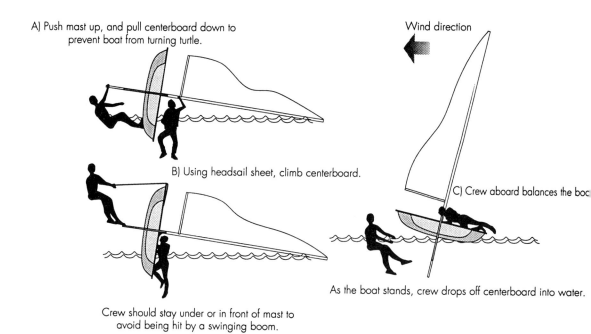

A) Push mast up, and pull centerboard down to prevent boat from turning turtle.

Wind direction

B) Using headsail sheet, climb centerboard.

C) Crew aboard balances the boc

As the boat stands, crew drops off centerboard into water.

Crew should stay under or in front of mast to avoid being hit by a swinging boom.

FIGURE 12.2 *Righting the boat after a windward capsize.*

it into the wind, right the boat as if it were a leeward capsize, as just discussed. Know, however, that turning a capsized boat into the wind is rarely easy. If unsuccessful you must recover from a windward capsize. It works this way:

Follow the steps one through three in recovering from the leeward capsize. One change, however, is that when recovering from a windward capsize, the lighter person goes to the centerboard, and the heavier person first supports the mast to keep the boat from turning turtle, and then is scooped aboard. Another change is that the person about to be scooped up should keep his head directly under or better yet slightly forward of the mast (see Figure 12.2B). This way, the swinging boom can't hit him.

As in Step 4, the person on the centerboard stands on the end of the board and leans back, using the jib sheet for support (see Figure 12.2B). However, as soon as the boat starts to stand upright, and the wind finds its way under the sail, the person on the board should let go and drop back into the water (see Figure 12.2C). Do this quickly if it is windy, less quickly if it isn't. Never attempt to scramble into the boat from the centerboard as there is a likelihood the boom will hit you.

The crew member now scooped into the boat remains on the windward side or the centerline—whichever is appropriate—to prevent a second capsize—this time to leeward. Again, the person who is scooped into the boat should keep his head far below the arc of the boom. Then follow Step 5.

Righting a Boat That Has Turned Turtle

If the boat has turned turtle, the mast is facing down (see Figure 12.3). To recover from this, take a long sheet over the hull and then to windward. If the centerboard has slid back into its trunk, keep your fingers away from the trunk, because if the board pops out, you can get hurt. Then the crew—more than one person if possible—should stand on the windward rail and at the same time pull on the sheet. The boat should turn on its side. Drop the centerboard, if it isn't already down, and continue the recovery as if this were a leeward capsize.

Note: If the boat won't spin, the crew members should move forward or back and stand on the gunwale using the sheet for support and for leverage (see the inset in Figure 12.3). This position and new angle of pull will often cause the boat to start to turn.

In the rare occurrence the boat turns turtle, and the mast sticks in the mud, the likelihood is that you're going to need assistance from another vessel. Try to attract the attention of the operator of a powerboat. Recall from Figure 4.1, page 46, that a commonly recognized distress signal is to wave your arms over your head. The higher out of the water you are, the easier you will be seen, so signal the other boat while sitting or even standing on the overturned boat if you can safely do that. If you have a choice, it is better to ask for help from someone in a small, more maneuverable motor boat than a large less maneuverable powerboat or sailboat.

Typically, the centerboard will lean to one side or the other. Ask the operator of the motor boat to approach the sailboat on the centerboard side. Tell the driver to be very careful of those in the water, as a spinning prop can be very dangerous. Better yet, have him remove the crew from the water. Definitely recover people if you suspect hypothermia. When you are recovering crew members from the water, the prop shouldn't be spinning; the engine should be in neutral. Then a person on the bow of the powerboat should grab the centerboard. While he is holding on to the centerboard, the boat under power slowly backs up. This should get the mast out of the mud.

A variation on this method is to place a line around the low-side shroud and then cleat it to the bow of the powerboat. Again, the powerboat backs

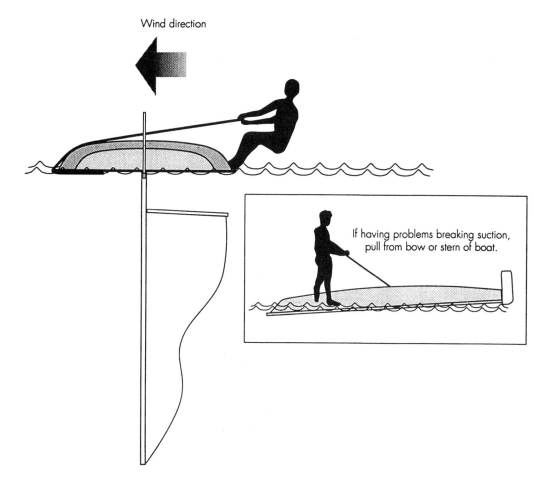

Wind direction

If having problems breaking suction, pull from bow or stern of boat.

FIGURE 12.3 *Turning a boat that has turned turtle on to its side. When this is accomplished, you right it as in a leeward capsize (Figure 12.1).*

slowly away. Then the boat is righted as if it were a windward or leeward capsize—whichever is appropriate.

Staying Aboard

Preventing emergencies is at least as important as responding correctly to one. A good safety harness, which can keep you aboard, is a requirement on larger boats (i.e., any craft with lifelines), in rough weather, or when there is the smallest chance of falling overboard. As with lifejackets, there must be one harness for every crew member.

You should clip yourself to the windward, or the high side of the boat and keep the tether short. Be careful, however, what you clip on to. Any through-bolted fitting should be strong enough, as should shrouds, cleats, winches, and the mast. Don't, however, attach to the lifelines, the stanchions that support lifelines, the pulpit, sheets, or cockpit-dodger supports. The harness should have two strong clips—one on either end. This way if you need to unclip yourself in an emergency, you can do it without having to climb to the high side. This can be difficult.

Man Overboard!

If someone should fall overboard, however, the Quick-Stop maneuver is my preferred method for recovering him—particularly if you have sufficient crew. This method was developed by the US SAILING Safety at Sea Committee, the U.S. Naval Academy Sailing Squadron, the Cruising Club of America Technical Committee, and the Sailing Foundation of Seattle. Its main advantage is that it keeps the boat closer to the man in the water than any other method of recovery. This is desirable because the spotter watching the victim from aboard the boat is less likely to lose sight of him.

This method also keeps sailhandling to a minimum, freeing crew members from this distraction. Also, the boat makes a circle around the man overboard, which is easy to remember. Other methods require more complex maneuvering, which can cause you to lose sight of the victim.

The Quick-Stop maneuver works this way:

One, as soon as someone falls into the water, shout the words, "Man overboard!" to alert other crew members to what amounts to an extreme emergency (see Position 1 in Figure 12.4). If there is another person besides the helmsperson on deck, this person should do nothing but keep his eye on the victim. If your boat has Loran or GPS, save your position immediately by pressing the MOB button. If alone, however, don't take your eye off the man in the water to do this. All crew should immediately come on deck to help.

Two, toss flotation devices, such as lifebuoys, buoyant cockpit cushions—they should be on deck—rolled up lifejackets, or life rings to the victim. The more of these objects in the water, the better.

One type of life ring, carried on the transom of some boats, combines a high-visibility location flag, strobe light, and whistle, as well as a drogue anchor, to prevent it from drifting rapidly away. A device such as this can be slow to deploy, however, so don't throw it overboard first. If sailing at night, an inexpensive personal strobe light and whistle, which should be securely worn by each crew member on deck, can be helpful in locating the man in the water. Every person on deck or in the cockpit at night must wear a harness.

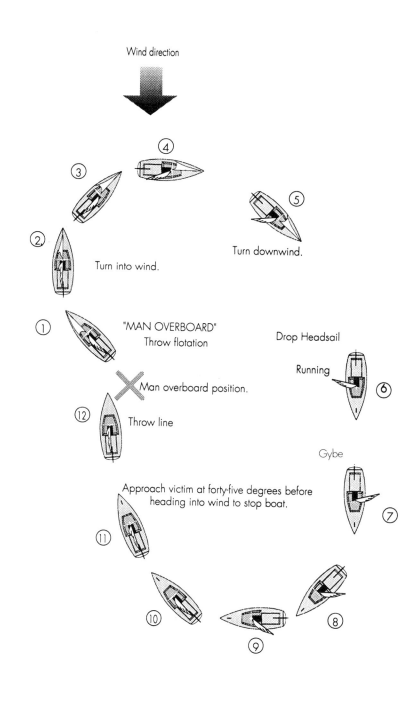

Wind direction

④

③

⑤

②

Turn downwind.

Turn into wind.

①

"MAN OVERBOARD"
Throw flotation

Drop Headsail

Running

⑥

✕ Man overboard position.

⑫   Throw line

Gybe

⑦

Approach victim at forty-five degrees before
heading into wind to stop boat.

⑪

⑧

⑩

⑨

FIGURE 12.4 *Recovering a man overboard using the Quick-Stop method.*

Three, immediately turn the boat into the wind to stop it (Position 2). This keeps the boat near the victim. (If flying a symmetrical spinnaker, ease the pole to the headstay when you turn into the wind. Without easing the sheet or guy, drop the spinnaker halyard and gather the sail on the foredeck. If flying an asymmetrical spinnaker with a sail-sock device, snuff the sail as you turn into the wind.)

Four, tack (Position 3). Don't, however, release the headsail; keep it trimmed on the wrong side, or "backed." Turn farther off the wind until sailing on a beam to broad reach (Positions 4 and 5).

Five, sail two or three boat lengths and then turn farther off the wind until you're running (Position 6). Drop the headsail.

Six, continue downwind. Once the victim is *aft* of abeam, or behind a right angle extending from the boat, gybe the mainsail (Position 7).

Seven, you should be sailing at a course of from sixty to forty-five degrees to the wind as you approach the victim (Positions 10 and 11).

Eight, stop the boat near the man overboard (Position 12) by turning into the wind. Make direct contact by throwing a line. For little more than twenty dollars, you can buy a throwing line in a bag. With this device, one can easily and accurately toss a line seventy-five feet upwind. (Obviously, buy this ahead of time. Also, keep the throwing line handy and make sure everyone knows where it is, as you might be the one who falls overboard. As stated in Chapter 4, the whereabouts of all safety equipment should be noted on a list and posted in an obvious place.) Before throwing the line, tell the man in the water what you are doing. When he has the line firmly in his hands, pull him carefully to the boat—don't pull so hard, however, that this person loses his grip on the line.

(Note that the use of an engine in effecting the rescue is debatable, due to the danger of the spinning prop severely injuring the victim or fouling a line. It might be a good idea to start the engine, but keep it in neutral until making your final approach to the victim. Shift back to neutral when, for example, a boat length away.)

Nine, getting the victim back aboard is a challenge in itself. Don't expect him to climb aboard or walk up a swimming ladder. In nearly all cases, the crew on deck must hoist the man back on the boat. A substantial block and tackle affixed to a strong boom of a keelboat can be helpful in this regard (see Figure 12.5). Keep the block and tackle handy for this emergency. Again, make sure the entire crew knows where it is.

Before attempting to hoist the victim out of the water, if using the boom as a crane, drop the mainsail. You will likely have to lift the boom with the topping lift or halyard so the victim is able to clear the lifelines.

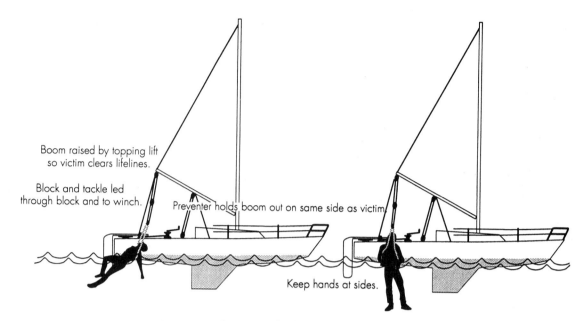

FIGURE 12.5 *Getting the victim back aboard following rescue with the Quick-Stop method.*

Also, the boom has to be eased out to the same side as the man overboard with the mainsheet and held out with a preventer (see Figure 9.4, page 139). Hoist the man where the freeboard of the boat is the lowest.

Without releasing the throwing line, help place a loop of thick (three quarter inch) line over the victim. The loop should go under his arms and around his back. Attach the other end to a block and tackle at the end of the boom. (A bowline [see Photo 5E, page 61] can be a handy knot in this regard.) Instruct the man overboard to keep his elbows at his sides. This way, the line won't slip off. Hoist him above the lifelines, with the line from the pulley that goes through a block and then onto a winch. Ease the preventer as you trim the mainsheet to bring him into the boat. Let him down slowly and under control.

Every person should know how to perform the Quick-Stop maneuver and the recovery. Like a fire drill, practice man-overboard drills. For such a drill, retrieve a buoyant cushion or something similar, not a person.

Lifesling

The Lifesling, a fairly recent man-overboard innovation marketed by the Sailing Foundation of Seattle and available worldwide, facilitates bringing the victim back aboard and making initial contact with him. It seems particularly appropriate if you sail shorthanded.

Rescue with the Lifesling is a variation on the Quick-Stop maneuver. It works this way:

As before, the crew immediately calls "Man overboard!" (see Position 1, Figure 12.6). Throw flotation to the victim, and, again, the more the better. If possible, one person should do nothing but keep his eye on the victim. Tack in Position 2 (Figure 12.6), but as before keep the jib on the wrong side so it is backed. This will increase the rate of the turn downwind.

After tacking (see Position 3) deploy the Lifesling, a buoyant, horseshoe-shaped device, by opening its bag. This is normally mounted on the stern pulpit. Drop the Lifesling into the water; its buoyant line pays itself

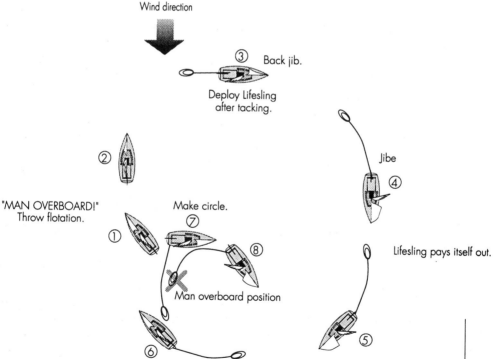

FIGURE 12.6 *Rescue with the Lifesling is a variation on the Quick-Stop method. It is particularly appropriate for shorthanded crews.*

out as you reach and then run in a wide circle past the victim (Position 4). Wait until the man overboard is aft of abeam before turning toward him (Position 5).

With the victim at first on your weather side, start making a wide circle around him (Positions 6 and 7). You will have to tack and perhaps gybe. (The Lifesling's line or horseshoe cushion makes the contact with the victim, not the boat, so don't tack or gybe too close to the man overboard, or make too tight a circle.) Similar to bringing the tow rope to a water skier, this circle, or a subsequent one, should bring the Lifesling to the man in the water.

After making contact, the man overboard puts the Lifesling over his head and then under his arms. He should at first face the boat and *face* the

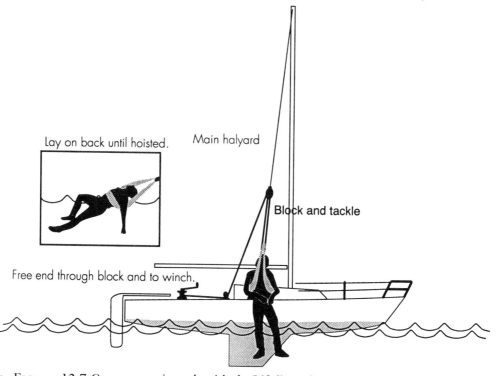

Lay on back until hoisted.

Main halyard

Block and tackle

Free end through block and to winch.

FIGURE 12.7 *Once contact is made with the Lifesling, the victim, facing the boat and facing the D-rings of the Lifesling, puts it over his head and under his arms (not pictured). The man is pulled to the boat and the sails are dropped. Note in the inset how he has turned around so he is now floating on his back and facing away from the D-rings. Finally, the man turns again so he is once more facing the D-rings in preparation for being hauled aboard.*

D-rings of the Lifesling. With contact, immediately stop the boat by turning it into the wind. Drop the headsail and mainsail. The crew pulls the Lifesling's line to the boat with the victim now floating on his back, or facing *away* from the D-rings of the Lifesling (see inset, Figure 12.7). A winch will probably be necessary to pull the man to the boat.

Don't stop pulling on the line until the victim is alongside the boat. Once there, the man in the water should turn in the Lifesling so he is again *facing* the D-rings. With his elbows held at his sides, he is suspended with his head and shoulders free of the water. The Lifesling's line is then cleated.

Next, attach the top part of a three- or four-part block and tackle to the main halyard (see Figure 12.7). In preparation for hoisting the man out of the water, raise the halyard to a height where the victim can clear the lifelines, or until it is about ten feet above the deck, and then cleat it.

Attach the bottom part of the block and tackle to the D-rings of the Lifesling. Take the free end of the block-and-tackle line through a block and to a winch. Use this line to hoist the victim over the lifelines and into the boat. Slack the Lifesling's cleated line after the block and tackle has begun to hoist the man on board.

An alternative is to attach the D-rings of the Lifesling to the main halyard, and use it alone to winch the man out of the water. This is possible if the winch is appropriately placed, for example, on the mast, and of sufficient power to accomplish the task.

Refloating a Boat After Running Aground

Draft, you will recall, is a measure of the distance from a boat's waterline to the bottom of its keel or centerboard. Simply considered, if the depth of the water is less than your draft, you're aground. While a theme of piloting a boat is to stay off the bottom, I have yet to meet a sailor who hasn't run aground.

In a centerboard or daggerboard boat, running aground normally isn't a big problem. Assuming the board is down, all you need to do is hoist it enough to get off the bottom and sail away.

A keelboat, however, doesn't lend itself to such an easy method of escape. If you run aground in a keelboat, first take measurements around the craft with a "lead line," used to measure depth, or a boat hook to determine where the deep water is. This information can help you plan an escape route. Obviously, it doesn't make any sense to try to go forward if that's taking you into even shallower water.

If you sail in a tidal area and the tide happens to be "flooding"—or rising—often all you need do is wait for the water depth to increase sufficiently and sail off. (That said, the longer you wait there the greater the chance the boat could be further damaged.) You can have a long wait, however, if the tide isn't flooding, or an interminable wait if the area where you're sailing doesn't have tides.

If stuck and awaiting the rise in tide, row or very cautiously swim out an anchor. (In the latter case, the anchor should be floated on a lifejacket. The swimmer should be wearing a lifejacket, as well, and be tethered to the boat.) Set the anchor (see Chapter 10), and keep strain on it until the tide rises, and the boat floats free. The anchor can prevent you from drifting and going aground again.

Heeling the boat with all the crew members on one side can also help to free you. This effectively decreases the craft's draft, and you might be able to sail or power off the shallow area. If there is wind, you can often overtrim the mainsail. This causes the boat to heel more. The crew should put their weight on the low side at the same time—causing the vessel to heel even more.

Another alternative is to drop the mainsail, pull the boom to the centerline, and cleat it with the mainsheet. Have crew members sit on the boom. The heaviest people should be at the back end. Then ease the boom out to the appropriate side; a preventer might be necessary to pull the boom outboard.

If your boat has an engine, try reverse gear at the same time as you heel it. Watch engine instruments, however, as you don't want the engine to overheat. This is more likely to happen when aground, as bottom debris, stirred up by the grounding, is brought in with the cooling water. Such debris can clog the cooling system. If reverse gear doesn't work, try forward; turn the wheel or tiller at the same time. If turning one way doesn't work, try turning the other way.

You can sometimes heel the boat further by tying the main halyard to another boat, an anchor (which will probably have to be placed using a dinghy or swimming), or even to something ashore if you are close enough. Then grind the main halyard up with a winch to heel.

What to Do in the Event of a Collision

Collisions occur (avoiding them is the subject of the next chapter), and boats are sometimes holed as a result. If your boat is holed, tack if appropriate so the opening is out of the water. Place all nonessential crew and other movable ballast (i.e., sails, tools) on the low side.

You can stem the flood of water by placing a collision mat over the hole. This is a square piece of heavy polyester with grommets in the corners. Tied or spliced to the grommets are lines, which can reach around the hull. The collision mat goes over the hole on the outside of the boat, then the lines are cleated. If you don't have a collision mat, you can try to use a small sail.

The hole should next be plugged from the inside. Mattresses, cushions, or even floorboards can be used to plug it from the inside. Obviously, they must be held in place with oars, fenders, or some similar type of ad-hoc solution. It can be a real test of ingenuity.

It is also possible to save a holed boat by running it purposely aground on soft sand or mud. Unless you prefer the fire to the frying pan, running it aground on rock or coral isn't usually appropriate.

Lightning

Take precautions if you find yourself out in a storm accompanied by lightning; don't panic, however, as not that many boats get struck by it. Also, most boats are grounded, which is a good but not infallible method of dispersing the energy from the mast, which will attract the lightning, to the water.

Lightning usually comes with some warning. Know that the time between the lightning flash and the clap of the thunder tells you how far from the storm you are. Sound travels at one-fifth of a mile per second, so a five-second interval between the flash and the thunder means the storm is about a mile away; three seconds equals a half mile. Such storms typically move fast, however—about 25 mph. Also plan a compass course, as there will be little or no visibility.

Use the time to reef or drop sails, in preparation for the increased wind that typically accompanies a thunderstorm or squall. Close hatches and put on safety equipment: lifejackets and harnesses. Turn off all electronics. Send all non-essential crew members below decks wearing lifejackets if you have that option. If you don't, sit low in the cockpit. Obviously someone has to steer and keep a lookout. When it is lightning, avoid touching the mast, boom, shrouds, halyards, or other electrical conductors. Further, stay out of the water.

Fire

The first rule is to prevent a fire before it starts. This means take the proper precautions when fueling (see Chapter 6), don't smoke in a bunk, don't turn on your gas stove and then start searching for a match.

Failing in prevention, act quickly to minimize the effects of a fire. Eliminate the oxygen that feeds it. To do this, close hatches, ports, or doors and turn off the blower if it is running. Fire extinguishers also help to eliminate the oxygen. They also can minimize heat, which further helps put out the fire.

Use a multipurpose fire extinguisher or else the appropriate type. (For advice on types of fire extinguishers see Chapter 4.) These will help douse flames involving flammable and combustible liquids: gasoline, alcohol, liquefied cooking gas, or paint. Again, never use water on this type of fire as it will cause it to spread. You can, however, use water to wet down areas adjacent to the fire to keep it from moving.

If a burner on your alcohol stove flames up, perhaps due to leaking fuel that has collected in a drip pan, cover it with a kettle or large pot filled with water. When cooking, keep either one handy for this possibility. As noted, don't dump the water on such a fire; turn off the fuel's shutoff valve—its location should be apparent. (You can, however, *spray* water on an alcohol fire. Keep a spray bottle handy for this contingency.) If an engine fire, turn off the engine before using the extinguisher.

While not essential but useful, a foam or dry powder fire extinguisher works on fires involving solid fuels, paper, curtains, mattresses, as does water—but plenty of it. The problem is, unless you are at a dock, near a hose, you won't normally have access to significant amounts of water. A bucket brigade is likely to be too slow. A BCF extinguisher works on electrical fires but this gives off dangerous fumes in confined spaces. Substantial amounts of water can also be used, though this is not preferred.

Note that each type of fire extinguisher requires a slightly different technique. You should be familiar with the technique *before* you need to use one. Some general rules: Get as close to the fire as possible. Aim carefully at the base of it and move the extinguisher back and forth. You should know that extinguishers empty quickly—in under fifteen seconds in the case of a 2.5-pound one.

If the fire is in the bow, turn the stern into the wind. Don't, however, move ahead, as this will fan the flames. If the fire is in the stern, turn the bow into the wind.

If all else fails, you may have to abandon ship. Put on lifejackets and launch life rafts. If possible, call in a Mayday with your position before abandoning ship. A portable VHF radio or cellular phone, which can be taken aboard a life raft, can be particularly handy in effecting a rescue.

13 | Rules of the Road

An old adage goes: A collision at sea can ruin your entire day. That, of course, is putting it mildly, as a collision at sea can ruin your life and that of your family and friends.

To avoid this, there are rules of the road in sailing as there are in driving. These regulations are spelled out in the booklet, "International Regulations for Preventing Collisions at Sea", published by the RYA. The "Collision Regs" are also detailed in the Macmillan's and Reed's almanacs.

For boats 39.4 feet or longer, this publication must be aboard. You should not just have it on your boat, but you should be familiar with it. It is, to be sure, tough sledding. For boats smaller than 39.4 feet, you need not have it aboard, but being familiar with it is still essential. A collision at sea is no less of an insult—or worse—for small boats than it is for larger ones.

This chapter focuses on rules of the road for those who sail during the day, in good visibility, and near shore. As such, it is a much-condensed version. If your aspirations are broader, buy the book and study it.

In the UK, the rules for inland and coastal waters are exactly the same as those for international waters, although many harbors, rivers and estuaries also have by-laws to be observed.

Give-Way and Stand-On Vessel

In most crossing situations, there is a "give-way" vessel and a "stand-on" vessel. The give-way vessel is the one that *maneuvers*—changes its course and speed—to avoid the other boat. The stand-on vessel is the one that *holds* its course and speed while the other boat maneuvers around it.

If you are the give-way vessel, be timely and obvious in your actions. Rule 8(a) says, "Any action taken to avoid a collision shall, if the circumstances of the case admit, be positive, made in ample time and with due regard to the observance of good seamanship." Rule 8(b) says, "Any alteration of course or speed to avoid a collision shall, if the circumstances of the case admit, be large enough to be readily apparent to another vessel . . . A succession of small alterations of course and speed should be avoided." To put this another way, subtlety has no place in close-quarter maneuvering.

If you don't understand what the other vessel is doing, sound at least five short (one-second) rapid blasts of a horn or whistle.

Even if you are the stand-on vessel—well armed by the rules—don't demand what hasn't been given. Don't assume the other captain of a vessel even knows the rules. Thus, if you need to make last-minute alterations to avoid a collision—even break the rules—do it. The last thing you want to be is right: dead right.

An old verse I recall hearing years ago says it better: "Here lies the body of Michael O'Day, who died while maintaining the right of way. He was right, dead right, as he sailed along, but he's just as dead as if he'd been wrong." The author, I believe, is H. A. Calahan.

You should know that in a collision between two vessels, both boats share the blame and responsibilities. Also, the rules are written for situations involving *two* vessels. When more than two meet, all captains are responsible for avoiding collision.

Three Important Questions

When passing near another boat, three questions are critical. They are: Are we on a converging course? Is the distance separating the two boats decreasing? And, what type of craft is the other vessel?

The best way to determine if you're on a converging course is to take bearings on the other boat with a handbearing compass. If a collision seems even remotely possible, sight the other vessel's bow from the cockpit of your boat (see Figure 13.1). Write down the bearing. A few moments later, take a second bearing from and to the same reference points. Also, note if the distance between you and the other vessels appears to be decreasing. If time permits, take a third bearing and again note the relative separation.

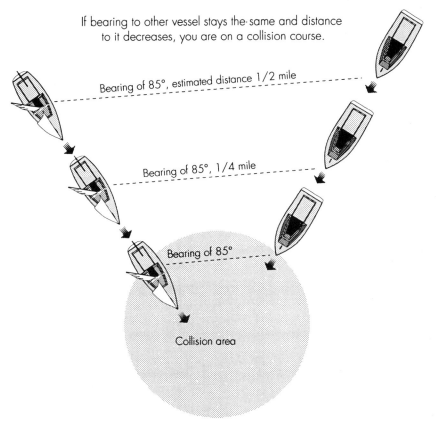

If bearing to other vessel stays the same and distance
to it decreases, you are on a collision course.

Bearing of 85°, estimated distance 1/2 mile

Bearing of 85°, 1/4 mile

Bearing of 85°

Collision area

FIGURE 13.1 *If you suspect you are on a converging, or collision, course with another vessel, sight it two or more times with a handbearing compass. The rule is that constant bearing plus decreasing distance (as in the figure) equals a collision.*

If the bearing *hasn't changed*, or *has changed very little* and the distance between the two vessels is *decreasing*, you're likely on a collision course. The old law of the sea goes: Constant bearing plus decreasing distance equals a collision. If the bearing *has changed*—is getting larger or smaller—or the distance between the two boats hasn't changed, you're probably not on a collision course.

While this works with most boats, it won't work if you're sighting an oversized ship, or with a vessel towing a barge or something similar. For me, might makes right when meeting a substantial vessel. A good rule is never to cross ahead of a significant ship. Give them plenty of room.

PECKING ORDER

As noted, the third question was: What type of craft is the other vessel? This is asked because there is a pecking order determined by a ship's position, mission, type, size, draft, or relative ability to maneuver. The order is:

One. **A boat being overtaken.** You are overtaking a vessel if your course is no more than 67.5 degrees off dead astern. That is an area of 135 degrees (see Figure 13.2, top). Rule 13 says that if there is any doubt that you are overtaking a boat, assume you are. It makes no difference if you're a sailboat overtaking a powerboat, as in the top figure. The overtaking vessel must give way.

You can signal your intentions by sounding one short blast on the vessel's horn, which means "I am altering my course to starboard," or by sounding two short blasts, meaning "I am altering my course to port." In an overtaking situation this makes it obvious to the vessel being passed which side you are going to pass him on. The vessel being overtaken should, with one or two short blasts, as appropriate, signal his agreement. But if your message is misunderstood or inappropriate for any reason, he may respond with the danger signal, which is at least five short blasts. This is a warning for you to abort the maneuver.

If you hear a signal of three short blasts, this means "I am operating astern propulsion."*

Two. **A vessel "not under command," i.e., broken down.** A boat in this category has experienced a substantial mechanical failure; maybe the

---

*The meaning of this is that the boat is in reverse gear, or slowing. It doesn't necessarily mean, however, the boat is moving backward.

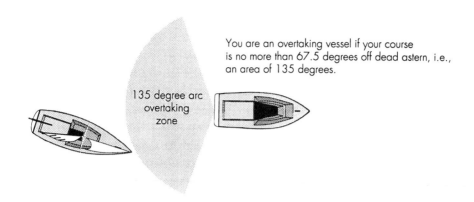

You are an overtaking vessel if your course is no more than 67.5 degrees off dead astern, i.e., an area of 135 degrees.

135 degree arc overtaking zone

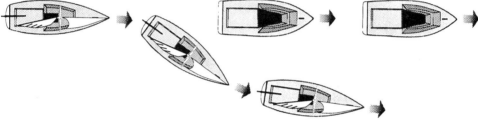

Overtaking boat has no rights, even if a sailboat overtakes a powerboat.

Two short blasts mean, "I intend to overtake you on your port side."
Sound one short blast meaning, "I intend to overtake you on your starboard side."

FIGURE 13.2 *An overtaking vessel, even if it is a sailboat under sail overtaking a powerboat, is the give-way vessel.*

propulsion is broken or the boat has lost steering. During the day, a boat not under command *should* show two black balls, one above the other, where they are most likely to be seen. (See Figure 13.3, middle-left, for this day shape.)* All other vessels must give way.

Vessels "restricted in ability to manuever" are also in this category. According to Rule 9, of the "Collision Regs", *all* sailboats and other vessels less than 65.6 feet shall not impede the passage of a vessel that can safely navigate only within a narrow channel or fairway. Such a vessel, restricted in ability to maneuver (RAM), should be delineated by a ball-diamond-ball displayed in a vertical line, where they can best be seen. This might be a

*While such signals are required, their use is not universal. At night, vessels display characteristic lights.

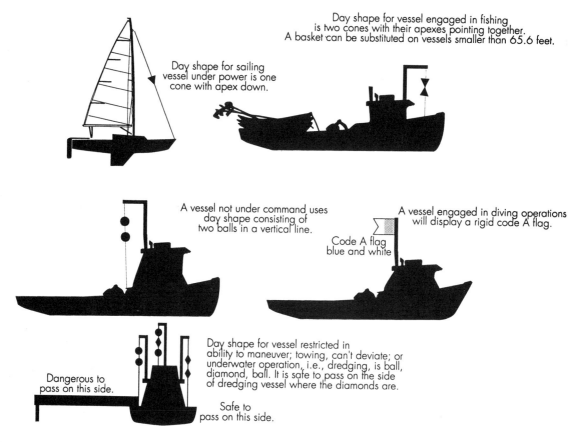

Day shape for vessel engaged in fishing is two cones with their apexes pointing together. A basket can be substituted on vessels smaller than 65.6 feet.

Day shape for sailing vessel under power is one cone with apex down.

A vessel not under command uses day shape consisting of two balls in a vertical line.

A vessel engaged in diving operations will display a rigid code A flag.

Code A flag blue and white

Day shape for vessel restricted in ability to maneuver; towing, can't deviate; or underwater operation, i.e., dredging, is ball, diamond, ball. It is safe to pass on the side of dredging vessel where the diamonds are.

Dangerous to pass on this side.

Safe to pass on this side.

FIGURE 13.3 *An important question in the rules of the road is: What type of craft is the other vessel? To help you in this regard, boats should display the following day shapes. Know, however, that not all boats do.*

large or deep-draft freighter, a ferryboat, or a tug boat pulling or pushing a barge. Common sense and the rules say if a vessel cannot operate outside a channel, do nothing to impede its progress.

These boats also have the right of way over a sailboat in traffic-separation schemes—the nautical equivalent of a dual carriageway. Traffic-separation zones—common in areas of high-density shipping—are marked on the chart by purple boundary lines and purple arrows showing the direction of travel.

If crossing a narrow channel or traffic-separation scheme, do it so as not to interfere with a vessel that can only navigate within the channel, fairway, or traffic-separation scheme. Also cross it at a right angle.

Obviously, don't anchor in a narrow channel or separation scheme. If traveling in a channel, stay as far to the right as possible.

Sailboats must also give way to working vessels, that is, those engaged in commercial diving (displaying international code A, or alpha flag, see Figure 13.3, middle-right), minesweeping, laying cables, launching or recovering aircraft, or dredging (ball-diamond-ball).

A dredge boat might also show two black balls over one side and two black diamonds over the other (see Figure 13.3, bottom). Don't pass on the side with the balls, pass on the side with the diamonds.

Three. **A commercial vessel engaged in fishing with nets or trawls.** The fishing vessel must also be "restricted in its ability to maneuver." Such a vessel should display two cones apex to apex, except that such a vessel less than 65.6 feet can instead display a basket. This category does not include, however, "...A vessel fishing with trolley lines or other fishing apparatus which do not restrict maneuverability." In the eyes of the rules, there is a difference between trawling (pulling a fishing net) and trolling (pulling a fishing line). Also generally not included are pleasure boats engaged in fishing. That said, the best advice is to avoid any vessel engaged in fishing, as an altercation just isn't worth it.

Four. **Vessels under sail.** Note, you must be sailing. If your engine is on and in gear, you're a powerboat—even if you have the sail(s) up and trimmed.

Five. **Pilot boats.**

Six. **Power-driven boats, including sailboats when motoring.** When powering, a sailboat should display a conical shape with its apex, or smallest part, facing down (see Figure 13.3, top left). While not often seen, this is a good idea for any size sailboat under power.

Seven. **Seaplanes.**

When a Sailboat Meets Another Sailboat

If a sailboat meets another sailboat, two rules apply: First, if the boats are on *different* tacks, the one on starboard tack has right of way (see the black boat in Figure 13.4, top). Recall that tack is a function of which side of the boat the wind strikes *first* (see Figure 2.9, page 22). Even more simply, if the boom is on the right, or starboard, side, you're on port tack. If the boom is on the left, or port, side, you're on starboard tack.

The rules say that if you can't determine which tack another boat is on, assume it is on starboard tack.

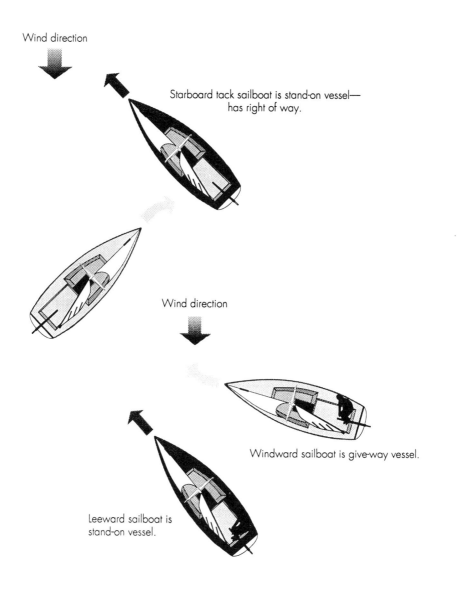

Wind direction

Starboard tack sailboat is stand-on vessel—
has right of way.

Wind direction

Windward sailboat is give-way vessel.

Leeward sailboat is
stand-on vessel.

FIGURE 13.4 *Two rules apply when a sailboat meets another sailboat: port-starboard*
(top) and windward-leeward (bottom). In both cases, the black boat is the stand-on vessel.
For those who sail on inland lakes, these two rules, plus the rule that says a sailboat has
right of way over a powerboat (i.e., a pleasure craft)—save when overtaking (see the
pecking order)—are probably all you need to know.

The second rule comes into play when two boats are on the *same* tack. In this case, the leeward boat (see the black boat in Figure 13.4, bottom) is the stand-on boat. The windward vessel is the give-way boat. As described in Chapter 2, leeward, or lee, designates farther downwind, while windward, or weather, designates farther upwind (see Figure 2.5, page 16).

What happens if a nonracing sailboat encounters racing sailboats? While not a rule, the racing boats are generally afforded the right of way, as a courtesy.

A Sailboat Under Power

As described, a sailboat under power—that is, with the engine running and in gear—is a powerboat. According to the pecking order, such a boat is the give-way vessel in every situation, save when meeting a seaplane, which, in my experience, doesn't happen very often. Even then, when *overtaking* a seaplane (see Figure 13.2), a sailboat is the give-way vessel.

Sound one short blast to pass port to port as illustrated, or two short blasts to pass starboard to starboard.

A) Crossing head on.

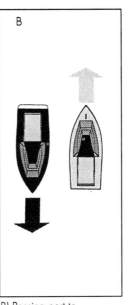

B) Passing port to port is preferred.

C) Continue on safe course.

FIGURE 13.5 *A sailboat under power is a powerboat. When two powerboats meet more or less head on, the boats should head to starboard—unless there is a reason to the contrary—so as to pass to port. Note the optional sound signals.*

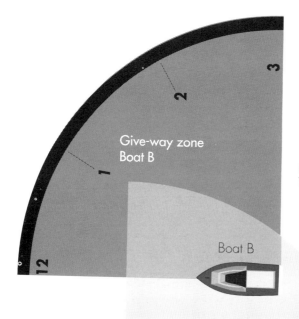

Boat B is in Boat A's "give-way zone."
Therefore, Boat A must give-way to Boat B.

FIGURE 13.6 *If one powerboat is crossing another powerboat (including a sailboat under power), the vessel crossing from starboard is the stand-on vessel, or has right of way. Perhaps the easiest way to think of this is to give right of way to a vessel that approaches you on a course from twelve to three o'clock. If you aren't sure if you are crossing another vessel or passing it* head on, *assume it is the latter.*

If, however, two powerboats meet more or less head on—or on reciprocal courses, or nearly so—both boats are the give-way vessel. (Again, this rule applies to sailboats when motoring.) Unless there is a reason to the contrary, both boats should head to starboard so as to pass port-side to port-side (see Figure 13.5).

Passing port-side to port-side is easy to remember as it is the opposite of how one drives down the road in the United Kingdom.

If crossing another powerboat, the one crossing from starboard is the stand-on vessel (see Figure 13.6). One way to think of this is that your danger zone in a crossing situation is from twelve o' clock to three.

If you aren't sure whether you are crossing another vessel or passing ahead of or astern of it, assume it is a head-on crossing.

Sound signals may also be used—as before, one short blast if turning to starboard, two short blasts if turning to port, and three short blasts if operating astern propulsion. A boat that does not understand another boat's intentions should sound five short blasts.

When the Rules Don't Work

The rules work well if both boats know the rules, abide by them, and, of course, can see one another. They don't work as well if these conditions aren't met or if more than two vessels meet.

In crowded harbors or congested waterways, act prudently, not legally. Move slowly. Allow yourself plenty of time to work out a solution to a potential collision situation. Pass aft of other vessels—that is the safest of all possible worlds.

Be warned, however, that if, when sailing, you pass to leeward of a large high-sided vessel, like a freighter, which according to the pecking order probably has right of way, you may lose the wind for up to several minutes. You could find yourself dead in the water, and as a result without steerageway and thus unable to comply with the rules, or even to avoid a collision. This is another reason to give such vessels plenty of room.

When Visibility Is Limited

While we've assumed you are sailing in good visibility, fog, for example, can occur at any time. When visibility is limited, due to fog or other atmospheric conditions (snow or smoke), no boat is the stand-on vessel—or has right of way.* When operating in such conditions, you should slow down, or even stop, until you've determined that the risk of collision no longer exists.

In times of low visibility, boats communicate by sound signals. For example, when visibility is limited, sailboats that are sailing, "shall sound at

---

*A clear, dark night doesn't qualify as a time when visibility is limited. At night, boats show distinguishing lights. See the "Collision Regs" for a list of lights and signals.

intervals of not more than two minutes, three blasts in succession; namely, one prolonged followed by two short blasts." This same signal is sounded by a vessel not under command; a vessel restricted in her ability to maneuver—whether underway or at anchor—a vessel engaged in fishing—whether underway or at anchor—and a vessel engaged in towing or pushing another vessel. Also, a power-driven vessel (including a sailboat under power), "making way through the water shall sound at intervals of not more than two minutes one prolonged blast." If that power-driven vessel, including a sailboat, is "underway but stopped and making no way through the water," it shall sound, "at intervals of not more than two minutes two prolonged blasts in succession with an interval of about two seconds between them." For other sound signals see the "Collision Regs".

School's Out

At this point, school's out. Doubtless, you found some of it challenging. I hope you found much of it interesting, too. As I've said often and in many ways, sailing is both challenging and interesting.

This book has, I hope, given you a good start in the sport. Now, I trust, you will keep sailing. Keep learning, as I do, forty-seven years after I happened onto this great pastime.

Bibliography

Videos

Coastal Piloting, Magic Lamp Productions, Hollywood Video Studios.

Come Sail with Us, Pearson Yachts, Portsmouth, Rhode Island.

Learn to Sail, Steve Colgate, Bennett Marine Video, 1983.

The Learn to Sail Series (sanctioned by USYRU now US SAILING), Sea TV, New Haven, Connecticut.

Michelob Sailing: A Complete Introduction to Sailing, Gary Jobson, Busch Creative Services Corporation.

Penny Whiting Sailing Video, Video One.

Rules of the Road, Charters West, Summerland-by-the-Sea, California.

The Sixty Minute Sailor, Invideo Production Company, Mill Valley, California, 1986.

This Is Sailing, Sea TV, New Haven, Connecticut.

Books

Altimiras, J., *Sailing Knots,* Arco Publishing, Inc., New York, 1984.

Bond, Bob, *The Handbook of Sailing,* Pelham Books, London, 1985.

Bond, Bob and Sleight, Steve, *Small Boat Sailing,* Alfred A. Knopf, New York, 1983.

Coles, Adlard, *Heavy Weather Sailing*, Adlard Coles Ltd., London, 1967.

Conner, Dennis and Levitt, Michael, *Sail Like a Champion*, St. Martin's, New York, 1992.

Dellenbaugh, David, *The North U. Cruising Course Book*, North Sails Group Inc., Milford, Connecticut, 1992.

Dent, Nicholas, *How to Sail*, St. Martin's, New York, 1979.

Dixon, Conrad, *Start to Navigate*, Adlard Coles Ltd., London, 1977.

Editors of the BMIF, *A Guide to Boating and Watersports Facilities in the UK*, The British Marine Industries Federation, Surrey, 1992.

Editors of *Cruising World, Safety at Sea Official Seminar Text*, Middletown, Rhode Island, 1992.

Editors of Macmillan Publishing Ltd., *The Macmillan and Silk Cut Yachtsman's Handbook*, Macmillan London Ltd., London, 1984.

Editors of the RYA, *Cruising Yacht Safety*, Royal Yachting Association, Eastleigh, 1986.

Editors of *Sports Illustrated, Small Boat Sailing*, J. B. Lippincott Company, Philadelphia and New York, 1972.

Editors of Time-Life Books, *Seamanship*, Time Inc., New York, 1975.

Editors of *Yacht Racing/Cruising* (now *Sailing World*), *Encyclopedia of Sailing*, Harper & Row, New York, 1978.

Farnham, Moulton H., *Sailing for Beginners*, The Macmillan Company, New York, 1967.

Franzel, Dave, *Sailing: The Basics*, International Marine Publishing, Camden, Maine, 1985.

Goode, John and Everitt, Dick, *Navigation Made Simple*, 1992; *Let's Do It Under Sail*, 1993; *Handling Emergencies*, 1993; *Handling Under Power*, 1994. All E. G. Publications, Poole.

Houghton, David, *Weather at Sea*, Fernhurst Books, W. Sussex, 1986.

Jarman, Colin and Beavis, Bill, *Modern Rope Seamanship*, International Marine Publishing Company, Camden, Maine, 1976.

Kinney, Francis S., *Skene's Elements of Yacht Design*, Dodd, Mead & Company, New York, 1981.

Larr, T. S., *Sailing Instructor Manual Dinghy,* United States Sailing Association, Newport, Rhode Island, 1992.

Ludins, George H., *Seamanship for New Skippers,* Banyan Books, Inc., Miami, 1980.

MacLeod, Rob, *Sailing Fundamentals,* American Sailing Association, Marina del Rey, California, 1984.

Mellor, John, *The Art of Pilotage,* David and Charles, Devon, 1990.

Moore, James and Turvey, Alan, *Starting Sailing,* Doubleday & Company, Inc., New York, 1974.

Myatt, John, *Effective Skippering,* Adlard Coles Ltd., London, 1992.

Nautical Terms Under Sail, Crown, New York, 1978.

O'Day, George, *Sail in a Day,* Grosset & Dunlap, New York, 1967.

Rousmaniere, John, *The Annapolis Book of Seamanship,* Simon and Schuster, New York, 1989.

Sleightholme, J. D., *This Is Basic Sailboat Cruising,* United Nautical Publishers S.A., Basel, Switzerland, 1976.

Toghill, Jeff, *Knots and Splices,* Fernhurst Books, W. Sussex, 1979.

Whidden, Tom and Levitt, Michael, *The Art and Science of Sails,* St. Martin's, New York, 1990.

Articles

Bernon, Bernadette Brennan, "A Man-Overboard Plan," *Safety at Sea Official Seminar Text, Cruising World* Publications, 1992.

Dove, Tom, "Mastering the Art of Gybing," *Sail* magazine.

———, "Steering by Compass," *Sail* magazine.

———, "Beyond Starboard over Port," *Sail* magazine.

Murphy, Tim, "Splash! Man Overboard! What Will You Do?" *Cruising World* magazine, December 1992.

Textor, Ken, "Sound Advice for Sailing in Fog," *Sail* magazine.

Wijsen, Louk, "Plan to Stay Healthy Offshore," *Sail* magazine.

Williams, Margaret, "Fire Prevention Framework," *Safety at Sea Official Seminar Text, Cruising World* Publications, 1992.

Index

f = drawing
p = photo
n = footnote